D1525555

BLACK MAN IN THE HUDDLE

SWAIM-PAUP SPORTS SERIES
Sponsored by James C. '74 & Debra Parchman Swaim
and T. Edgar '74 & Nancy Paup

BLACK MAN IN THE HUDDLE

Stories from the Integration of Texas Football

ROBERT D. JACOBUS

Foreword by Annette Gordon-Reed

This paper meets the requirements of
ANSI/NISO Z39.48–1992 (Permanence of Paper).
Binding materials have been chosen for durability.
Manufactured in the United States of America

Library of Congress Cataloging-in-Publication Data

Names: Jacobus, Robert, author.
Title: Black man in the huddle: stories from the integration of Texas
    football / Robert D. Jacobus; foreword by Annette Gordon-Reed.
Description: First edition. | College Station: Texas A&M University Press,
    [2019] | Series: Swaim-Paup sports series | Includes bibliographical
    references and index. |
Identifiers: LCCN 2018045050 (print) | LCCN 2018046343 (ebook) | ISBN
    9781623497521 (ebook) | ISBN 9781623497514 | ISBN 9781623497514 (cloth:
    alk. paper)
Subjects: LCSH: Football—Texas—History—20th century. | Discrimination in
    sports—Texas—History—20th century. | African American football
    players—Texas—History—20th century. | Texas—Race
    relations—History—20th century.
Classification: LCC GV959.52.T4 (ebook) | LCC GV959.52.T4 J33 2019 (print) |
    DDC 796.332/6309764—dc23
LC record available at https://lccn.loc.gov/2018045050

To Eva with gratitude, for your love, support, and constant dedication

Contents

Foreword

"Friday Night Lights" occurs after a day begun with pep rallies filled with cheers and songs. Then, later, long lines of school buses venture out on the highway along with fans piled into cars and trucks, forming a caravan to football stadiums across the state of Texas. These are familiar sights for millions who have grown up in the Lone Star State, where high school "football is king." Even people outside of the state know how devoted many Texans are to the game and the rituals that surround it. For it is not just the young men on the field who make the sport what it is. The players have a supporting cast—cheerleaders, pep squads, twirlers, the band—giving diverse parts of the student body a chance to participate in and actually help make the spectacle. High school football is intensely social. The phenomenon of fanatical support continues into the college years, with teams having diehard fans who may not have even attended the university to which they have established a strong allegiance.

For the most part, people have forgotten—or conveniently tucked away in their memory banks—that this entire social system used to be divided along racial lines. Up until the late 1950s and early 1960s, the experience of football as a force that brought communities together was a segregated one. African Americans experienced the thrill of the game, the pep rallies, the band, the cheerleading, and pep squads in one set of schools, and whites experienced them in another. The same was true for colleges in Texas. It took many years after the Supreme Court's 1954 decision in *Brown v. Board of Education of Topeka* began the process of dismantling de jure segregation in the United States for blacks and whites to play on the field together.

Because they are so driven by the idea of merit and the drive to win, sports have been seen as a natural training ground for dissolving differences. If a player can run fast, block well, and catch passes—if he can help his team *win*, the story goes—then that player should be accepted. However, as the long-held institution of segregation was winding down in America, it was not so simple, particularly because of the social significance of the game. Bringing blacks and whites together on the field, in the stands, and in the schools challenged the expectations of racial separation in Texas society. White fans may have wanted to win, but many were also frightened of the changes in society that integration of the beloved past time would entail. Many blacks were concerned about losing their sense of community as well. At the end of the day, black and white players on the field could be a reality only if blacks and whites went to high school and college together.

The law, of course, stepped in to answer the question about black and white football players and black and white schools—at least as a legal matter. Although de facto segregation remains a real phenomenon, people are used to seeing black and white players on the field together, black and white cheerleaders, and members of integrated marching bands. It is worth remembering that this was a hard-fought battle and knowing the names of the people who personally traveled the journey from the legalized segregation of the past to the much more inclusive system of today. *Black Man in the Huddle: Stories from the Integration of Texas Football* tells this fascinating and important story, making it clear that the history of those times should never be forgotten.

Annette Gordon-Reed

Author's note: Annette Gordon-Reed, winner of the 2009 Pulitzer Prize in history for her book The Hemingses of Monticello: An American Family *is a native Texan and in 1965, as a first-grade student, was the first African American to enroll in the Conroe Independent School District.*

Preface

Black Man in the Huddle: Stories from the Integration of Texas Football focuses on the significant number of young African American males who dealt with the sometimes-flawed efforts of the integration of Texas football fields in the 1950s and 1960s. The focus becomes sharper and zeros in on how these players rose from segregation, both de jure and de facto, to achieve a measure of success, both in athletics and in their later careers in spite of the odds against them. My thesis was based on the Texas experience, since history shows high school football has always been an obsession for Texans. In the era of early integration, African American football stars were limited if they "stayed home" to play college ball. They went outside for opportunities in the Big Ten, Big Eight, and at colleges on the West Coast. Then, as now, the Lone Star State historically sends more players to the pros than any other state. Rare is it that any NFL team fails to have at least a few players from Texas.

A segment of my first book, *Houston Cougars in the 1960s: Death Threats, the Veer Offense, and the Game of the Century*, examined how before Warren McVea came along in 1964 to integrate the University of Houston football program, African American football players in the Lone Star State, because of segregation, typically played at a historically black college or university (HBCU), such as Texas Southern University or Prairie View A&M, if they stayed in-state. If not, they had to leave Texas if they wanted to play at a major (i.e., white) college. I interviewed several players and their family members about their leaving Texas for better opportunities, like Junior Coffey, from the Panhandle city of Dimmitt; Ollie Matson, whose family left Texas while he was still in high school to move to California for more opportunities; and Bubba Smith and Gene Washington, from the Texas Gulf Coast, who went on to All-America status at Michigan State.

However, I started thinking about expanding my research from that chapter to look at the integration experiences of other African American high school and college football players in Texas. There were so many stories that hadn't been told, or needed to be told. There were many unanswered questions. What were their experiences with integration? What was it like growing up in a totally segregated environment and transitioning to an integrated environment? Were there any specific examples of de facto segregation in their new school or on the football field? How did they get involved in sports? How were the facilities, both academic and athletic, at their all-black schools, compared with their new white schools? What colleges recruited them out of high school? What was it like integrating a high school in, say, San Antonio or Corpus Christi not long after *Brown v. Board*? What was it like being recruited by an HBCU, or a college outside of Texas, and ultimately, by a four year traditionally all-white college in Texas?

The result of my effort is an oral history told by the young men who lived through segregation and the transition to the gradual integration process throughout Texas in the 1950s and 1960s. The main focus is on the high school and college football experience, the coaches and influences involved, and details about the difficult social adaptation to suddenly attending a predominately white school with a locker room filled with white players. I interviewed players from all corners of Texas so all regions of the state would be represented and their experiences could be compared with those from other parts of Texas. The players experienced various levels of segregation in different regions of Texas, and the same held true for integration.

Just like my research experience with *Houston Cougars in the 1960s*, I found many players had similar experiences when it came to integration. However, I also found that many of their experiences and stories were unique. I also found through pouring over many newspaper clippings from this transitional era that very little specific information existed that detailed the integration experience, because newspapers in cities all over Texas, as well as the South in general, virtually ignored the black community in the days of Jim Crow. I also discovered that this integration topic had never been examined in detail, either in book form or otherwise. Following my previous research path, I decided to set out to interview as many people as I could to learn these details. An oral history was about the only way to tell this compelling story. That's when I decided to write a comprehensive book about the integration of high school and college football in Texas.

The number of interviewees grew to almost 250. Wow, and what a who's who of Texas high school football made up this list, as well as college football and the All-Pro and Hall of Fame ranks who starred in the 1950s and 1960s. The interviews herein include four members of the Pro Football Hall of Fame, and fourteen inductees to the College Football Hall of Fame. Forty-six are members of their respective college's athletic halls of fame. Twenty-four players were named to college All-America teams. Twenty-eight were the first to integrate their high school or college team. Several players, one example being Sid Blanks, integrated both their high school and college teams.

Out of the pros in this distinguished interview group, twenty-one were named first team All-Pro and played in more than one hundred Pro Bowls. Six of these individuals were named NFL/AFL Rookie of the Year. One of the players interviewed, Green Bay Packer wide receiver Boyd Dowler, was named for the NFL's Fiftieth Anniversary team in 1969, while another—Houston Oilers and Washington Redskins safety Ken Houston—was chosen for the NFL's Seventy-Fifth Anniversary team in 1994. Dowler was also named to the 1960s All-Decade team, as were Tommy Nobis, Clem Daniels, and Miller Farr. Daniels also ranked as the AFL's all-time leading rusher and was named to the all-time AFL first team. Ken Houston and Mel Renfro were named to the 1970s NFL All-Decade team. Two players interviewed were the number one overall pick in the NFL draft: Tommy Nobis (1966) and Bubba Smith (1967). These interviews also documented other trends in the integration process. By the late 1950s and early 1960s, smaller Texas institutions of higher learning, such as Texas A&I, West Texas State, and North Texas State, integrated their football programs. Then, by the mid-1960s, major college football programs in the state of Texas such as UH, Baylor, and SMU integrated their teams.

The story begins with the epic tale of Ben Kelly, the first African American to integrate a college football team in the former Confederate states when he suited up for San Angelo College in San Angelo, Texas, in August 1953, almost nine months before the landmark *Brown v. Board of Education* Supreme Court case in 1954.

The tale continues with high schools and colleges throughout the state slowly integrating, from San Antonio to Corpus Christi Schools integrating not long after *Brown v. Board of Education*, the decision by the Supreme Court in 1954 that struck down segregation in public education. The book also discusses resistance to integration at the same time in these two areas, as well as other parts of the state.

Another early effort at college football integration in 1956 was the well-known story of Abner Haynes and Leon King, when they tried out for the North Texas State football team. *Black Man in the Huddle* delves into that same year and the not-so-well-known story of Louis Kelley, who along with four of his high school teammates from Abilene Woodson High School, integrated Cisco Junior College the same year, 1956. The book continues with the gradual integration of high schools in other parts of Texas, such as the Rio Grande Valley and parts of Central Texas, and the continued resistance to integration in East Texas. Two groundbreaking high school teams, the 1960 Corpus Christi Miller Buccaneers, which was the first integrated team to win a state title, and the 1962 San Antonio Brackenridge Eagles, who became the first inner-city minority team in Texas to capture a state championship, are also chronicled in these pages.

Other smaller Texas colleges and their tales of integration in the early 1960s continue the story, such as Texas A&I College in Kingsville, West Texas State College in Canyon, and Lamar College in Beaumont.

Here we also examine college players leaving Texas for better opportunities to play football elsewhere and their exploits, both positive, such as Bubba Smith and Gene Washington leaving Texas for glory at Michigan State, and negative, such as the experience of Lewis Ritcherson at the University of Wisconsin, before more than just a handful of Texas colleges had integrated.

Finally, the book concludes with major colleges in Texas integrating in the mid-1960s, such as the University of Houston with Warren McVea, Baylor with John Westbrook, and SMU with Jerry Levias, and how that led to the final integration of high schools in East Texas in 1967.

To a lesser degree, the secondary theme is geography and demographics. Even though these players in areas of Texas appeared to have it easier than players in parts of Texas like, say, Houston or Dallas, sometimes being the first came with its own set of problems. Some of the early integration pioneers were on an island, sometimes being the only black person or one of the few black people in their school.

In addition, the book discusses how the Texas experience appeared to provide evidence of the Lone Star State being a model for school integration in the South. Texas schools were some of the first to integrate. By

1964, Texas alone accounted for 50 percent of desegregated school districts in the South and for more than half of all blacks integrating in the South.

However, these figures were misleading. School integration in Texas was mostly geographic, and somewhat demographic, in nature. For example, East Texas, the Dallas/Fort Worth Metroplex, and the Greater Houston area remained heavily segregated until the mid- to late 1960s, because of their close proximity to Louisiana and the rest of the Old Confederacy. Other parts of Texas, like the Coastal Bend area around Corpus Christi, the Rio Grande Valley, and the San Antonio area, integrated in 1955, about a year after *Brown v. Board*. In the Texas Panhandle, some of the smaller towns, like Borger and Dimmitt, integrated early on, whereas the two largest cities, Lubbock and Amarillo, waited until later in the decade. Integration in Central and West Texas varied from city to city. Former players from all of these areas were interviewed.

Their recollections testify that demographics also played a role in the integration of Texas. For example, the areas where early integration took place had smaller population percentages of African Americans. To wit, most towns in the Coastal Bend and Rio Grande Valley had less than a 1 percent African American population—except in military towns like Corpus Christi, Kingsville, and Del Rio, where black populations could approach 5 percent. However, in East Texas, where segregation was more rigid, in some cases towns could have up to a 50 percent black population. What set Texas apart from the other Southern states was its sheer size. Instead of the whole state continuing to be rigidly segregated after 1954, like Mississippi, Alabama, Georgia, or Louisiana, different regions of Texas integrated very early. Then we see that East Texas and the Dallas and Houston areas remained segregated until the 1960s.

In spite of the odds, many of these players rose up to remarkable levels of success not only in college and pro football, but also in other endeavors outside of football. Many of the athletes interviewed were not just integration pioneers, but were successful in other areas outside the sporting world. Some were pioneers in other niches of football: Charles Garcia became one of the first African American scouts in professional football in the late 1960s, while fellow Texan Carl Jackson became one of the first African American assistant coaches at both the college and professional level during the 1970s and 1980s.

Joseph Searles III, who helped integrate Killeen High School, went to Kansas State University to play college football, and played briefly for the New York Giants. After his football career, Searles worked for New York Mayor John Lindsay in the late 1960s and New York Governor Nelson Rockefeller. In 1970, Searles became the first African American member of the New York Stock Exchange.

Brady Keys grew up in segregated Austin before moving to Los Angeles to become a star at Polytechnic High School. He played football at Colorado State before joining the Pittsburgh Steelers in 1961. He played eight years in the NFL, making All-Pro as a defensive back. After his football career came to a close, Keys became the first African American to own a fast food franchise in America, and later owned more than one hundred Kentucky Fried Chicken restaurants throughout the United States.

The players were split on the effects of integration. The aforementioned players mostly felt integration was necessary to advance as far as they did in their careers. Segregation was holding them back. A large number of interviewees, however, lamented the passing of their segregated schools. They tell of an environment of caring teachers and administrators who made sure they got the proper education. Many of them felt that integration got rid of their traditions and schools that they could take pride in.

The stories each of these players told were unique. Just because a player lived in a less segregated part of Texas, like West Texas or the Rio Grande Valley, or a part of the state that desegregated soon after *Brown v. Board of Education* in May 1954, like Corpus Christi or San Antonio, didn't mean they were free and clear of any obstacles to overcome. In East Texas, players were still part of rigid segregation until the mid- to late 1960s, and the races for the most part remained separate, in everyday life, in school, and on the athletic fields. Players in less restrictive and integrated areas had their own obstacles, like being the only black person or one of a few blacks in their new all-white school environment. The same held true on the athletic gridiron. These players needed to gain the acceptance of their new teammates, coaching staffs, and white teachers. So, in the end, no matter what part of Texas players hailed from, they each had their own sets of challenges.

Ultimately, the stories contained in *Black Man in the Huddle* are told by these courageous players, mostly in their own words, and detail how they had to overcome obstacles in their Texas towns, large, medium, and small, to achieve a measure of success in high school football and beyond, whether it be in college or pro football, or in other facets of life. Lastly, the book contains direct interviews with Texas high school and college football players from the 1950s and 1960s, partially done to preserve the authentic history and to tell the story from that time period before it was too late. Sadly, since I started this book in 2015, more than twenty of the interviewees (about 10 percent of the total contacted for interviews) have passed away. Luckily, many of their words are captured in the pages of this book, and their legacy and experiences as to what happened in that era are preserved for future generations to study and enjoy.

BLACK MAN IN THE HUDDLE

1

A Black Man in the Huddle

Coach Bum, I want to play football for San Angelo College.
—Ben Kelly to San Angelo College Head Football
Coach Max Bumgardner

Max Bumgardner was feeling good. After a memorable road trip in 1953, he must have felt like he beat the Texas heat that blistered you and squeezed the sweat out of you in a fiery August, just like it does today. Bumgardner, the head football coach at a modest two-year institution of higher learning in the West Texas town of San Angelo, had just won the season's first football game. He did it on the road—in Wichita Falls, 236 miles to the northeast, in what was then known as the Oil Bowl, which annually pitted high school all-star football players from Texas against their counterparts from Oklahoma across the Red River. The narrow win was three days behind him, and Bumgardner now focused his concentration on the upcoming fall training for his San Angelo College team. His assistant, Phil George, sat across the desk in the coach's office. The first day of practice was just a week away.

Suddenly and unexpectedly, a young man appeared outside their door. The coaches recognized him as Ben Kelly, whom coach Bumgardner and his assistant knew as a star halfback at San Angelo Blackshear High School. In 1950 Kelly led Blackshear to the state title with a 32–0 win over Huntsville's Sam Houston High School. Initially the two coaches were puzzled by the sudden appearance of Kelly. He was older than most San Angelo students—at the age of twenty-two. A few years prior, Bumgardner and George were known to head over to Blackshear a couple of times a year to take in one of Kelly's games. They had especially recognized his talents on the football field. "I think that's why he came to us," George said years later. "He felt comfortable with us because he knew us."

After his 1951 graduation, however, Kelly went off to play football at the University of Illinois, much in part because he was so well thought of in the community that two San Angelo businessmen, Homer Nickle and

Earl Horn, raised enough money to send Kelly to play on a team in the Midwest. "That's how much people around here thought of him," George recalled. After just a semester, however, Kelly left school to join the army. He served two years.

After his military stint was up in 1953, Kelly reflected, "I could have gone back to Illinois and played. It was just too cold, though, and it was so far away from San Angelo. If I played here, I wouldn't have to make those sacrifices."

When Kelly came into that coaches' office on that hot August day in 1953, Phil George remembered, "You could tell there was something on his mind. He kept rocking back and forth like he wanted to say something."

Ben Kelly remarked years later about that moment: "I was concerned that the coaches would tell me no. You don't know until you ask, so I took a shot."

Phil George described what happened next. Kelly looked at Bumgardner and uttered, "Coach Bum, I want to play football for San Angelo College." Bumgardner, a former defensive back at the University of Texas and 1948 first round draft pick of the Chicago Bears, had heard this same request from several prospects over the years. But with Ben Kelly, it was different and it was unusually problematic.

Max Bumgardner, San Angelo College Head Football Coach, 1954. Courtesy of Angelo State University.

You see, this was August of 1953, almost nine months before the historic May 17, 1954, US Supreme Court decision *Brown v. Board of Education of Topeka*, where Chief Justice Earl Warren and the other eight judges unanimously struck down segregation in public education from elementary school all the way through college. Ben Kelly, who made the request to play football at all-white San Angelo College, was African American.

Coach George, who in 1968 became the athletic director at Angelo State University, nee San

Angelo College, recalled, "Coach Bumgardner was taken aback. He finally said to Kelly, 'Ben, that's fine. We'd like to have you, but you know we can't have you. We're a segregated school and there's no way I could let you come here and play football for the Rams.'

"Kelly then asked Coach Bumgardner, 'Then who would have the authority to allow me to go out for your team?' Bumgardner replied, 'The president of the college, Rex Johnston, would be the one who had to make that decision.' Bumgardner then took Kelly outside and pointed him toward the administration building."

"When Kelly started heading over to the president's office, Coach Bumgardner tried to call the president's secretary, Virginia Feist, to give her advance warning that a young black gentleman was heading over to their office. However, the line was busy."

When Kelly arrived at the president's office, he asked Virginia Feist if he could see President Johnston but did not tell her the reason for his visit. Once admitted, Kelly must have made an impassioned plea to play football for the Rams. For President Johnston finally said to his visitor, "If I felt as strongly about it as you do, I'd go over to the registrar's office and enroll." Johnston then called the registrar's office and said he was sending a young man over to fill out the proper paperwork.

George recalled, "President Johnston then called us back over at the coaches office and said to Coach Bumgardner, 'I think we just integrated our school. Ben Kelly is going to play football for you.'"

These steps taken by Ben Kelly, the football coaches, and the school president set into motion the integration of athletics at Texas high schools, colleges, and—for that matter—the former Confederate States of America.

Yet, technically, Kelly was not the first black student to attend San Angelo College. During World War II, blacks from Goodfellow Air Force Base had attended night classes there as part of their service at this non-flying base dedicated to cryptologic and intelligence training. But Kelly officially was the first African American to actually enroll at the college.

Before Ben Kelly entered San Angelo College, however, there were a couple of events in Texas in the three years preceding his enrollment that paved the way for him to become an integration trailblazer.

In 1950, a Supreme Court decision that was a precursor to *Brown v. Board* helped open the doors for integration in Texas and the rest of the South. In *Sweatt v. Painter*, Houston resident Heman Sweatt had in

1945 applied to the University of Texas Law School. Since Sweatt was African American, his application was turned down, prompting Sweatt and the NAACP to file a lawsuit seeking his admission. In an attempt to appease these plaintiffs, the Texas Legislature in 1947 created a new four-year college in Houston, now known as Texas Southern University, complete with a brand new law school for blacks. Not satisfied, Sweatt and the NAACP continued with their lawsuit. In 1950, the nation's highest court ruled in Sweatt's favor, thus admitting him to the UT Law School. This decision opened the door for other public education institutions to integrate, not just in Texas but throughout the South.

Ben Kelly was not the first African American to integrate a Texas college, either. Del Mar College in Corpus Christi, another two-year college, had in July 1952 enrolled the first black students at a previously all-white college in Texas, thanks in large part to the *Sweatt v. Painter* decision and the work of both civil rights activist Henry Boyd Hall and Del Mar President E. L. Harvin.

Coincidentally, San Angelo President Max Johnston, who was just a little more than a year into his tenure, had written a letter to President Harvin of Del Mar College in August 1952, in anticipation of San Angelo College's possible integration. In part, the letter inquires, "How do you handle the registration of Negroes who applied for admissions to Del Mar? Mr. Barnes tells me you were very effective in your treatment of the Negro situation. Since I wish to take the matter up with my Board next Wednesday, I shall appreciate you answering my letter as soon as you can."

Once Kelly enrolled at San Angelo College for the 1953 fall semester, what now remained was his acceptance as a player on the football team. At the first team meeting of the semester, the players learned that they had a new teammate. Phil George recalled, "When the players came in the following week for the start of fall practice, they had not been forewarned that Ben was part of our team. At the first team meeting they found out about Ben. All of a sudden, standing in the middle of them was this strong black guy with a big grin on his face. Well, that was pretty traumatic for some of these kids. But by the end of the first week of practice, they were all singing Ben's praises."

More than one of Kelly's surviving teammates underscore the accolades. One of them was lineman George Bookout, who hailed from Wichita Falls, where he played for the legendary Coach Joe Golding. Bookout helped the Coyotes gain a state title in 1950. "Ben was a fantastic guy and a great football player," he said. "We had no racial problems on our San Angelo team. Everyone was treated as an equal. I remember when Coach Bumgardner introduced Ben to the team. He was very well-received by the players."

Another teammate was Jimmy Gafford, a lineman from Lubbock High School, where he made the all-state team twice and helped lead the Westerners to state crowns in 1951 and 1952. Gafford said, "Ben was a super guy. He was a hard guy to get down. He was big for a runner back then but not that

BEN KELLY

Ben Kelly, San Angelo College, 1954. Courtesy of Angelo State University.

fast. He would run over you rather than around you. One time we were watching a film, and on one play I swear it took nine or ten guys on the other team to get Ben to the ground.

"Ben being on the team wasn't a big deal. I don't remember there being any bad feelings toward him by the other players. Sometimes we had to do things a little different with Ben when we went on the road. Ben couldn't stay with us at the hotels, so Coach Bumgardner would give him five or ten dollars so he could get a room and meals in the black part of town. We would then see Ben at practice and at the game. We didn't break through all the barriers with Ben, and for that I have some bad feelings. When someone did make a racial remark to Ben during a game, however, we would knock that player into the dirt to get back at him."

Receiver Loman Jones came to San Angelo via Brownfield, about thirty miles south of Lubbock. When asked about Ben Kelly, he thought back to an away game against Paris Junior College to end the 1953 season. "Paris was ranked in the top ten, and if they beat us they were going to go to a bowl game," Jones recalled. "Our season had been disappointing. We won our first four games but then we had three or four key players get hurt, including our quarterback, Gene Henderson. We lost five games in a row heading into the game with Paris.

"Well, Gene Henderson played after being out for a few games, and we upset them, 21–20. Us beating Paris kept them from their bowl game. The game was played in the fog, and you could barely see down on the field. We were trapped in our end of the field and we kept giving the ball to Ben, and he led us downfield for the game-winning touchdown. During the drive, however, one of the Paris players got rough with Ben and started twisting Ben's ankle when he was in a pileup. It made us angry, and it made us more determined. It also made us appreciate Ben more.

"Ben was a great addition to our team. He was a great running back. He was a big boy. He ran over more people than he ran around. He was something. Ben was one of us. We never excluded him from anything. He was even named class favorite in the yearbook. We played with and for Ben Kelly.

"There's one incident, when I look back upon it, that probably wouldn't have been accepted in most places in 1953. Ben was nursing an ankle injury and he had to get whirlpool treatments on it. Well, Ben would just get into these big whirlpool tubs we had in the training room and share it with a bunch of us white players. Sharing water with a black person probably wouldn't sit well with too many white people back then. We honestly didn't think about it. We all loved Ben.

"When we played other teams, they would intentionally try to hurt Ben. Sometimes players on the other team would try and hit him high and low. Ben was tough, though; he took it. He was also a man about it. I never saw him get mad or show emotion. He never said anything, nor did he complain about the treatment he was receiving. I'm sure he was mad on the inside. He stayed calm and level-headed. You had to stay that way to be a black player in an all-white environment. It took a lot of courage to do what Ben did."

One of Kelly's teammates who eventually became his close friend was Paul K. "Buddy" Horne, who hailed from the tiny town of Lohn (population: 200), sixty miles east of San Angelo. "Lohn is a very small town," Horne said years later. "No blacks lived there. Meeting Ben was a whole new experience. I remember Coach Bumgardner saying to the team at our first meeting that Ben would be the first Negro to play at a previously segregated school south of the Mason–Dixon Line. I didn't know if that was true, but that's what he said.

"As it turned out, Ben was very easy to get along with. If you closed your eyes on all this and let him do what he did, you would never know what color he was. Everyone liked him, and he liked us. To us, he was just a football player. Ben lived at his parents' house in San Angelo, but he would come over to the dorms to hang out. We became friends."

Kelly added, "Those were some of my favorite football memories—hanging out in the dorms, and being able to talk and discuss things with the guys."

Once the games started, Kelly faced the anticipated obstacles. He took most of them in stride. His historic first game was on September 19, 1953, at Bobcat Stadium in San Angelo. The Rams defeated Phoenix College 26–0. All during the season, Kelly faced abuse during and after plays. Buddy Horne said, "Ben got some bruises in games. He got punched a few times. Remember, there were no facemasks on helmets yet. We knew what was happening, and we tried to protect him. To Ben's credit, he never fought back and never said a word."

Coach George added, "Ben used to get his hands stepped on, spit on, called names, and get punched in the face. I asked him one time, 'How do you go through this humiliation week in and week out?' Ben said, 'My mother always told me to never let someone else's problem become my problem. They have a problem, not me.'"

Also, when the Rams were on the road, they faced conflicts with hotel arrangements and eating establishments. "Ben couldn't eat in the cafés or stay in the majority of hotels on the road," George said. "He would have to go back into the kitchen to eat at restaurants. One of his teammates would go back there with him to eat."

Horne was that teammate. "When we got to stay at a hotel that allowed blacks," he said. "Ben would be my roommate. When the team had no choice but to eat at restaurants that did not allow blacks in the main dining area, I would go back into

Phil George, San Angelo College Assistant Football Coach, 1954. Courtesy of Angelo State University.

the kitchen to eat with Ben. I didn't mind, though. Turns out, Ben and I probably ate better than anyone on the team. Most of the cooks were the same color Ben was."

Years later Kelly said, "Changes, obstacles, football—they're all just one of those parts of life that you get knocked down and get up and move on. My first year was a tough year. Once we started to get to know each other, my teammates accepted me, once they realized I just wanted to do my job. After a while, when there were problems—for example, on road trips—my teammates rallied around me and showed support."

Kelly, however, did not see himself as a trailblazer, nor was that his intent when he enrolled in San Angelo College. In an interview just months before his death on November 15, 2014, at the age of eighty-three, Kelly said, "Being a pioneer didn't dawn on me. I wasn't going out there for that. I just loved football and wanted to be on the team."

Kelly's widow, Alvetta, concurred, saying, "Ben just liked football. His teammates accepted him. In not too long, before games they would have team luncheons and Ben and I would go to them." In fact, Ben Kelly was so accepted by his teammates and his classmates at the college that by the end of his freshman year, he was voted "most popular." Phil George said, "That tells you everything you need to know about Ben Kelly."

Kelly shined on the football field. He was named All-Pioneer Conference two years in a row, as he helped the Rams to a 10–8–1 record during his two seasons. When he finished school, he had opportunities to play in the NFL with the San Francisco 49ers and New York Giants. But after two years, he had to think about supporting his family. Kelly worked for the Boys and Girls Club of San Angelo, eventually rising to executive director before retiring in 1996. In 1994, the gymnasium at the club was named in his honor.

On December, 7, 2013, Ben Kelly was inducted into the Texas Black Sports Hall of Fame in Dallas. The following January he was inducted into the Angelo State University Hall of Honor. And on May 1, 2014, Angelo State University renamed the Center of Human Performance in honor of Kelly.

The naming and renaming didn't stop there. On May 12, 2014, the weight room in the Junell Center/Stephens Arena was renamed the Ben and Alvetta Kelly Weight Room. The Ben and Alvetta Kelly Football Scholarship Endowment was also created, which annually awards a scholarship to a member of the San Angelo State football team.

What Ben Kelly unknowingly did in the early 1950s—when the Jim Crow laws affected the makeup of football teams in Texas and throughout the South—was to set into motion the historic desegregation. This, in turn, led to the integration of high school sports, and eventually more Texas college athletic programs as well. Eventually other African American high school and college football players in Texas experienced what Kelly did: being accepted, sometimes begrudgingly, into a previously all-white society. Like Ben Kelly, each of these young men had their own stories to tell, and their stories of perseverance in the midst of a tumultuous time are inspiring.

On the surface, Texas would appear to be the South's model for school integration. Not long after *Brown v. Board*, the small Texas Panhandle town of Friona was the first school district in Texas and one of the first in the former Confederacy to integrate.

In September 1954, the family of Robert Walker Jr. moved to Friona. Walker, a migrant farmer, had three sons—Robert, Ray, and Jimmy. There was only one elementary school in town, and building a new elementary school for just three black children would be cost-prohibitive. Thus Dalton Caffey, the Friona superintendent, chose to enroll Walker's children in the all-white elementary school, thus quietly achieving the first integrated public school in Texas.

Caffey informed the local school board of his decision, and the integration went fairly smoothly for the school and the new students. The Walkers moved away during the school year, but in the spring of 1955, three more African Americans were enrolled in the school system. Caffey received threats from as far away as Georgia and Alabama, and there were threatening phone calls from local parents. But the fact remained that there was no violence in Friona.

Other Texas school districts desegregated in the 1955–56 school year. Cities that adopted immediate, across-the-board integration were San Antonio, Corpus Christi, Lubbock (postponed until 1960s), San Angelo, El Paso, Crystal City, Carrizo Springs, La Ferria, Mission, and Brownsville. Austin, which had planned to integrate, held off until 1956, and then only partially integrated with grades 10–12. School districts that began in 1955 with partial integration, usually at the high school level and then with a staggered schedule for the lower grades, included San

Marcos, Robstown, Bishop, Port Lavaca, Brownwood, Kerrville, Weslaco, Harlingen, Sinton, Amarillo, Kingsville, Rockport, Aransas Pass, Karnes City, Kenedy, and Runge.

Using Austin as an example of staggering integration by grades, the city integrated high schools in 1955, junior highs in 1958, grade 6 in 1961, grade 5 in 1962, and all other grades in 1963. With larger Texas cities that integrated, like Austin, San Antonio, and Corpus Christi, the black high school in those communities remained open until the late 1960s, and in Austin's case, its Anderson High School remained open until 1970. African American students in San Antonio could go to an integrated high school or remain at Wheatley High School. In Corpus Christi, they could choose between the predominately white schools or Solomon Coles High School.

Once again, on the surface, Texas appeared to be the model of integration for the former Confederacy. Numerous Texas schools were some of the first to integrate. By 1964, Texas alone accounted for 50 percent of desegregated school districts in the South and for more than half of all blacks integrating public schools in the South. These statistics were somewhat misleading, though. Because Texas is such a large and diverse state, both demographically and geographically, school integration was mostly by regions, which were in some cases demographic in nature.

In Houston, Dallas, and East Texas, since they were in closer proximity to the former Confederate South and had a higher percentage of African Americans in the general population, no school districts integrated early on. Texas Citizens Councils, similar to anti-integration organizations in Mississippi, sprang up in East Texas areas. The Dallas and Kilgore Texas Citizens Councils pledged to "fight integration by every legal means."

In the early to mid-1950s, the black population in Dallas and Houston was between 25 and 30 percent. Even in 2017, two-thirds of blacks in Texas live in the Dallas/Fort Worth Metroplex or in the Greater Houston Metropolitan Area. Full-scale integration of schools shortly after *Brown v. Board* would have meant larger numbers of African American students mixing with Anglos than in other Texas towns with a much smaller black population.

In general, the farther west, north, or south one went from the Louisiana/Texas border, the integration of Texas school districts varied and was more frequent in nature. Once again, there was a lower percentage of blacks living in areas other than the eastern part of the state. In all other parts of the state, there were fewer than 10 percent blacks living in cities. In the Panhandle, Lubbock's black population was about 8 percent and Amarillo's was 6 percent. In Central Texas, both Austin and Abilene had a black population of about 8 percent. In West Texas, Midland had about 7 percent, Odessa 5 percent, San Angelo 4 percent, and El Paso 3 percent. South Texas had the least amount of African Americans, with Corpus Christi's black population being 4 percent, Kingsville's 4 percent, Del Rio 1.5 percent, and Brownsville's 0.4 percent.

When Texas started the implementation of integration plans in 1955, the Coastal Bend area in South Texas, with Corpus Christi being the main city there, was the most progressive. Not coincidentally, this was one of the areas of Texas that had the lowest percentage of blacks in school.

Once Corpus Christi announced its plans to desegregate in 1955, other school districts in the Coastal Bend followed suit. In Nueces County, where Corpus Christi is the county seat, out of eighteen school districts, seven ordered desegregation, nine had no black students, and one district, Sundeen Independent School District, voted not to integrate. The Sundeen school board also unanimously voted to prohibit any football games in 1955 against teams that had black players, forcing them to immediately cancel two games. One Nueces County superintendent, formerly from an East Texas school district, said, "We cannot force a Negro to pay taxes, send him to war, and then tell him, in many ways, he is a second-class citizen."

While geography and demographics were factors in the individual football players integration experiences, in the end they all had a variety of obstacles to overcome, no matter what part of Texas they resided in. Some players, in the eastern part of Texas, appeared to have the deck stacked against them much more so than players in other parts of the Lone Star State. Most of the time, their all-black schools were inferior to their white counterparts. The same held true in athletics. Players at the black high schools suffered from substandard equipment and facilities. The East Texas players also had to deal with strict segregation, both de facto and de jure, well into the 1960s, and in general, a less tolerant society as East Texas was closer in proximity to the old Confederacy and its attitudes toward race.

While the road may have seemed easier for players in areas of Texas far away from East Texas, they too had their own variety of issues. In many cases, some of the African American players in places like South Texas or the San Antonio area were the only African American, or one of very few, in their new all-white school when it came time to integrate. Fostering friendships and carving out any type of school social life was sometimes difficult. For many of the players in this part of Texas, when they went on the road to play their opponents, since in many cases were the only African American on the field, they were singled out for abuse and, in some cases, faced cancellation of games.

What had started back at San Angelo College back in 1953 became a common theme for these integration trailblazers. It didn't matter what part of Texas a player played in: West, East, South, Central, or West Texas, each of these integration pioneers had their own set of obstacles, and had to learn how to press on and overcome them.

So, with Ben Kelly of San Angelo College integrating college football in Texas in 1953, the *Brown v. Board of Education* Supreme Court decision in 1954, and the partial integration of Texas school districts in 1955, Texas high school football began to undergo some major changes. For years, white schools and black schools were segregated into their own separate leagues, the white schools playing in the University Interscholastic League (UIL), which was founded in 1910, and the black schools playing in the Prairie View Interscholastic League (PVIL).

The PVIL started in 1920 as the UIL decided to establish a separate Negro division. It was officially named the Texas Interscholastic League of Colored Schools (TILCS). From the beginning in the black community, it was called the Prairie View Interscholastic League (PVIL), or the "Negro League," because the state track meet was held each spring at Prairie View A&M University.

The guidelines for deciding state champions in sports like football were loosely defined, since there were no playoffs. This left the door open for more than one school to claim a state championship. This is how the TILCS was governed until 1939.

In 1940, Andrew "Pat" Patterson, a young coach at Houston's Jack Yates High School, created the new structural organization for the TILCS. The state was divided into districts, and there would be bi-district, semifinals, and state finals to determine a state champion. On December 24, 1940, I. M. Terrell High School out of Fort Worth beat Austin Anderson High School 26–0, to become the first state football champion under the new setup.

From 1920 until 1963, the Texas Interscholastic League of Colored Schools (TILCS) remained the official name of the governing body for African American schools. The name was officially changed to the Prairie View Interscholastic League (PVIL) in 1964, and remained that way until 1970.

At first, after the *Brown v. Board of Education* decision, school districts that integrated in all areas except East and Southeast Texas started having an influx of blacks into the UIL and previously all Anglo American high schools. In the East Texas, Dallas, and Houston areas, segregation remained until 1967, when the UIL absorbed teams from the PVIL into its organization. The PVIL ceased to exist in 1970.

Even though integration started in the 1950s, African American high school football players in Texas still faced many obstacles. While some got to play in the UIL, the majority remained at segregated high schools in Dallas, Houston, and East Texas, where most of the black population resided. Although "separate but equal" had been overruled in 1954, black players still faced inferior classrooms, poor athletic facilities, prejudice, and de facto and de jure segregation while growing up in their respective towns.

In spite of these roadblocks, many of these players overcame all odds in the 1950s and 1960s to make it to college and play football and, in some cases, the American Football and National Football Leagues. These young men achieved their dreams in different ways. Some players played for historically black colleges and universities (HBCU) in Texas, like Prairie View A&M University and Texas Southern University, or HBCUs in other states, such as Southern University and Grambling College in Louisiana or Tennessee State University in Nashville.

Other African American players in Texas, with the major colleges in the state being segregated until the mid- to late 1960s, left Texas to play for colleges in the West, such as Arizona State, UCLA, or Washington. Some players went north to play in conferences like the Big Eight or the Big Ten.

Also, after Ben Kelly broke the segregation ice by integrating San Angelo College in 1953, in 1956 four-year colleges like North Texas State (now the University of North Texas), West Texas State (now West Texas A&M), and Texas A&I (now Texas A&M-Kingsville) began integrating their football teams. This trend continued throughout the 1960s, when major colleges like the University of Houston integrated with Warren

McVea in 1964 and Southern Methodist University (SMU) with Jerry LeVias in 1965, integrating the old Southwest Conference (SWC).

Unfortunately, because of the obstacles many of these players faced in growing up in 1950s and 1960s Texas, many African American players never got the opportunity to further their education or football careers in the home state. Gene Washington grew up in the segregated town of LaPorte, on Galveston Bay about twenty-five miles southeast of Houston. Washington became an All-America player at Michigan State University in 1965 and 1966 and went on to become an All-Pro wide receiver with the Minnesota Vikings. He became a member of the College Football Hall of Fame in 2011.

"I wouldn't have accomplished all I did without leaving segregated Texas," Washington said. "I owe a lot of things in my life to my going to Michigan State. Fortunately, I was one of the lucky ones. There were so many great black players I went up against who never got the chance I received. I don't know where I'd be or what I'd be doing if I hadn't got the chance so many didn't. I'm very grateful."

The chapters that follow will serve to explore the stories and legends of these great black players. Yet before we can examine the different paths they took to college, the NFL, and other forums for achievement, we must learn what it was like growing up among the seemingly endless obstacles created by segregation in the years before the arrival of Ben Kelly at San Angelo College in 1953 and the *Brown v. Board of Education* decision in 1954.

2

The Hand-Me-Downs

As it was pretty much everywhere in Texas for blacks, we received hand-me-downs from the white school, both in the classroom and in athletics.
—JOHN PAYTON, LIVINGSTON, TEXAS, CIRCA THE 1940S

Before Ben Kelly integrated San Angelo College in the fall of 1953 and the landmark *Brown v. Board* decision a year later, the state of Texas was like the rest of the former Confederacy—completely segregated. This applied to society in general as well as the athletic programs at high school and college levels. It didn't matter if it were in South Texas or West Texas—where the number of African Americans was low—or in the eastern third of the state, where those numbers were considerably higher. These factors later showed that the African American segregation experience in the Lone Star State was different during the decades preceding the painful integration era of the fifties and sixties. However, while different, it didn't matter which part of Texas the African Americans players were respectively from. They each had their own unique story when it came to segregation.

Lufkin is an East Texas town 120 miles northeast of Houston. Today its population is 35,000, considerably larger than the 5,000 people in 1921, the year Ralph Allen was born there. Allen eventually went to Texas College in Tyler, an HBCU, and played football there. He went on to a long and distinguished coaching and school administration career in Texas towns like Henderson, Temple, Nacogdoches, and LaMarque.

"Actually, segregation was OK," Allen said, describing his experiences. "It wasn't as bad as you think. There were times we were mistreated. You know, though, throughout life I've been mistreated by both blacks and whites. We pretty much knew our place as a black. We were allowed to shop in the white businesses in Lufkin; we could even go borrow money at the local bank. We had separate facilities like drinking fountains and bathrooms. For the most part, though, we stayed in our part of town and the whites stayed in theirs.

"It was crazy at times. I was the star running back at the black high school, Dunbar, and I tried one time to get into the Lufkin High School game against rival Longview High School on a Friday night. That's when the white high schools got to play. They wouldn't let me into the stadium. I had to go stand outside the stadium behind the end zone and watch the game from there. I had to stand the whole game because there were no seats."

Another incident from Ralph Allen's childhood stuck with him: "When I was a kid, I stayed in a garage apartment that was owned by whites. There was a restaurant in town called Eat-a-Bite. There was only one door to get in and out of the place. The whites that owned our apartment ordered me one day to go down to the restaurant to get them some burgers. I had to go through the front door because it was the only way in or out of there. I walked in, and the owner said, 'What do you want, boy?'

"He had a skillet in his hand. I was scared he might hit me with it. I somehow ended up getting the burgers, and I got the heck out of there and ran the four blocks back to the garage apartment. When the apartment owners found out what happened, they went back to Eat-a-Bite to go cuss out the owner for the way he treated me. Now *that* really scared me. I thought the restaurant owner might take it out on me and retaliate.

"There was only one time I was upset about my situation, and that was after my last college game on January 1, 1943. My school, Texas College, played Tuskegee in the Vulcan Bowl in Birmingham, Alabama. We won 13–10. I threw a touchdown pass early in the game, and then, with forty-three seconds left in the game, I ran seventy-one yards for the winning touchdown. I felt I could have gone on and played pro football from there, but I couldn't because the NFL hadn't been integrated yet. I wish I could have had that opportunity." (For the record, Allen did score the winning touchdown, but it was *sixty-one* yards right before halftime. The second half was scoreless.)

Livingston is forty-five miles south of Lufkin. John Payton grew up there in the 1940s when the town's population was a little less than two thousand. Payton ended up being an All-America running back at Prairie View A&M College (later University) from 1952 to 1955, and then went on to a long and decorated coaching career in Woodville and Beaumont before he was chosen in 1970 to be the first black assistant coach in any sport at Lamar University. He was the running backs' coach.

Payton's recollections remained vivid over the years: "I went to Livingston Dunbar High School and graduated in 1952. Obviously we had a white school and a black school in Livingston. As it was pretty much everywhere in Texas for blacks, we received hand-me-downs from the white school, both in the classroom and in athletics.

John Payton, circa early 1950s. Courtesy of John Payton.

"In Livingston we did have a 'black' part of town. It was kind of across the tracks. We pretty much stayed in our part of town. There were not many black-owned businesses in town. My uncle had a little café but that was about it. We could go to the white side of town, but there were restrictions. We could buy clothes at the white store, but we couldn't try them on in the store. At restaurants it was pretty typical of the day—we had to go back to the kitchen to be served. At the local movie theater, it was par for the course; we had to sit in the balcony. I found out later my upbringing in Livingston was pretty typical of other black people's experiences in their hometowns."

Charles Brown's experiences were similar to John Payton's growing up in nearby Montgomery, sixty miles southwest. Brown grew up in the late 1930s and early 1940s. After a football career at Texas College, a few years after Ralph Allen roamed the gridiron there, Brown went on to a distinguished coaching career with stops at Shepard and Livingston. From there, Brown became head coach at Conroe Washington High School in 1960, where he took his team to the PVIL state championship game in 1960, 1961, 1963, 1964, and 1965. His teams won state titles in 1960 and 1965.

Brown recalled, "Montgomery was very small back then. I think there were only about three hundred people living there. Segregation was the normal thing for that time. We had our place and that's where we stayed. There was no real 'black' section of town. There was a black café but not much else. There were no other black-owned businesses. We did get to shop in the white stores but we had to go to the bigger towns in the area like Conroe or Navasota to do it. Those towns were also pretty typical of the day. They had separate drinking fountains, and we had to use outdoor bathroom facilities.

"We didn't have a movie theater in Montgomery; it was so small. We did have 'tent movies,' though. Those were like the circus. In the 1930s and 1940s, they would travel to small towns all over and set up a tent just like the circus, but they would show movies. When we went to those, we had to sit or stand in the back of the tent."

Brown then brought up something that was mentioned by many of the former players. "The thing is, we weren't aware of the difference between the way whites and blacks were treated growing up. We just kind of kept to ourselves. It was later, after I got out into the world, I found there was a difference in the way we were treated."

Percy Hines grew up in the deep East Texas city of Orange, just across the Sabine River from Louisiana. With Port Arthur and Beaumont, Orange formed what became known as the Golden Triangle. When Hines was growing up in Orange in the 1940s and early 1950s, the population grew from about seven thousand to twenty-one thousand, mostly because of a military base that was installed there. Hines played football at Orange Wallace High School for legendary coach Willie Ray Smith Sr., father of football great Bubba Smith. After playing football at Tennessee State in the mid-1950s, he too went into coaching and had his greatest success at Lubbock Estacado High School, where he was offensive coordinator under head coach Louis Kelley. Hines was also head track coach, and his teams won state titles in 1981, 1982, and 1986.

"Segregation wise, I had a pretty good life in Orange," Hines recalled. "We didn't think of it as much of a problem. Blacks lived all over Orange. We did have the separate restrooms, water fountains, etc. We realized what was going on. We didn't rebel, though. We knew our family could get into trouble with the whites if we did.

"I do remember one incident growing up. My friends and I went to go get a burger one day, and the owner told us we had to go around to the back to order. What we decided to do after that was every day we would go to the front to order a burger. When we were told to go to the back to order, we would order our burger, but when it was ready, we would tell the owner, 'Naw, we don't want anything.' Within a week, they took down the signs that told us to go to the back and order, and from then on we were able to order from the front just like the whites. I guess it was our little victory over segregation."

Rosenberg, Texas, is situated about thirty miles southwest of Houston. In the 1930s and 1940s it was home to future PVIL and UIL coaching legend Joe Washington. Washington played running back at Prairie View from 1948 to 1950 and began his coaching career at Bay City's Hilliard High School. Washington coached there until 1966, winning a state championship in 1959. From Bay City he went on to become the head coach at Port Arthur Lincoln High School and helped the school integrate with the UIL in 1967. He remained at Lincoln until his retirement in 1994. He is the father of Joe Washington Jr., who was an All-America running back at the University of Oklahoma from 1972 to 1975, and went on to a Pro Bowl NFL career with the Colts and Redskins, winning a Super Bowl ring with the Redskins in 1982.

Percy Hines, circa early 1950s. Courtesy of Percy Hines.

The senior Washington recounted his growing-up years: "I was born in 1929 and grew up in Rosenberg, Texas. I lived 'across the tracks' on Third Street. Rosenberg was segregated by the railroad tracks running through town when I was there in the 1930s and 1940s. We mostly stayed across the tracks in our part of town.

"Sometimes we did go into downtown Rosenberg to go shopping and maybe go to the movies. The big department store in Rosenberg was Blasé Dry Goods. I used to go there to buy my school clothes. We were allowed to enter through the front door of the store, but we could not try on clothes in the store. If we got home and they wouldn't fit, we couldn't return them. I actually interviewed for a job there. I worked for one day there when I was thirteen, but after that one day I decided to go across the street to the Eagle Café. I ended up working there for three or four years, all the way through high school. If I or other blacks wanted to eat there, we had to enter through the kitchen in the back.

"Right across the street also from Blasé Dry Goods was the Cole Theater. If we wanted to use the bathroom at any of the businesses in downtown Rosenberg, we had to use a separate restroom that was outside. If we went to a movie at the theater we had to sit in the balcony. Every once in a while, however, they would show an all-black movie. I remember seeing in the 1940s *Cabin in the Sky* and also *Stormy Weather*, starring Lena Horne.

"Rosenberg was for the most part pretty calm. It wasn't like there were lynchings on the street every day. Not that it was all peaches and cream, though. I remember as a boy seeing the Rosenberg police manhandle some black citizens. Nobody really bothered me that much growing up. I had an attitude growing up where I didn't take any back steps from whites. There was one time, though, when I was a kid when I went to the white high school football game in Richmond, right next to Rosenberg. We had to sit in the end zone to watch the game. Sometimes, though, we would climb some trees in the end zone so we could see the game better. A couple of times, the white kids threw rocks at us."

Washington also remembered the lack of quality facilities and athletic opportunities: "The athletic situation for us in Rosenberg was not good in the 1940s. I went to A. W. Jackson High School, which was over on our side of the tracks. One thing, though—the Hispanics also lived on our side of town. However, they got to go to the white school. Our only real organized team was basketball. A couple of guys ran track. It was not a great athletic program by any means. Right across the street from Jackson High School was a white semipro baseball diamond. We used to get to play on it sometimes.

"They eventually moved the baseball field, and they put an outdoor basketball court in its place. We had a good basketball team. In 1945, I think it was, we got to go to Houston to play in a basketball tournament at Booker T. Washington High School. It was significant because that was the first time we had played indoors.

"For football at Jackson, it was slim and none. In 1945 we talked our principal into letting us play a couple of games against the black high schools in Richmond and Sugar Land. We didn't have much in the way of equipment. We got the old stuff from the white high school. You have to remember, the school districts back then didn't appropriate money to the black schools, especially for athletics."

Washington also recalled other growing-up experiences in Rosenberg. "Back in the day, we had strong role models in the black community we could look up to. In Rosenberg growing up, my principal, A. W. Jackson, had a tremendous influence on me. He encouraged me and guided me; he didn't really counsel me. Mr. Jackson basically told me what you needed to do, like, 'Get an education!' There were no negotiations with him. I didn't get into trouble a lot of times as a teenager because of Mr. Jackson. If I got involved in something I wasn't supposed to be and he found out, I would be in big trouble.

"Unfortunately, though, segregation was habit-forming. Out of habit you did things, or conformed to things. For example, if we went to Houston and got on the bus, out of habit you went to the back of the bus. You didn't question it."

"While I'm thinking of it, another example of segregation or giving in to segregation happened in Bay City in the mid-1950s when I was the head football coach at Hilliard High School. There was a youth baseball team I think from Refugio that had a black player on it. The town of Bay City asked me if I would put him up at my house while they were in town. Out of habit, I agreed to it. After this happened, though, my conscience bothered me. I felt that I was contributing to the situation."

Another Rosenberg native who grew up in the 1940s and early 1950s was Charles Garcia. Garcia would go on to play football at Prairie View. After coaching high school football for a few years in the late 1960s, Garcia became one of the first black scouts in pro football. "Growing up in Rosenberg," Garcia said, "We thought that's the way life was until we left. We didn't know anything else, and we didn't know any better. We had the same problems with whites as most other places. At our school we got-hand-me-downs or had things rationed out to us. Of course, we got the old school books from the white school. I also remember one time we had to go over to the white school to pick up ten or twelve rolls of toilet paper for us to take back to our school. They had to dole them out to us.

"In downtown Rosenberg my dad was a cook at the Eagle Café, the same restaurant that Joe Washington worked at. We used to go into the white businesses down there on Third Street. I used to buy my school clothes at Blasé Dry Goods. I remember one time there they wouldn't cash a company check for me. I had been working for a car dealer on Highway 90A in Rosenberg. I went with my brother Herbert, who also worked there, to Blasé Dry Goods to cash it. They said they couldn't cash it; they had to call the car dealer to make sure the check was good. The people at Blasé's knew my father and my family. We decided to take our business elsewhere. We went to Houston to buy our clothes.

"One time, talking about how things were back then, Rosenberg had a police chief by the name of Bill Somebody, a mean-ass white man. We had an old family dog we kept on a leash in the front yard. The chief drove by our house one day and just shot that dog for no reason. We had to hold back my grandfather from retaliating."

Garcia made another observation about growing up in the Jim Crow era. "One thing about back then—women had to take care of business. Anything that was sticky or could lead to controversy, a man couldn't stand up for himself. He could get beaten up and, in some cases, even lynched if he spoke out against something. I remember my uncle had to leave town one time and catch a train to Fort Worth because he knocked the shit out of a local white businessman, whose name was Geick, because he had taken advantage of him."

Rufus Granderson gave some insight in what it was like being African American and growing up in Central Texas. Granderson was raised in Temple, thirty-five miles southwest of Waco, which was considered to be "the Heart of Texas." After graduating from Temple Dunbar High School in 1955, Granderson went on to become an All-America tackle at Prairie View in 1958. He was the first African American from Temple to be drafted into the NFL when the Detroit Lions took him in the nineteenth round in 1959. A year later, Granderson became one of the first African American football players for the Dallas Texans of the AFL, when Dallas was still a segregated city.

"The fact is," Granderson said, "you grew up in the South, in Texas, and in Temple knowing you were not being treated as an equal. The whites thought they were better than we were. I later found out, once we left segregation, that they were no better than we were.

"My folks had menial jobs in Temple. One job was picking cotton; others were washing dishes in a restaurant or making beds for whites. Temple was not a real small town—it had about twenty-five or thirty thousand people back then. We had black-owned businesses there. We even had our own movie theater, but we would also go to the white movie theater on occasion. Of course, we had to sit in the balcony there.

"As far as our school and athletics were concerned, our school was actually newer than the white school. Of course, we got the used books and used sports equipment from the white school. Our school did have a gymnasium and football field. For the time period, our facilities were pretty good. We didn't look down upon what we had. We didn't get to play against the white school, of course. I felt that our team was better. I would have loved the opportunity to play them."

"Rufus was one of the best pass-blocking tackles there was," Granderson's Prairie View teammate and star pro football running back Clem Daniels recalled. "Unfortunately, with run-blocking, not so much. Rufus had bad knees that hampered him."

Daniels hailed from the city of McKinney, thirty miles north of Dallas, with a 1950s population of twelve thousand. Daniels left McKinney in 1955 to play running back at Prairie View. He caught on with the Dallas Texans in 1960, becoming Rufus Granderson's teammate again, while also helping integrate this pioneering American Football League team and the city of Dallas. In 1961 Daniels went to the Oakland Raiders, and he retired in 1968 as the AFL's all-time leading rusher. He was voted to the all-time AFL first team as a running back.

Daniels reflected on the 1940–50s McKinney: "I think one of the keys to success is how you overcome your conditions. When you're growing up and you're poor, you don't realize you're poor. We took what we had and made the most of it. Our practice field in McKinney was dirt, and we were a small school. We only had fourteen kids on the team. We learned to play both ways. In spite of these obstacles, we made it to the semifinals my senior year. I've also never backed down from things. If you want things to change, you have to ask, and in some cases, demand change."

Soon after graduating from McKinney's all-black Doty High School in 1955, Daniels experienced something that made him want to make things better for his mother and everyone else. "My mother, Ida, was a housekeeper for Gibson Caldwell, a bank chairman and civic leader and one of McKinney's wealthiest citizens," Daniels said. "I was asked to come to his house after I graduated from high school. I went over, rang the bell to his front door, and I was escorted by a black servant who took me into Caldwell's study.

"Mr. Caldwell got up from behind his desk, shook my hand, and congratulated me on getting a scholarship to Prairie View. I thanked him and left, again out the front door. When I got home that evening, my mom told me Mr. Caldwell had come to see her to tell her that if I came to the house again to make sure and come to the back door. When I looked at her, there were tears streaming down her face. I had to console my mother, and I vowed to myself then and there to make things better for her and all of us, for that matter.

"A few years later, after I'd signed with the Texans, I bought a new car in McKinney, but the manager of Mr. Caldwell's bank said I needed to get my mom to co-sign. I ended up taking my business to the bank across the street. It was my own little victory for my mom and myself."

Co-Captain Clemon Daniels '59

P. V. — Jackson Battle to 14–14 Deadlock

The Prairie View Panthers and the Jackson College Tigers battled to a 14-14 deadlock in Jackson, Mississippi, on September 7, in a Southwestern Conference encounter, the season's opener for both teams.

The Panthers scored early in the first quarter following a successful 28 yard pass thrown by quarterback David Webster to Frank McKee which moved the ball to Jackson's 3-yard line. Halfback Calvin Scott plunged over for the score.

Clem Daniels, 1959. Courtesy of Prairie View A&M University.

Yoakum, Texas, was the home for Marvin Douglas until college. Yoakum was home to about five thousand people in the 1930s and 1940s when Douglas was growing up there. Yoakum is situated about 130 miles southwest of Houston and about 100 miles southeast of San Antonio.

Douglas recalled, "I was born on April 19, 1926. My family came to Yoakum from Mississippi. I'm not real sure why they moved to Yoakum from Mississippi. My parents were Alfred and Ethyl Douglas. My dad's father, Stanford Douglas, had been a slave. I knew him just a little bit before he died. I was the youngest of seven children.

"Yoakum wasn't that bad of a place in terms of segregation. It was at first a railroad town and later a farming community. It was settled by the Germans and the Czechs. Blacks lived all over town, not just in one spot. "I grew up one block from town. I had no money growing up, and most of the people in Yoakum, black and white, were in the same situation. We learned to get along with each other. The interaction with the whites was mostly good. Now we did have our separate facilities, and we had to sit in the balcony at the movie theater. We obviously had separate schools. I went to Yoakum Colored High School.

"We had used books and equipment at our school, but our teachers made sure we learned," Douglas said. "Truth be told, I didn't know that much about segregation and discrimination until I moved to Austin, Texas, in 1943 to play football and get an education at Tillotson College. Remember, back in Yoakum, everyone depended on everyone. Our only real restrictions were social stuff."

Marvin Douglas's wife, Morene, to whom he has been married for seventy-two years, recalled a couple of examples of Jim Crow during this

Tillotson College, Austin, Texas., football team 1945—note Marvin Douglass, front row, seventh from left, and future Pro Football Hall of Famer Dick "Night Train" Lane, second row, fourth from left, while still a high school student at Austin Anderson High School. Courtesy of Marvin Douglas.

time period in Austin. Mrs. Douglas said, "I too didn't know much about discrimination and segregation until I got to Austin. I grew up in Central Texas around Temple, and I took the train to Austin so I too could go to Tillotson College. My mom pinned forty dollars on me, and I was to use it to buy a coat when I got to Austin. I went to Scarborough's Department Store, which was on Sixth Street and Congress. I walked in and grabbed a coat off the rack and tried it on. I didn't know you weren't supposed to do that. It turns out they fired the clerk because she let a black try a coat on in the store.

"Also, after college we were starting our family here in Austin in the 1950s, and I was at Zales, which was a store in downtown Austin between Sixth and Seventh Streets. My oldest daughter, who was about five or six at the time, had to go to the bathroom. The clerk said, 'We don't have a bathroom here for you people! You have to use the colored restroom!' Well, the closest restroom for us was on Tenth Street, about four blocks away. I told my daughter, 'Just go tee-tee on the floor.' The clerk then rushed over to pick up my daughter and rushed her to the white restroom in the store."

Unlike Marvin and Morene Douglas, who moved to Austin to attend college in the mid-1940s, Leroy Bookman Sr. was born and raised in the capitol city. Bookman was a 1946 graduate of Austin L. C. Anderson High School, a legendary PVIL school. The Anderson Yellow Jackets won PVIL state football titles in 1942, 1956, 1957, and 1961. Bookman, who was quarterback for the 1943–45 teams, said, "We had some great teams. I think our best team in Anderson history was our 1944 squad. We were disqualified in the playoffs because we had an ineligible player. We also made it to the state finals when I was a senior."

Two of Bookman's teammates were future Chicago Cardinal and Houston Oilers defensive back Julian Spence and Pro Football Hall of Fame cornerback Dick "Night Train" Lane. Spence, who died at age sixty in 1990, integrated the Houston Oilers in 1960 along with teammate John White. In 1961, he clinched the AFL title for the Oilers with a fourth quarter interception in the Oilers 10–3 victory over the Los Angeles Chargers. Spence later coached at Grambling and ended his career at LaMarque High School, about forty miles south of Houston.

Austin Anderson had other famous attendees throughout its history. One early Anderson student was baseball Hall of Famer Willie Wells Sr., who was a Negro League star from 1924 to 1948. His son, Willie "Zipper"

Wells Jr., was a star end on the 1942 Anderson state champion team. In the 1942 state title game, a 40–0 win over Paris, Wells caught a record five touchdown passes.

Another prominent Anderson football player was defensive back Brady Keys, who would have been a teammate of Bookman, Spence, and Lane, but moved to California from Austin after his freshman year. Keys went on to play eight seasons in the NFL, making one Pro Bowl. More significantly, in 1967 Keys became the first African American to own a fast food franchise in America, when he opened All Pro Fried Chicken in San Diego. Keys eventually owned numerous Kentucky Fried Chicken franchises in the Southeast.

Leroy Bookman Sr. recalled his days growing up in Austin and playing for Anderson High School. "I grew up on the east side of Austin in what was considered the black part of town. I never really felt the segregation. We played with white kids growing up, down on Second or Third Street. It was a mixed neighborhood. When I was a kid I just didn't know that much about segregation and discrimination. We were young, and we really didn't think about it. By my teens, though, I started to realize that we were treated differently—for example, like when we went to the white stores downtown to shop. There were 'colored' bathrooms and water fountains. We also couldn't try on any clothes in the stores.

"One thing that I don't think many people know about—we used to scrimmage every once in a while against the football team from all-black Samuel Huston College here in Austin. They eventually merged with Tillotson College in 1952 and became Huston-Tillotson College. We beat them in the scrimmage. That shows you how good we were. One time, though—and most people won't believe this—we got to scrimmage against the University of Texas Longhorns in 1943, I think it was. They came over to our field at Anderson and played us there. I remember it was low scoring, but we beat them."

Roland Harden graduated from Anderson in 1944 and then attended Samuel Huston College. His experience with whites was somewhat different from Leroy Bookman's. "We had very little contact with whites in Austin," Harden remembered. "We were on the east side. They were everywhere else. Sometimes we would play a little sandlot ball with the whites, but that was about it. If we went to downtown Austin, we couldn't eat at the lunch counters there. There was also a department store on Sixth and Congress, called Scarborough's. They wouldn't let us try on clothes. We also had to go to the basement of the store to shop. I remember their slogan was, 'Are you being served?' I guess that only applied to the whites, or us if we were in the basement. We had a black movie theater called the Harlem Theater on Twelfth Street on the east side. If we went to the white theater on Sixth Street, called the Ritz, we had to sit in the balcony.

"Obviously we didn't play high school ball against the whites. It's a shame because in 1942 Anderson had a great team that won state that was led by Willie Wells Jr. Austin High School, the white school, also won state that year. It would have been great to see those two schools play. The teams right after that were great too. They were led by Leroy Bookman, Richard Lane, and my best buddy, Julian Spence. To show you how good they were, 'Night Train' Lane was second string. Julian, who also played in the NFL, was backup quarterback to Bookman.

"Julian and I were best friends. We went into the army together. After high school we both went to Samuel Huston College. Julian played football, and I played basketball. In 1948, though, we joined the army. We were sent to basic training in Fort Knox, Kentucky. It was the same as Texas—segregated. Not long after we joined up, though, the military integrated. We were among the first troops to do so.

"Night Train Lane also went into the army about this time too. He started playing on the military football team, and he did well there. It wasn't too long after he got out that he hooked up with the Rams. One day I was reading the paper, and it said he was playing in the NFL. I couldn't believe it. Remember, he was second string at Anderson. He was a really nice guy. He got along with everyone.

"After Julian and I finished up basic training at Fort Knox, I was shipped to Japan and he went to Germany. I got out of the army after two years. Julian signed up for two more years and didn't get out until 1952. When he got out, he went back to Austin and played for Huston-Tillotson College. Samuel Huston and Tillotson had merged in 1952. Julian played two or three years there. He was joined on the team by Jimmy Hill from Dallas. He played running back. When Jimmy left Huston-Tillotson, he went to the NFL with the Cardinals, and he played defensive back there and went to the Pro Bowl several times. It turns out Night Train and Julian ended up with the Cardinals too. Those two had played football together in the military at Fort Ord. After Night Train went to the Cardinals before Julian got out of Huston-Tillotson, he got them to eventually pick up Julian. I think he also got Jimmy Hill to come there too."

Harden did not play football at Anderson, but when he got to Samuel Huston College, he did play basketball his freshman year of 1944–45. This was important because of who his coach was. It has almost been forgotten through time that Jackie Robinson, the man who integrated Major League Baseball in 1947, was the basketball coach at Samuel Huston College for the 1944–45 season before he went on to play for the Dodgers. The legendary Robinson ended up in Austin as a favor to the president of Huston at the time, Karl Downs. Downs had graduated from Huston in 1933 and made his way to California, where he encountered Robinson. Downs established himself as a Methodist minister in Pasadena, where Robinson grew up, and became Robinson's pastor and mentor.

In 1943 Downs became president of Samuel Huston College at age thirty-one. At the same time, Jackie Robinson was stationed in the army just sixty miles up the road at Fort Hood in Killeen. Robinson in his downtime would travel to Austin to visit Downs. When Downs needed a basketball coach for the 1944–45 season, Robinson, who had just received an honorable discharge in November 1944 because he had refused to move to the back of a bus in Killeen, accepted the job as a favor. Robinson said, "There was very little money involved, but I knew that Karl would have done anything for me, so I couldn't turn him down."

Roland Harden described his experience playing basketball for a civil rights legend. "I got to play basketball for Jackie Robinson in 1944–45 at Samuel Huston College. In the fall of 1944, I was watching the basketball team practice and I said, 'I can play as well as those guys!' So Jackie said to me, 'Well, come on out for the team then.' I tried out and I made it. I even got a partial scholarship that covered my tuition. My mom was happy about that!

"We knew all about Jackie. He was famous from his days of playing at UCLA. He was some athlete. He was only about twenty-five when he coached us, and he would work out with us many a day. Jackie could play just about any sport. He beat me easily at table tennis, and I was pretty good. He was also a great tennis player. He was a good coach, though.

"He made us behave, and he had us wear a suit and tie on road trips. We also ran a lot as a team, so that was fun. Jackie did have a temper, though. That's why he got kicked out of the military in the first place, because of his temper. I was kind of surprised he stayed under control when he went to play for the Dodgers. I guess Branch Rickey knew what he was doing when he chose Jackie to integrate."

Marvin Douglas also encountered Jackie Robinson while he was a student and playing football at Tillotson College. "I met Jackie when he came to coach Samuel Huston," Douglas said. "They would practice over at Anderson High School. When I first saw him, I said to my friends, 'That's Jackie Robinson.' We in the black community knew all about Jackie from his UCLA days. His biggest problem back then was controlling his temper. Things ended up working out for him with the Dodgers, though."

Decades after these stories of the problems segregation posed for these great black athletes from Texas, we must reflect on a great "what-if" in history. What if more of these individuals had been allowed to integrate the all-white teams of the era in Texas and the rest of the South? At this stage in history, the experts in the field of sports can only speculate. But they have the strongest empirical evidence possible—the experiences of African American athletes who moved out of the South to the more welcoming athletic environs of the West, the East, and the Midwest. It was there they were welcomed not only in stores downtown but also on the college football fields of some of the nation's most prestigious colleges and universities.

3

Go West, Young Blacks, Go West!

If you knew anything about Texas back then, you would know why we moved. It was a horrible place. We left for better economic opportunities and a better life.
—JOHN WOOTEN, TWO-TIME PRO BOWL GUARD IN THE NFL AND NATIVE TEXAN

Sometimes—sensing better opportunities and less racial problems elsewhere, and attempting to overcome the experience of segregation—a number of black families moved from Texas before their athletic sons reached high school or college. This way, they would have more options for the future, both for their sons' athletic careers and for the family's welfare in general. In some instances, a family would send a son on his own away from Texas and segregation to take advantage of more promising opportunities. In many cases, the most promising land of opportunity proved to be California, which had been integrated for years and was more tolerant of African Americans.

One player who moved there with his entire family was Olympic silver medalist and future Pro Football Hall of Fame member Ollie Matson. Matson starred at the University of San Francisco and led his team to an undefeated 1951 season. Ironically, it was the last year the school put a football team on the field. What should have been a storybook final season was spoiled by the fact that the team was turned down for a bowl game in the South because two blacks were on its roster, Matson and teammate Burl Tolar.

It is not well-known that prior to his college years, Matson grew up in the East Texas town of Trinity until he turned eleven years old and his family moved to Houston. He eventually attended Jack Yates High School, where he played football his freshman and sophomore years. Matson played left end on offense and defense, and even scored a touchdown in 1945 against the Temple Lions in an 87–7 Yates victory. Unfortunately, as a sophomore that same year, Matson's football season ended at the halfway point, when he suffered a broken ankle. Ollie Matson's sons, Bruce and Ollie Jr., and his twin sister Ocie, have vivid recollections of why the Matson family left Houston for San Francisco in 1945.

Bruce Matson, who became a Houston dentist, recalled, "My grandmother decided to go to California to teach and get married. Another reason she went was that she wanted my dad to be a dentist, and she figured it would be easier for him in California. From what I understand, when the family moved to California, my dad was only about 150 pounds. It took him a little while to fill out, and that's one reason he went to San Francisco Junior College before he went to the University of San Francisco."

Ollie Matson Jr. remembered, "My dad wanted to be a boxer. My grandmother sent him to San Francisco. She did not want him to go to an all-black college. Some of my dad's sisters and brothers were already in California. He had broken his ankle and had missed half of the 1945 season at Yates High. They left Houston, and Dad ended up going to Washington High School in San Francisco his last two years.

"The family left Houston because of segregation. Back then there were two Houstons—the black part and the white part—and the races rarely mixed. The family had come down from the family farm in Trinity. We used to have dairy cows. We did OK during the Great Depression, but my grandfather got a job with the railroad in Houston. My grandmother had wanted to be a funeral home director in Texas, but she couldn't be. In California she could be anything. She ended up teaching school and marrying a dentist. People didn't get along in Texas like they did in California."

Ocie Thompson, Ollie Matson's twin sister, recalled, "My mother thought there were more opportunities in California than in Houston. Ollie was tall but thin. Most of his best football days were ahead of him in California. At the time in Houston, we didn't go to school with the white kids. We pretty much had very little contact with whites at all."

Another native Texan also left to go west to California before the *Brown v. the Board of Education* Supreme Court decision in 1954. Brady Keys hailed from Austin. He claimed to have a different reason for why his family migrated to California in 1952. "I'm from the east side of Austin—1912 East Twenty-First Street," he explained. "I went to Kealing Junior High. My mom worked as a cafeteria worker at L. L. Campbell Elementary, which I had attended. There were a couple of reasons we left Texas. My stepdad, Garland Franklin, went to Los Angeles partly because of work. He got a job in one the foundries there. Once you got to LA, you got into the mix there. You could go to any school you wanted. It didn't matter what your race was; schools were integrated. I attended Polytechnic High School in Los Angeles. It's probably best I left Austin and the east side with its segregated schools. I tended not to fit in with the status quo and I liked to question things. I probably would have gotten into trouble."

Keys then mentioned what he thought was the main reason his stepdad took the family West. "My family moved from Texas because my stepfather, Garland Franklin, was run out of town by some white folks in Texas. During those days, it was common for white folks to plant drugs on black people. The cops would plant things, and they planted something. I can't remember what it was, because I was young at the time. They told him they would give him twenty-four hours to leave. He and my mom didn't wait twenty-four hours; they left in seven. They left because they were going to put him in prison. They left me behind. It was February, and I stayed in Texas to finish out the school year."

John Wooten had a unique case. Wooten, an offensive guard, and a member of the College Football Hall of Fame, played varsity football for the Colorado Buffaloes from 1956 to 1958. He then played nine seasons with the Cleveland Browns from 1959 to 1967, twice being elected to the Pro Bowl before concluding his career with the Washington Redskins in 1968. He was known as the pulling guard that led legendary Browns running back Jim Brown on those fantastic sweeps that often resulted in first downs or touchdowns. Wooten later served as an NFL scout, including sixteen years with the Dallas Cowboys. He presently is chairman of the Fritz Pollard Alliance, an organization that promotes diversity and equality of job opportunities in the coaching, scouting, and front office staffs in the NFL.

He escaped Texas as a youngster when his family left for better economic opportunities and to escape the racism present in Red River County, only to return to face segregation in Texas as a teenager playing football for Carlsbad, New Mexico, High School. In West Texas, New Mexico high schools regularly played Texas schools like Pecos, Monahans, and the El Paso schools. Some New Mexico schools like Carlsbad integrated even before *Brown v. Board* in 1954. Traveling into Texas with an African American player on its team presented a problem for Carlsbad in 1952—for Wooten and his family couldn't seem to get away from racism by moving to New Mexico. They got another dose as the visiting team on a Texas football field.

Wooten recalled the experience. "I was born in Riverview, Texas. It doesn't exist anymore. It was in the northeast corner of Red River County up by the Texas/Oklahoma border. Clarkesville was the closest town. We moved to Carlsbad, New Mexico, when I was two or three. If you knew anything about Texas back then, you would know why we moved. It was a horrible place. We left for better economic opportunities and a better life."

"When we got to Carlsbad, schools there were segregated. I went to the black high school in Carlsbad, Carver High School, until 1952, when I was in the tenth grade. I had gone to Craft Elementary and Alta Vista Junior High, the black schools in town. I would never have gone to Carlsbad High School if not for Superintendent Tom Hansen, Principal Guy Wade, and my coach, Ralph Bowyer. This was over two years before *Brown v. the Board.* In the spring of 1952, these three men called for an assembly at Carlsbad High. At the assembly, they asked the student body, 'Would you be opposed to having Negroes go to your school?' The students said, 'Yes, they can come; we have no problem with it.'

"Integrating Carlsbad High School opened doors for me. I had never played football before. Coach Bowyer was a catalyst. He was a Tom Landry type, who I had worked for years later with the Cowboys. They were both Methodists, the sons of preachers. They both talked and acted like Christian men. What Coach Landry showed me with the Cowboys and Coach Bowyer back in high school was how to be a top quality person.

John Wooten, circa 1956. Courtesy of the University of Colorado.

"Coach Bowyer protected us in high school. He was also our basketball coach. We won state all three years I was there (1952, 1953, and 1954). Coach Bowyer would check out restaurants ahead of time and made sure we ate at places that allowed blacks. He did the same with motels, too. Coach Bowyer said, 'When people stand up for what is right, it becomes right.' Carlsbad is dear to me. The people there gave me opportunities. I would have never made it to college and the NFL without them. I don't want to paint the picture that everything there was a bed of roses, but you can't be bitter about things."

In 1952, after thinking he had escaped racism by leaving Texas as a youngster and then going to integrated Carlsbad High School, Wooten instead jumped headfirst into controversy when Carlsbad scheduled two games against segregated high schools in El Paso. New Mexico high schools from towns such as Carlsbad, Hobbs, and Roswell regularly came to Texas to play. Carlsbad was to play El Paso Bowie High school to open the 1952 season on September 13 at R. R. Jones Stadium. Wooten said, "The people in El Paso wanted myself and my black teammate, Joe Kelly, to stay home. Our school administration told the El Paso people if Joe and I couldn't come, they wouldn't play the game. Well, we played the game, which we won." However, this experience resulted in a change the next time Carlsbad had a game against an El Paso high school. Officials at El Paso's Bowie High agreed to change the venue to Carlsbad. El Paso officials claimed it was because of a conflict with a college game in El Paso that same night.

Then, after the season, the El Paso public school system ended their twenty-year tradition of playing Carlsbad High School. That change in scheduling came in a letter to the Carlsbad superintendent of schools, Irvin P. Murphy, stating that the reason was the desire to confine non-district scheduling to schools in Texas. That wasn't the real reason, of course. Jim Crow was still playing on those Texas football fields. A local Carlsbad businessman had school system connections on both sides of the Texas-New Mexico border. He asked to be quoted directly for a story in the *El Paso Herald Post* on December 10, 1953, stating, "El Paso cancelled the gridiron series because of Carlsbad's insistence to field Negro athletes on El Paso's football fields."

Furthermore, *Herald Post* sports editor Bob Ingram said in his column, titled "EP's 'Color Line' Cause of Break with Carlsbad," dated December 13, 1952: "There's no use trying to camouflage the issue or beat around the goal posts. The real reason for the rupture of the pleasant football relations between Carlsbad and City high schools is the racial problem. Carlsbad has a star Negro player and the New Mexico school wants him to play when the Cavemen come to El Paso. The El Paso school board's long-standing policy prohibits it. The reason for the break isn't the fact that El Paso schools want to concentrate on Texas opposition . . . it's because it's a polite and diplomatic cover-up for the antiquated policies of the school board here."

Like John Wooten, there were other native Texan African Americans who left the state before they completed high school. Besides leaving to escape the segregation and Jim Crow laws of Texas, there were other reasons players and their families relocated.

Some left Texas when they were infants. One such player was Marv Fleming, who played tight end for the Green Bay Packers in the 1960s and the Miami Dolphins in the 1970s. Fleming became the first NFL player to appear in five Super Bowls, two with the Packers and three with the Dolphins. Fleming hailed from Longview, Texas. "I only lived in Longview for two days before we moved to California," Fleming said. "My mom's brothers were already out there and my mom was real close to them, so she moved out there. I'm not real sure if there were any other reasons why we moved. Most likely it was to be with family and to have a better way of life. Getting away from segregation may have had something to do with us leaving, but I'm not real sure." Fleming eventually ended up in Compton, California, and went on to play college football at the University of Utah.

Ironically, there were two other football players from Compton High School in the late 1950s and early 1960s who made it to the NFL, and they also had Texas roots. One was Marv Fleming's first cousin, wide receiver Roy Jefferson. Jefferson was a sophomore at Compton in 1958 when Fleming was a senior. Like Fleming, Jefferson also went on to play college football at Utah. After college, Jefferson was a Pro Bowl wide receiver with the Steelers, Colts, and Redskins. He won a Super Bowl ring with the 1970 Baltimore Colts and played in the 1973 Super Bowl with the Washington Redskins.

"I was born at home at my house in Texarkana, Texas," Jefferson said. "My sister was born in a hospital on the Arkansas side of Texarkana. I think that's why it says I was born in Arkansas, but I really was born in Texas. I spent two years in Texarkana, and then Mom, Sis, and I moved to Oakland. Part of the reason we left Texas was because my dad died. My mom managed a breakfast and lunch place in Texarkana until he passed. We went to California and Oakland because my mom had three brothers living there. Eventually two of them relocated to Los Angeles, and my mom remarried and moved to LA too. We went when I was in the sixth grade. We moved to Watts. In eighth grade we moved to Compton. I'm not sure, but I think part of the reason we left Texas was because of the segregation there. I think the biggest reason, though, was my mom wanted to be close to her brothers because she revered them."

Sandwiched in between sophomore Roy Jefferson at Compton and senior Marv Fleming in 1958 was junior wide receiver Walter "The Flea" Roberts. Like Jefferson, Roberts was born in Texarkana, Texas, and eventually made his way to Compton. After his senior season in 1959, Roberts went to play college football at San Jose State. He then had a six-year NFL career as a receiver and kick return specialist. Roberts was a member of the 1964 NFL champion Cleveland Browns.

"I was born in 1942 in Texarkana, Texas. I wasn't there long, only about six or seven months," Roberts said. "We moved to Mesa, Arizona. We were looking to get out of Texas to have a better life. We settled in Maricopa County. Back then, it was a rural area and a fair amount of blacks lived there. I went to Booker T. Washington Elementary School. Things were segregated in that part of Arizona. I had all black teachers. By the early 1950s, when my younger brother and sister went to school, things were integrated. We went to Bakersfield, California, for a little while when I was twelve or thirteen. Frank Gifford was from Bakersfield. He was my early hero. We felt like we knew him. When we moved to Compton, I would go watch him at USC. When I was a kid, I would sell programs at the Los Angeles Coliseum and usher the games there. I was eventually recruited to play at USC, but I went to Compton Junior College to play for a year, and then I decided to go to San Jose State."

One of Walt Roberts's teammates at San Jose State who got his start in Texas but made a name for himself not in the NFL but in the coaching ranks was Cass Jackson. Jackson grew up in San Jose, California, and ended up playing football at San Jose City College before ending up at San Jose State. A halfback, Jackson played in the Canada pros for three seasons before returning to San Jose State as the freshman coach in 1968. He eventually became the defensive backs coach at San Jose State, and then, in 1973, Jackson made history when he became the first African

American football coach to become a head coach at a predominately white college—Oberlin College in Ohio. In his two years at Oberlin, Jackson compiled a 9–9 record. He is the only head coach at Oberlin in the past eighty-five years to have a .500 or better record. He had other head coaching stops at Morris Brown and Southern University. Art Shell, the first African American head coach in the NFL, said of Jackson, "Thanks to you for helping to open the doors for the Denny Greens, the Ray Rhodeses, the Tony Dungys, and many others who followed in the path that you blazed."

Baseball Hall of Fame member Frank Robinson, who in 1975 became the first African American manager in Major League Baseball, was another who left Beaumont, Texas, as a youngster to move to California for a better life. Reflecting on Cass Jackson, he said, "You were to black coaches as Jackie Robinson was to black athletes. Thank you for paving the way."

Cass Jackson said of his journey to California from Texas, "My family was from Terrell, Texas. We were one of the early families to move from Texas to California. Sometimes circumstances create opportunities or reasons for moving. We were looking for a better life. I was only two years old when we left. My mom had gone to Langston College in Oklahoma. After college, she stayed in Oklahoma and taught school. We eventually left Texas because the segregation was so bad. My mom wanted to get away from there. There was a big migration West by blacks during World War II. There were a lot of jobs in the shipyards. My uncle worked at one in Oakland, and that's how we ended up in San Jose.

"Now I did go back to Dallas one time to visit relatives when I was seven. I remember seeing a drinking fountain in Dallas that said, 'colored.' We didn't have those in California. I thought it was Kool-Aid, and so I tried to drink out of it. I just didn't know any better."

Besides Marv Fleming, Roy Jefferson, Walter Roberts, and Cass Jackson, another African American who left Texas at a very young age was future Dallas Cowboys Pro Football Hall of Fame defensive back Mel Renfro. Renfro was born in Houston on December 30, 1941. "We moved from Texas for health reasons," Renfro said. "My older brother had sinus problems, and his doctors recommended we move to a place with a better climate. We decided to move to Oregon. There was also the prospect for a better job on the West Coast. So we moved when I was only two. I can't say for sure whether the segregation or Jim Crow laws had anything to do with us leaving Texas—not to my recollection anyways. But, to be honest, I've never really asked anyone about it, either."

After starring at Jefferson High School in Portland as a running back and defensive back (the quarterback for Jefferson was future Heisman Trophy winner Terry Baker of Oregon State), Renfro attended the University of Oregon. There he played mostly running back, becoming a two-time All American. He was elected to the College Football Hall of Fame in 1986 and the Pro Football Hall of Fame in 1996.

In Renfro's junior year of 1962, he returned to Texas twice—first to play the Texas Longhorns in Austin on September 22 in their season opener. Oregon lost, 25–13. Three weeks later, on October 13, Renfro returned to the town of his birth, and the Ducks defeated the Rice Owls, 31–12. Renfro had perhaps his greatest game at Oregon. Playing offense and defense, he rushed for 141 yards and a touchdown, caught two passes for 17 yards, and returned a kickoff for 25 yards. On defense, for good measure, Renfro intercepted a pass and returned it 65 yards. During the game at Rice Stadium, which had seen very few African Americans play there, Renfro received applause several times from the home crowd. After the game, Rice Coach Jess Neely said of Renfro, "I don't know when I've seen a better back. He can run, block, tackle, play defense, and he does everything a back is supposed to do."

Since there were still members of the Renfro family in Houston, some of them attended the game. In 1962 Rice Stadium was still a segregated facility, but university officials allowed the Renfro family to sit in the white section at the thirty-five-yard line.

One of Renfro's teammates, Ron Jones, described the trips to Texas. "We were very naïve about the horrible racial discrimination down South," Jones recalled, "so when we traveled to Texas to open the season, it was quite a shock to witness that personally. We had black players on the team, and I remember the day before the game Mel Renfro was with us and was thrown out of a soda fountain. They also weren't going to let Mel and the other black players stay at the team hotel. Our coach, Len Casanova, said, 'If you're not going to let one of our players stay with us, then we are going home.' It was extra special when a few weeks later, we went back to Texas to Houston to play Rice and Mel Renfro had his best game."

Another player who got his start in Texas but moved to California at an early age was Benny Barnes. Barnes ended up in Richmond, California, north of Oakland. After graduating from Kennedy High School in 1968, Barnes went to Contra Costa College before transferring to Stanford University. A defensive back, Barnes played on the Cardinals' Rose

Bowl winning teams in 1971 and 1972. Barnes then played eleven seasons with the Dallas Cowboys, appearing in three Super Bowls, winning a ring with the 1977 champion Cowboys.

"I'm from Lufkin, Texas," Barnes said. "I moved to California when I was six or seven months old. My dad got a job in the shipyards in Vallejo, just up the road from Richmond. A lot of blacks did this—go to the West Coast, a better job, a better life. There was never really an explanation as to why we went to California. Leaving because of segregation and Jim Crow may have had something to do with it. Hey, we ended up in California, and that in the end was OK by me."

Running back Reggie Sanderson was a teammate of Benny Barnes at Stanford and he, too, came to California from Texas. Sanderson came to the Bay Area by way of Galveston. Sanderson graduated from St. Francis High School in Mountain View, just down the road from Palo Alto, the home of Stanford. After his last season at Stanford in 1972, Sanderson spent part of the 1973 NFL season with the Chicago Bears. The reason Sanderson's family moved to California from Galveston was one that most would not suspect.

Sanderson discussed life in Galveston in the 1950s and early 1960s, and explained why his father moved to California in 1962: "There wasn't one set place where blacks lived in Galveston back then. Some lived on the east side; some lived on the west side. We did have contact with the white kids. We would play sandlot ball—football, baseball, basketball. The white kids would bring a team down to play us. We could never play without fighting after the games. It never failed. Some things were separate between the races in Galveston, like the churches. St. Patrick's church was for whites and Holy Rosary was for blacks. Sometimes the congregations would get together for a big event. One time the archbishop came, and we went to see him. We would always meet at St. Patrick's, though. The blacks would then have to sit in a certain section of the church. After a while, when we got older, we began to question those things and notice things—like why did we have to go to the white church? Why did we have to sit in a certain area?

"My dad was a policeman in Galveston. It was one of the few good jobs a black could have back in those days. When I was twelve, though, my dad moved us to California. My dad was a good athlete. Back when he was just seventeen, he briefly played baseball in the Negro Leagues for the Kansas City Monarchs. One of his teammates was Satchel Paige. He moved us to California because he got hooked on golf and wanted to be a golf pro. California was the home of golf, so that's where he wanted to be. When we first got there, he did odd jobs while he was trying to make it as a pro. He also gave golf lessons to help make ends meet. We didn't have much. I have six siblings, two sisters and four brothers. My dad eked out a living. He was pretty much a self-employed golf instructor. In fact, I didn't have my own bed until I went to Stanford.

"When we got to the Bay Area, it was culture shock. I went from an all-black school to an integrated one. In Galveston, the Catholic nuns wouldn't take any shit from us. We would get beatings. In California, the white kids would disagree with the teachers and nothing would happen to them.

"In retrospect, my dad left Texas because he felt the opportunities would be a lot better for himself and his family in California. He was right. Not only did I graduate from Stanford, but so did my youngest and oldest daughters. The old man made the right move."

What Sanderson said rang true for many of the blacks that left Texas to escape Jim Crow and search for a better life. Many did have better opportunities by moving west, mostly to California. For most African Americans living in Jim Crow Texas, however, most did not leave their surroundings for various reasons. After the *Brown v. Board* Supreme Court Decision in May 1954, schools gradually desegregated, presenting new opportunities for black athletes in Texas—potentially, anyway.

4

Integration Year of the Forfeits

*I remember when Yoakum refused to play us that first game . . .
we weren't really angry, just disappointed . . . the whole town was
disappointed.*
—WILLIE JONES, STAR FULLBACK FOR ROBSTOWN HIGH SCHOOL
IN TEXAS, 1955

With Ben Kelly playing football for San Angelo College in 1953, the *Brown
v. Board* Supreme Court decision on May 17, 1954, and the subsequent
integration of the Friona, Texas, school district in the fall, the door opened
for the integration of schools and football programs, not only in Texas but
throughout the South. East Texas and the Houston and Dallas/Fort Worth
areas remained mostly segregated until the mid- to late 1960s. The rest of
Texas varied in its integration, both in grades and level of integration. As
with the earlier African American football players that had to deal with
segregation growing up, this new breed of integration groundbreaker
had to overcome many obstacles when integration came to Texas private
schools in 1954 and public schools in 1955.

Some private Catholic schools in Texas had started accepting black
students and eventually black football players by the fall of 1954–55
school year, the first full school year after *Brown v. Board*. This came
despite the fact that private schools were not bound by the monumental
decision. By the time the fall term began, however, Catholic schools in El
Paso, Marfa, San Antonio, Austin, Fort Worth, and Corpus Christi were
accepting African American students.

One Catholic school, boys-only Corpus Christi College Academy,
admitted four African Americans that fall. Three of them—Charles Wynn,
Freddie Winn, and Timothy Sterling—wound up playing on the football
team. On September 10, the academy opened its season against Freer
High School and lost 46–13. With Wynn, Winn, and Sterling taking the
field against Freer, a Class 2A powerhouse that made it into the state semifinals that season, they became the first African Americans to play against

a Texas public school. College Academy also played games against Donna, San Antonio Edgewood, San Benito, and Laredo Martin that season, while also playing other Catholic schools for their remaining five games.

The three black players for College Academy caused little fanfare among members of the Texas Interscholastic League (TIL), now the University Interscholastic League (UIL)—the governing authority for public school football in Texas. There was a scant mention of Freddie Winn appearing in the Monday, October 25 edition of the *Corpus Christi Caller-Times*, in an article about College Academy defeating St. Edwards of Austin, 28–13. The article said, "Freddie Winn, probably the first Negro to ever play on a South Texas high school team . . . was outstanding on the Cavalier defense."

A couple of Anglo American teammates of Wynn, Winn, and Sterling at Corpus Christi College Academy recalled playing beside them in 1954. Victor Benys was a 172-pound tackle. Benys recalled, "We had a decent team in 1954. We had three black guys on the team and about five on the team in 1955. We had no problems with the guys being at our school or on the team. First of all, the Benedictine fathers wouldn't have tolerated them being treated badly.

"Now, I do remember a couple of problems on the road. A lot of times when we played out of town, we slept in our opponent's gym because that was the only way we could all stay together. In 1955 we went to Brownsville to play, and it was rough. First, people were throwing rocks at the windows of the gym where we were sleeping to keep us awake. Then, I'm convinced someone put a laxative in our food, because a lot of our guys got sick. And then, when the game was over, we had to get a police escort out of town."

Another teammate of the three African Americans was Donald Tansey, who said, "I came to Corpus Christi College Academy from Houston. I went to St. Thomas High School in Houston for part of my freshman year. I cheated on the entrance exams, and they put me in advanced classes. When they found out I couldn't handle it, they kicked me out. I then went to Milby High School in Houston. I got kicked out of there for fighting. My parents ended up sending me to Corpus Christi College Academy, because Houston Independent School District wouldn't let me attend any of their schools. I attended Corpus Christi with a friend of mine and spent my last three years of high school there. The school was a monastery, too, and had full-time students training to be Benedictine monks and then high school kids like me that were boarding there. We had about two hundred students there. There were nuns on-site. They did all of the cooking for us and made sure we stayed in line.

"I ended up playing football, and I was a defensive end and captain of the team. We had three black players in 1954. Charles Wynn, he was a big kid, he was physically gifted—an extremely good player. He was a nice guy too. They encountered no problems at the school. They were accepted by the guys. If you went to that school, you didn't question things. I really can't tell you why there were no problems. I think the leaders at the school wouldn't accept it, and also as Catholics we were taught to be accepting of everyone. There were never any racial tensions. I think another reason was that the students were from all over. There were guys like me, from other places in Texas. There were also a lot of students who were Mexican Nationals, and we had a guy from South America and another from Holland. We all just got along.

"About the only racial problem we had at Corpus Christi College Academy was my senior year. I somehow was coaching the baseball team, and we went to Houston for a tournament. We had a couple of blacks on the team, so we weren't allowed to stay in any hotels. The team ended up staying together at my parents' house."

When public schools and their football programs started integrating in Texas—mostly in the fall of 1955—the town of San Saba in Central Texas and several cities in the Corpus Christi area (Robstown, Refugio, and Sinton to name just three) were among the first in the state to integrate.

Blackshear High School in San Angelo was a school of firsts in the football world. The aforementioned Ben Kelly, the first African American to play college football at a previously all-white school when he suited up for San Angelo College in 1953, was from Blackshear. One of Kelly's teammates and friends at Blackshear was Rommie Loudd. Loudd played at Blackshear until he moved to California in 1950 to finish out high school. After high school, he played linebacker at UCLA, where he helped the Bruins win a national championship in 1954. After college, Loudd played in Canada until 1960, when he joined the Los Angeles Chargers of the new American Football League. After his AFL career concluded with the Boston Patriots in 1962, Loudd became the first African American assistant coach in AFL history when he coached linebackers with the Patriots, starting in 1966. Loudd eventually became the first African American executive in pro football when he was named the

Patriots' director of player personnel in 1968. In 1974, he became the first African American owner in pro sports when he took over the Florida Blazers of the new World Football League.

A third integration trailblazer to attend Blackshear was William Storms. Storms attended Blackshear until his senior year in 1955, before he returned to his hometown of San Saba, Texas, to attend the newly integrated school there. Storms, along with several others, became one of the first African Americans to integrate a previously all-white UIL high school football program.

San Angelo Independent School District integrated in 1955, and Blackshear High School, where integration pioneer Ben Kelly had attended just five years earlier, was shut down and converted into a junior high school. African Americans in San Angelo would now go to San Angelo High School. Once there, however, they were not given the same opportunities as white students. William Storms said, "Many of the black kids who went to Blackshear were like myself, from a town surrounding San Angelo that didn't have a black school, so they were sent to San Angelo to go to school. I was from San Saba, and when they integrated I went back there for my senior year. When schools desegregated, many of those black students went back to their hometown to attend school. Those that lived in San Angelo went to the high school. The ones I was the closest to told me they were separated and sent to different parts of the campus, so they hardly ever saw each other. Only two or three of them got to play sports. It was devastating to them. My one friend, Theodore Donally, got to run track, but he ran into some problems when he couldn't stay in the same hotel as the rest of the team."

Storms's experience once he went back to San Saba to integrate the high school there was mostly positive, with but one exception. "I was born in San Saba," he said. "We lived there for a while, but my dad, a World War II veteran, moved us from there. My mom eventually convinced him to move back to San Saba. The schools were not integrated there yet, and so I went to San Angelo to the black school from seventh through eleventh grade. It was east, over one hundred miles away, so I had to live with my mom's sister there. I wished my parents lived there. I would go home a couple of times a month. I had a family member who was a minister in San Angelo, and he would go back to San Saba a few times a month.

"I had played football at Blackshear for Coach Thomas. I didn't play much as a freshman, but I started as a sophomore and junior. We were pretty good. We played black schools from all over that part of Texas—Abilene, Midland, Odessa, Lubbock.

"When I left Blackshear to go back to San Saba, it was a very difficult thing for me. I lost a lot of friends and relationships. Once San Saba integrated, though, I went home to go to school there. I really didn't want to be at San Saba High School. San Saba was a much smaller town than San Angelo, only about three thousand people, and the school was much smaller. The facilities at San Saba High School were worse than at Blackshear. Blackshear was a newer school. San Saba High School was really old with wooden floors. We had good teachers, though. They did the best they could with what they had.

"For the first couple of months at school, I wasn't a nice person to be around. Eventually I came out of it, though. Things blossomed for me. I got out of my shell, and I developed some beautiful relationships with the people there. The people there were nice to me, and if you think about it, they really didn't have to be.

"Now, football-wise, it wasn't a good year. I wasn't used to losing. We only won a single game on the field." Storms and San Saba, however, did win one game off the field, and it made Texas high school history. The Armadillos had started off their season with just one win in their first five contests, a 13–12 victory over Llano High School on September 23. San Saba was scheduled to play Rockdale High School in their last non-district contest on October 14. Ten days before the game, however, San Saba received word by telephone that Rockdale was planning on cancelling the game. The reason given: San Saba had a Negro on its team. Rockdale School Board President W. P. Spurlock Jr. said the decision "was keeping with the policy of 'going slow' on the integration question."

There was some thought of William Storms possibly not playing in the game. San Saba Coach Ben Hardy put that suggestion to rest when, at a Lions Club meeting in San Saba the Tuesday before the scheduled game, he said, "I will not sideline a boy who works out with the team and is good enough to be out there playing with the team. They will have to play our entire roster or forfeit." Hardy's words were met with a round of loud applause by the Lions Club members in attendance.

San Saba School Superintendent S. G. Boynton then said on October 12, two days before the scheduled game, that, under University Interscholastic League rules, that Rockdale could be forced to play the game as scheduled or meet demands that would make the proposed cancellation acceptable to San Saba. Failure to do one or the other could lead to Rockdale's losing membership in the UIL. San Saba requested that Rockdale pay San Saba $200 for expenses. In the end, Rockdale cancelled the game. The Wednesday after the scheduled game between San Saba and Rockdale on October 14, a check for $100 was received in the mail as forfeit money for breach of contract as a result.

Some of Storms's teammates recalled years later what they remembered about Storms joining the team and the forfeit by Rockdale. John Felts, whose brother Dick was on the coaching staff at San Saba, and after high school went on to play football at Abilene Christian University, said, "I knew William a little bit before he came back to San Saba to play his senior year. We accepted him with open arms. Willie wasn't a star player, but he was pretty good. One thing I remember was an early game we had scheduled at Goldthwaite High School. I remember Goldthwaite had a sign in town that was common in some towns back then, which basically warned blacks to 'don't let the sun set on your ass.' I was kind of worried how Willie would be treated there. Turns out, the town and their players treated Willie really well. It made us feel good.

"As far as the forfeit by Rockdale, I remember the coaches told us that we weren't going to play and explained the reason to us. The coaches were embarrassed that another high school in the state of Texas would do that. It was maddening. We were just kids. We wanted to play ball.

"I really don't remember William saying much about the game being cancelled because of him. I think he, too, was embarrassed by the whole situation."

Billy Don Everett, another teammate, said, "I really didn't know William growing up because he was off in San Angelo going to school. I knew his momma and daddy real well, though. I don't recall being upset that we didn't play against Rockdale. We didn't like it, but what could you do? I do remember joking with William that he won that game for us."

When asked about how he felt about Rockdale cancelling the game, Storms said, "I remember it was at practice and coach was getting us prepared to play on Friday. Coach Hardy said, 'We're not playing the game because of the Rockdale administration.' Word was all over town in less than five hours. I was seventeen years old, and I couldn't believe it. All the other schools we had played up to that point had been very nice to me. Rockdale of all places. Eventually when I went off to college at Prairie View A&M, my best friend was Frank McKee. Our future wives were roommates at Prairie View. Frank was from, of all places, Rockdale. Remember, Rockdale was segregated, and Frank had gone to the black school there, Aycock High School.

"Well, they were a powerhouse that year in the PVIL. They won state in both football and basketball, and Frank was one of the stars of that team. In fact, he was at Prairie View on a football scholarship. When I told him at college about how the white high school in Rockdale had cancelled the game with us because of me, he couldn't believe it. In Rockdale the people there had kept it very quiet. It was never an issue with Frank and me. In fact, we got past the whole thing in about ten seconds."

The African American community in Rockdale in 1955 apparently never got word about Rockdale High School cancelling its game with San Saba because they had a black player on their roster. This incident was a prime example of how the races rarely mixed in southern towns in the 1950s. Billy Ray Locklin was one of the stars on the Aycock football team that won state. Aycock ran roughshod over its Class A competition that fall, outscoring their opponents 629–51 in fourteen games. Included in that run were a 156–0 win over Snook High School, a 104–6 win over the Waco Moore B team, and a 78–0 victory over Lockhart in the playoffs.

Locklin went on to play guard and tackle at New Mexico State, where he was a part of the Aggies' 1959 Sun Bowl championship season. He then went on to a long career in the Canadian Football League, being named three times to the All-Pro team. Locklin said he knew nothing about Rockdale cancelling its game with San Saba. Many years after the incident, Locklin said, "The principals and teachers at Aycock must have kept it from us. We also really didn't have any contact with the whites in town. There is a Bible verse that says, 'People will perish for a lack of knowledge.' That's why I think we didn't mix. The whites didn't really know anything about us or have any kind of knowledge about us or the way we lived.

"Growing up in Rockdale, we never played against the white school, obviously. I do remember one time our coaches at Aycock tried to get a scrimmage against the high school. It was kind of a touchy subject, and the scrimmage never came off. Rockdale was about four or five thousand people back then. The dividing line between whites and blacks in town was the railroad tracks. As far as I know, there was only one black I grew up with who lived on the white side of the tracks, and that was Leroy. About the only time you went to the white part of town was to go shopping. When you spend money, people have no color. We were welcome to go in just about any store because we were spending money.

"We did have to sit in the balcony at the movie theater, and when we went to a restaurant, we had to go to the kitchen to eat. I could never understand that. If you don't trust me enough to sit up in the front of your restaurant, then why do you put me in the kitchen where all the food is? You know, all of this inspired me to become more vicious on the football field. It gave me the drive to play harder and the inspiration to really hit some people. It was all within the rules, though."

The "Leroy" that Billy Ray Locklin mentioned that lived on the white side of the railroad tracks in Rockdale was Leroy Wright, the quarterback on the state championship Aycock football team in 1955 and then the star player on the basketball team, as Aycock won state there too. After high school, the six-foot-nine Wright focused on basketball and played at the College of the Pacific. While there, Wright was the nation's leading rebounder, averaging 25.1 rebounds per game as a junior and 22.4 as a senior.

A second round draft pick of the Boston Celtics in 1960, Wright ended up playing semipro basketball for a few years before catching on with the Pittsburgh Pipers of the new American Basketball Association (ABA) in 1968, and helped the Pipers to the ABA title. The next year, when the Pipers moved to Minnesota, Wright played in ten games and then moved into the role of assistant coach for the remainder of the season. Wright thus became the first professional African American assistant basketball coach during the same period in which Bill Russell of the Celtics was the first black NBA head coach in 1967.

"I came to Rockdale from Rosebud, Texas in 1948," Wright said, "and I went to school in Rockdale from the fifth to twelfth grade. I was part of one of the two black families that lived on the white side of the railroad tracks, which was the north side of town. The blacks lived on the south side. I never really had any problems living on the white side of town. I did have to walk three miles to Aycock every day and pass the white high school on the way. Once again, I had no problems. It probably helped that I walked or ran to school with my three brothers.

"I was pretty much welcome in the white part of town. I could shop in the stores. Our money was just as green as a white person's. We couldn't eat in the café, though; we had to go to the kitchen. The white football and basketball players at Rockdale High used to come and watch us play our games. Even though I lived on the white side of town, I had no idea Rockdale High School cancelled that game way back then because San Saba had a black player."

Some players at Rockdale High during this time period spoke of their reactions to the San Saba game cancellation. Hal Stanislaw, later a head football coach at Cameron and Somerville high schools in Texas, spoke of his experiences. "Growing up in Rockdale," he said, "I had some contact with the blacks. My dad knew all of the black people in town. He owned a service station on the first street out of town, and all of the blacks would come fill up their cars and their tires. I knew all of the guys at Aycock, like Leroy Wright.

"We used to go watch them play on Wednesday nights. There was always a running joke with the black guys. They said they should be the ones getting their names in the newspapers, not us. They probably should have. They won state in football and basketball, and we weren't very good. However, the newspapers usually didn't report the black high school scores in the paper. I really don't remember much in the way of racial stuff in town. To me, there was no bigotry or hate among us peers—it was coming from somewhere else. We used to play sandlot ball against each other. In fact, one of my friends, Billy Buetow, used to go over to the black side of town to play pickup games.

"As far as the game being cancelled against San Saba, I think the people of Rockdale used not wanting to play against a black person to get out of the game. I think if the Rockdale folks thought we could have won the game, we would have played it. It wasn't really racial; they just didn't want to be embarrassed and beaten by a team with a black player on it. We weren't very good. We didn't win a game. We tied Smithville that year 6–6. The only game we won was against St. Mary's of Taylor, Texas. They were a small, private school that we scheduled at the last minute to take San Saba's place on the schedule."

Billy Buetow did frequent the black part of town in Rockdale growing up. Buetow said, "I was nicknamed by the black guys, 'Gray Boy.' It meant I wasn't black or white; I was kind of in the middle. I grew up with the black kids. I used to load watermelons in the summer with the black kids. I would also work the fields with them. My dad used to have a Humble filling station on one end of town that a lot of the blacks would go to. Hal Stanislaw's dad had a filling station on the other end of town.

"I knew all the guys on the team at Aycock High School. There was

Leroy Wright, the first black coach in the ABA, and Billy Ray Locklin—he played football in Canada for a long time. And Mickey McKee, he went to play at Prairie View and had a tryout with the Dallas Texans. Another guy at Aycock was Joe Louis Wilson, a running back. He only had one eye. His mom was a cleaning lady in town. Joe was going to go to Cisco Junior College in Cisco, Texas, to integrate it, but he decided against it and went into the marines.

"I didn't run with the black guys during the week because of the segregation in Rockdale. I would go over to watch Aycock play their football games on Wednesday nights. On Sundays, though, I would go over to the black side of town and play basketball over at the Aycock gym. Sometimes I would bring my best friend, John Yoakum, with me. After a while, I got to know the people in the black part of Rockdale pretty well. A guy named Mr. Robinson ran a diner, and I could get a hamburger there. There was also a lady named Miss Lucy who had a bar in the black part of town. I used to be able to go in there while I was still in high school to drink beer.

"As far as the game with San Saba being cancelled because they had the black player, it was the school board that made that decision. We really didn't have a choice, and there was nothing we could do about it. It was kept quiet by the white community in Rockdale. I never realized until many years later that my black friends didn't know we had cancelled that game because San Saba had a black player."

The forfeit by Rockdale to San Saba because they had an African American player was not the first occurrence of its kind in the state of Texas. During the first week of high school games for the 1955 season, there were a limited number of games throughout the state scheduled for Friday, September 2. One game of interest in the Coastal Bend area was the scheduled matchup between Robstown and Yoakum. Robstown, just outside Corpus Christi, had six African Americans on their roster, including future Purdue all-conference fullback Willie Jones, who also played briefly in Canada and for the Buffalo Bills in the old AFL. Jones was admired and revered in South Texas by both Anglo and African Americans. Bobby Smith, who in 1959 became the first African American to be named first team all-state while a running back at Corpus Christi Miller, said, "Willie Jones was my idol. He was a heck of a fullback."

Jones also inspired a young adult novel written in 1966 by Jim McKone, a sportswriter and later Sports Information Director for Pan

Willie Jones, Robstown High School, 1956. Courtesy of Robstown ISD.

American University in Edinburg, Texas, from 1969 to 1999. While he was still in college at the University of Corpus Christi, McKone was a sports reporter for the *Corpus Christi Caller-Times* from 1954 to 1956, focusing mainly on high school football. He reported on many of the early games that were integrated in the Coastal Bend area. He also knew and wrote about Willie Jones when he played for Robstown. The book McKone wrote was titled *Lone Star Fullback*, which closely mirrored Willie Jones's experiences. In the book, the fullback is named Robert Lee, from the fictional South Texas town of Sangre de Cristo. Lee integrates the Sangre de Cristo football team and leads them all the way to the state finals. Jones said many years after the book was written, "Jim McKone told me after he had written *Lone Star Fullback* that I was the inspiration for the book."

McKone wrote about the prospect of African Americans taking the field against Anglos as the 1955 football season was about to get underway. In the August 21, 1955, issue of the *Caller Times,* McKone wrote, "Something new will probably be added this season. A dozen or more South Texas high schools have desegregated, and racially mixed football has already been approved by the Texas Interscholastic League.

"If integration gets the final OK from the state's school financing, some Negroes appear certain to be playing on some starting lineups in South Texas. Most of the coaches in this area, if not all of them, have said that Negro players would be judged solely by their ability when they came out for football."

McKone then gave a possible reason why so many teams were willing to integrate. Much of it had to do with demographics, or the percentage of African Americans in the general population. "However," McKone posited, "the proportion of Negroes to the total population in South Texas is so small that integration is unlikely to change the overall preseason predictions of which teams are strongest."

Anticipation ran high for the first integrated public school football game in Texas history. Just days before the game, McKone wrote an article about history that was to be made when Robstown and Yoakum collided on Friday, September 2, 1955. His article, titled "Robstown to Make Football History," said, "Texas football history will be made here (Robstown) Friday night. Negroes and whites will play together on a public high school team for the first time.

"Three or four Negroes will be in the starting lineup for the Robstown Cotton Pickers when they tackle the Yoakum Bulldogs in their season-opening game. Ends Louis Smith and George Epps, halfback Floyd Henderson, and defensive tackle Harold Winn will all start against Yoakum. Fullback Willie Jones, who got a late start at practice because he had been working, would also see a lot of action for the Cotton Pickers.

"As a dramatic unveiling ceremony for school desegregation, as well as the kickoff for the 1955 season in the Corpus Christi area, the game is certain to draw a capacity crowd of 6,000."

McKone went on to point out in the article that Robstown Coach Mark Culwell said desegregation had gone over "as smooth as it can be. Our colored boys are popular . . . and they've worked hard and just fitted in.

"The people in Robstown favor the new setup almost unanimously . . . even cafés have agreed to feed other integrated teams, such as Refugio, when they visit here. After progress like this, 1955 may be remembered as the year when the only 'race problem' in South Texas sports became how fast a boy could run the 100-yard dash."

The anticipation and excitement of the Robstown/Yoakum matchup crumbled just two days before the game. Yoakum notified Robstown they would be cancelling their game. Yoakum's school board voted 7–0 on August 31 not to play Robstown. The reason given was that Robstown was racially integrated while Yoakum was not. Yoakum School Superintendent George P. Barron said they had asked Robstown to remove the Negro players from their team. "When they (Robstown) refused, we decided not to play in view of the fact that we're not integrated," Barron said. "They contracted with us over a year ago when they were a white school. They have since become a Mulatto school."

Robstown Superintendent B. C. Banks, in response to Yoakum asking not to play the African American players, said, "Our boys are eligible, and since they made the team, they are going to play."

The Texas Interscholastic League then upheld Robstown's request for a forfeiture and said any other schools refusing to play integrated teams would have to forfeit. The forfeit cost Yoakum a $100 guarantee.

With the last minute cancellation, Robstown tried to schedule a game against the Corpus Christi Ray High School "B" team, but the Texas Interscholastic League refused to permit the game.

Yoakum High School faced the prospect of cancelling at least three other games later in the season. The Bulldogs were in District 26AA, along with Edna and Cuero, who were also segregated, and Port Lavaca, Refugio, and Beeville, who were integrated. Yoakum was scheduled to play Port Lavaca in Yoakum on October 14, at Refugio on October 21, and Beeville on October 28 at Yoakum. Forfeiting three district games would almost certainly ruin any chance to win the district title and advance to the playoffs.

Not coincidently, segregation in District 26AA was geographic in nature, similar to the conditions in the district involving San Saba and Rockdale. Rockdale was 130 miles east of San Saba, closer to the heavily segregated rural areas of East Texas. This represented a trend: the closer a small town school was to East Texas, the more likely it was to be segregated and less willing to compete against integrated schools.

Following this trend, the three 26AA schools closest geographically to Houston and East Texas were Yoakum, Cuero, and Edna—all segregated. Conversely, the three schools closest to Corpus Christi, which was more open to integration because the demographics, were Robstown, Refugio, and Beeville—smaller recently integrated schools that were farther away from Houston and East Texas. And each of these schools had a higher concentration of African Americans.

Superintendents Carl Chilton of Port Lavaca, E. M. Brice of Refugio, and Floyd M. Parsons of Beeville said they would contact Yoakum to see if Yoakum officials would forfeit those games.

After facing the cancellation of these three games and possibly more, the Yoakum school board hurriedly adopted a temporary policy of completing their football schedule in 1955, but announced a future policy that mandated a schedule consisting of only all-white schools—as long as Yoakum High School operated on a segregated basis. The Yoakum board also voted to ask officials of the Texas Interscholastic League to place Yoakum High School "in a district for the ensuing year where the high schools are segregated."

Yoakum did not have a game scheduled for the following Friday, September 9, and on Monday, September 12, the school board met until almost midnight. Parents of nineteen of the approximately thirty players who were on the Yoakum team came to the meeting and differed on what should be done. Nine parents didn't want their boys playing against blacks, seven said they wouldn't object, and three were against it but said they would let their sons decide.

Then, on Friday, September 23, Yoakum Superintendent George P. Barron issued his written, three-page statement that summed up the attitudes of many during that time period. He charged that some football coaches induced integration to add "swivel-hipped" Negro athletes to their teams in hopes of winning a district championship. "There have been two kinds of forced integration brought on by the whites—the economic type of integration and the athletic type," Barron said. Furthermore, he said that the football type of integration was the most pernicious of all because a victory-hungry coach suddenly becomes very considerate of the educational needs of the Negro athlete and induces the superintendent and the school board to integrate the high school, regardless of what the Negroes think about it. "This type of integration is quite successful, for the Negro boys suddenly become captains of the team or president of the senior class in the integrated school," he said.

Barron then commented that the economic type of integration occurred when a school district was either unwilling or unable to provide a satisfactory school for Negroes. He claimed that in such instances, Negroes were forced to go to the white schools and found themselves quite unhappy in an undesirable, unwelcome environment. Then he went so far as to suggest yet a third type of integration—"a free choice deal where Negroes can either go to their own schools or go to a white school." He then claimed that in Austin—the capital city of the Lone Star State—where this system was used, "Only thirteen chose to change from their fine Negro school to the white school."

As for the local system under his charge, Barron said, "In Yoakum, where adequate facilities for the Negro children have been provided, not a child from the colored school has asked to be admitted to the white school."

The Yoakum superintendent then surmised, "There are a bunch of very unhappy Negro boys and girls attending integrated schools. They want to be among their own people where a Negro girl can be crowned queen of the football team. They want to be among their own people where the grid-iron hero can be accosted by his lady love after the game and be awarded a hug and a kiss for his magnificent performance. This is all denied them. They are about as happy as I would have been if I had been sent to school with the Vanderbilts, the Rockefellers, and the Astors."

People in Robstown, both black and white, gave their recollections of integrating Robstown High in 1955, along with what they recalled about the game Yoakum forfeited to the Cotton Pickers.

Raymond Hoelscher, a white player, said, "Nineteen-fifty-five was my senior year, the year we integrated. I had always wanted to play football but my mom would never let me. I finally went out for the team and I really enjoyed it. I was the defensive right tackle. We had no incidents with the black guys. They were such a happy, friendly group of guys. They were very talkative, and they sang all of the time. I was used to blacks already. We used to pick cotton with them. My dad was an electrician and he used to work some in the black part of town. We were happy to get those guys from Solomon Coles—they really helped our team. I used to play alongside Harold Winn, one of the black players. We would pull all kinds of stuff like stunts so we could make tackles and disrupt things.

"I don't remember the Yoakum incident. The reason is I hadn't gone out for the team yet. I didn't play until our fourth game of the year against Kingsville. Although I went out for the team late and I only had a week of practice, I made the lineup."

Another defensive lineman playing alongside Harold Winn and Raymond Hoelscher was defensive end Dale Bullock. He said, "Integrating was quite an experience. 1955 was my sophomore year. It was a good experience, though. I remember when the black players came. Even though Robstown was a small town, we really didn't know them. There was the black side of town and the white side of town, and we pretty much kept to ourselves. When the guys came to the team, they brought a lot of spirit. Everyone benefitted from the experience." Bullock had no recollection of the Yoakum forfeiture.

Jerry Williams was the Robstown quarterback in 1956 when Willie Jones was a senior and led the Cotton Pickers to the state quarterfinals. He said, "I really didn't know about the Yoakum game being cancelled that year. I started out 1955 on the B-team, so I wasn't on varsity yet. I do know we played them in 1956."

Williams did offer opinions about Willie Jones and integration. "Willie was a very fine person. He was popular too. I believe he was voted 'Most Popular' at Robstown High. He was an outstanding player. He never seemed to get tired. Willie was also very well-mannered. In fact, all of the kids that came from Solomon Coles were that way. They were just normal people. We had respect for each other. Race was never an issue.

"I believe integration in Robstown went pretty well. Football and sports was the avenue for us to get acquainted with each other. Robstown was also about 50 percent Mexican American back then. We had gone through integration with them a few years earlier, so it made things a little easier. The city of Robstown also got behind the team and I think that helped too. You know the old saying, 'The last one out of town turn out the lights?' Well, that was Robstown.

"Everything wasn't perfect, though. I remember one time Willie ran about forty yards for a touchdown, and I said, 'Willie, I'm gonna buy you a steak!' The problem was that when we went to go get it, Willie had to eat it in the kitchen. About a year after Willie left Robstown, things were integrated, though.

"Also, by our senior year, before some home games my mom would have the team over for lunch. Everyone was there—blacks, whites, Mexicans. We really didn't think anything of it."

The Robstown quarterback in the integration year of 1955 was Marshall Lawrence. Like the others, he said, "I don't really remember the Yoakum forfeit. I do, though, remember integration. 1955 was our first integration year. I didn't know Willie and the others beforehand—it was a different time. The races didn't really mix. The blacks lived in their part of town, and they still had to eat in the kitchen, that sort of thing. It was a completely new thing for everyone. There were a few minor problems with integration, but nothing huge.

"One incident I remember was in the halls at school one day and Willie, by chance, called a girl 'honey.' He didn't mean anything by it. She was a cheerleader and she came running down the hall and said to me, 'Willie just called me *honey*!' I told her, 'Get over it!'

"Willie was a great player. He had a small waist and huge thighs. The other black guys were great as well. We used to go into Corpus Christi on Thursday nights to watch Solomon Coles, the black high school there, play. The blacks in Robstown played there before integration because there wasn't a black high school in Robstown. They would put on a show.

My center my senior year was Herman Belford, who came from Coles. I'll never forget when we broke the huddle for our first play of the season, Herman, as he was jogging up to the ball to get ready to snap it, turned a somersault on his way from the huddle to the ball. Apparently Herman had done that all the time when he was at Solomon Coles. He had never done it in any of our preseason practices; he waited until the game. Our coach, Mark Culwell, said, 'No more!'

"One time our team went to Austin to go watch Baylor and Texas play football. We tried to go eat at a soda fountain at a drugstore there, and they refused to serve us. We walked out, and we went as a team over to the black part of Austin to eat. There was one other incident. I grew up in the poor part of Robstown. I was out cutting the yard one day, and one of the black guys came by my house. He asked me, 'Can I come up in your yard?' I couldn't believe it. That was the times we grew up in, though. Blacks had to ask permission from whites to do certain things."

Gwen Culwell, the wife of Robstown Coach Mark Culwell, recalled the events surrounding the integration of Robstown High School and the Yoakum forfeit. She said, "When integration happened in 1955, my husband Mark was all for it and was delighted it happened. It helped that all of the boys that came over from Solomon Coles were good kids. And Willie Jones, what a joy he was! It also helped that they were good players.

"I also remember the game Yoakum forfeited. Everybody was quite incensed. Mark started getting anonymous letters. Many of them were ugly. I remember one postcard he received that said, 'Why don't you go coach at a nigger school? You should be kicked.' It was such a hectic time, and it was somewhat of a shock. The one constant positive that year were the black kids and the help they brought to the Robstown team."

Willie Jones had memories of his own, saying, "I remember when Yoakum refused to play us that first game. Our principal said, 'We play the game with our black players or not at all. Let's cancel the game.' So we did. That Yoakum game. We were just so young. We weren't really angry, just disappointed. There was a lot of hoopla leading up to the game. It was a sellout. When I played at Robstown, we always played in front of large crowds, both at home and on the road. We were filling stadiums like never before. So many good things had happened integration-wise up to that point. I was looking forward to playing. The whole town was disappointed. I remember the black community in Robstown didn't protest. They had been part of the hand-me-down system for years, so this was nothing new for them.

"Integration for the most part was good. The schools were segregated. Grade school in Robstown was tough. 'Separate but equal' was not the case. I went to Solomon Coles High School in Corpus Christi my freshman and sophomore years because we didn't have a black high school in Robstown. My junior and senior year, I went to Robstown High School. It was a big step up in facilities for us.

"Overall, integration went well. It was a little awkward at first. It was a small school with a small number of kids. We were accepted. We were a little apprehensive at first. People were amazed at how well integration went. We were kind of the model for Texas for integration. There were a couple of factors, I think. One was we had a lot of Mexican Americans in Robstown, and their integration earlier helped. The other factor was sports. It brought us together. Robstown was pretty dismal in sports before we came."

In Yoakum, people there handled integration and the prospect of having to face African Americans on opposing high school football teams much differently. Mertes Culak, whose late husband, Billy, played on the 1955 Yoakum team that cancelled the Robstown encounter, said, "Billy and I were high school sweethearts. I was there and I went to all the games. After the game with Robstown was cancelled, they played the rest of their schedule, but some of the parents still didn't want their kids playing against blacks.

"What they did was when the other team put black players in the game there were certain players on the Yoakum team that had to come out of the game because their parents didn't want them playing against blacks. It was sad to see them out there every week trying so hard. We didn't win a game. It caused a lot of hardship for the guys who still got to play. Most of the guys on the team didn't care about the other teams having black players. They just wanted to play, and their parents wouldn't let them."

Judy Soehnge's future husband, Charles, was on the 1955 team. She recalled, "There were certain parents that wouldn't let their kids play. The kids said, 'Please let us play!' There were meetings and some parents said no. Any time a black player on the opposing team went into the game, certain Yoakum kids had to go to the sidelines. The other teams figured that out, and they would keep their black players in the game. Most of the time we were shorthanded because of this. My future husband, Charles, got injured one time, and he had a cut on his nose that needed stitches. He had to go back into the game because the coaches had no one else to put in."

Wilbert "Red" Mueller was an all-district tackle for Yoakum in 1955. Mueller said, "It was the school board in Yoakum that forfeited that game, not us. We wanted to play. After the Robstown forfeit, it was decided we would play the rest of our games. Where the players on our team went out of the game when the other teams put black players in, that went on for a while. The teams that didn't have black players on them, we kept those games fairly close.

"Then we played Refugio and Port Lavaca back to back. Both teams had black players. We lost to Refugio 40–0 (African American running back James Lott for Refugio scored six touchdowns), and Port Lavaca beat us 75–0. After the Port Lavaca game, the rest of the parents relented and they let their kids play against blacks. There were still some people that complained after that, mostly some parents. I actually had one person call me on the phone and say, 'You don't want to play against them.'

"I really don't remember much in the way of incidents between whites and blacks growing up in Yoakum. The blacks lived in a certain area of town and we lived in our area. Sometimes I would interact with blacks when my dad would hire some to pick cotton on our farm.

"One time I do remember us mixing was in my sophomore year of high school. I was playing for the basketball team, and our coach had us scrimmage against the black high school in Yoakum. The white parents found out about it and gave the coach some flak. The next day, coach came into the locker room and said sarcastically, 'I brought some extra soap today in case any of them rubbed off on you.'

The cancellation of the San Saba/Rockdale and Robstown/Yoakum games could only slightly delay the integration of football in Texas but could not call a halt to it. Throughout the state in 1955 and beyond in varying degrees all over the state of Texas, schools and their high school football teams began integrating, with the exception of the Houston, Dallas/Fort Worth, and East Texas areas of the state.

That year, however, African Americans found acceptance in some big-city schools and on their football teams in 1955. Like their previous counterparts, they had to overcome many obstacles when public school integration came.

5

The Flood Gates Open

After the game, the Cuero guys walked up to me and Moses Clay and Floyd Robinson, the three black players, and they shook our hands but not the white players' hands . . . They said to us, "If it hadn't been for you guys, we would have won."
—VON FORE, PORT LAVACA PLAYER IN A HISTORIC
INTEGRATED GAME

Although the Robstown/Yoakum and San Saba/Rockdale games were forfeited because of a black player on a roster, there was no stopping the gradual integration of Texas high schools and their football teams from 1955 and beyond. The week after Yoakum forfeited to Robstown, more integration history was made. It happened in the Coastal Bend region during a string of September 9 games. Robstown, the victim of the forfeit against Yoakum the week before, took on Refugio High School, another integrated school. The other game pitted Sinton (integrated) against Cuero High School (segregated). Since there were instances where the African American players were often the only people of their color on the field, they had to learn to adapt to and to overcome the challenges that were thrown their way. Whereas in the segregated part of Texas, African Americans played within the PVIL with its inferior equipment and facilities, early integration opened up new problems.

There had been talk that host team Cuero would forfeit, or that at least players should anticipate problems at the game. But the Cuero school board decided to let the game take place. This South Texas town is located just seventeen miles from Yoakum, home of the previous forfeiture. Residents there shared segregation in common with their neighbors in Yoakum. The Texas Interscholastic League, concerned about potential problems in Cuero, dispatched directors Rhea Williams and Rodney Kidd to witness the game. An Associated Press story said Williams and Kidd were "very satisfied" when they found no sign of trouble in Cuero, especially considering the Pirates shut out the Gobblers

24–0. They were complimentary of the sportsmanship of the football players, the band, and Superintendent E. B. Morrison of Cuero. Kidd and Williams reported "no incidents involving the Negro players," who saw action about 50 percent of the time. Sinton coach Murray Stephenson also reported, "There were no incidents due to the Negro players."

The Pirates had two African Americans: defensive tackles Treilis Smith and Willie Reed. Kenneth Varnado was a teammate of Willie Reed at Sinton. He said, "I knew Willie. I had very little contact with blacks in Sinton before we integrated because they lived across the tracks on the south side of town. Willie was huge. Everybody loved him, though. We didn't have any racial tensions. I think if there had been racial tensions in Sinton, we wouldn't have integrated. About the only thing I remember segregation-wise growing up, there were a couple of restaurants on Highway 77 in Sinton, The Steak House and the J&A Café. At both of those places there was a window out back where blacks could order food. That's just the way it was back then."

Another Sinton player who knew Reed and his black teammate Treilis Smith was quarterback Billy O'Barr, who recalled more than six decades later, "There ended up being eight blacks in my graduating class. I found out later that East Texas didn't integrate until the late 1960s. We were a lot earlier than that. I used to go over to the black school before we integrated

Willie Reed, Sinton High School, 1955. Courtesy of Sinton ISD.

and watch Willie and the other guys play. Willie was a big guy. He was not only a good football player but an excellent shot putter. He was second at the regional meet in Kingsville, and he made it to state. I remember sometimes we would go places and they didn't accommodate us. We couldn't eat at certain places because Willie and Treilis were on the team.

"Now Treilis Smith was not as big as Willie. He was about five-foot-eleven, and Willie was about six-foot-three. Treilis, though, was one of the strongest athletes I've ever seen. Being a defensive tackle, he would play right over the center on the other team. He had unbelievable strength. I do remember playing Port Lavaca that year. It was a 13–13 tie, and we ended up going to the playoffs. They had an integrated team too."

The positive reports from the Sinton game did not absolve the Gobblers of incidents against other integrated teams that season. Willie Jones of Robstown discussed the problems he faced playing at Cuero. Jones said, "I got kicked out of the game. Their players were rough—they were punching me and gouging me after they tackled me. After a while, I learned to get up quick to avoid that stuff. One time late in the game I jumped up and the referees accused me of jumping up and being aggressive and trying to start a fight. That wasn't true.

"Nonetheless, they kicked me out of the game. They threw a flag on me and tossed me. I found out years later the referees and my coach, Mark Culwell, did it on purpose. They got together to get me thrown out of the game on purpose to protect me. So, in reality, I really didn't get thrown out of the game. I was pulled out. Coach Culwell told me this at our class reunion forty years later."

Gwen Culwell, the coach's widow, confirmed Willie Jones's account: "It's true what happened at Cuero, Willie being 'ejected' from the game. I was there in the stands. My husband Mark and the referees got together to get Willie thrown out of the game so he would be protected. When Willie got kicked out, I remember the Cuero fans were furious."

Floyd Robinson also reported there were problems when his integrated Port Lavaca team played at both Cuero and Yoakum. Robinson said, "The south side of Port Lavaca was for blacks. There really weren't any problems in 1955 when we integrated the high school. Most of us kids had grown up and worked together. We worked the cotton fields. We all knew one another. Guy Hays was our football coach. He always said, 'If you can play, you can play.' I was fifteen when we integrated. My parents didn't let me get involved with a lot of the issues facing us back then. I only recall one incident at Port Lavaca High School. A non-football player called my teammate Ray Leonard the 'N' word. They got into a fight in the halls.

"There were a couple of incidents at away games that first year in 1955. One was at Yoakum. They hadn't integrated there. We beat them 75–0. They took us off their schedule after that. After the game, we couldn't go to any of the restaurants. We had to eat our hamburgers on the football field after the game. When we played Cuero at their place, they were also still segregated. When we were playing, you could hear the crowd. I scored all of our touchdowns that game. I think we won 38–7. You could hear them in the stands chanting, 'Stop the nigger, stop the nigger!'

"There's a couple of other incidents I remember. We also played at Refugio that year in basketball. They had integrated their school, but Ray Leonard and I couldn't eat in the dining area of the restaurants in town. Our coaches were good about it. They asked, 'Would it be a problem eating in the kitchen?' Ray and I didn't mind. So we ate in the kitchen.

"Now Victoria, which was less than thirty miles northwest of us, didn't integrate for another seven or eight years. When I was a senior in 1957, we played them, and they were favored by thirty points. I ran for ninety-something yards, and we upset them 13–6."

Moses Clay was an African American teammate of Floyd Robinson at Port Lavaca. Describing some of his integration experiences, he said, "I was a senior in 1956. We didn't have any real problems when our school integrated. At Yoakum we didn't have any problems. When we played at Refugio, though, we had to eat in the kitchen at the restaurant.

"I also ran track. I went to Austin to state in the 440 relay. I couldn't stay in the motel with my white teammates. I stayed in the black part of town.

"Now, growing up in Port Lavaca, I wasn't the kind of guy that ran the streets. I pretty much stayed at home and stayed out of trouble. At the picture show in town, we had to enter through a side door and go up to the balcony. There were no bathrooms up there. If we had to go, we went to the local filling station that had 'colored' restrooms.

"We also didn't get to go to the soda fountain in town. There were some 'colored' drinking fountains in town. I remember there was one in the old courthouse. There was also a whites-only fountain in there too. Sometimes we would cut through the courthouse and sneak a drink from the white fountain."

Another African American who integrated the football team at Port Lavaca was Von Fore. He also spoke of Cuero, but in a slightly different way. He also spoke about race relations and the positive effects of school integration in Port Lavaca. He said, "I remember going to Wilkins Junior High and High Schools, which were the black schools, up through my freshman year in 1954–55. Then in 1954 the order for integration came to Port Lavaca.

"So for my sophomore through senior years starting in the fall of 1955,

I went to Port Lavaca Calhoun, the white school. We were for the most part well received. At that time, there was not a lot of animosity and conflict and craziness in Port Lavaca. It was nothing like it was up in Arkansas in Little Rock. We used to read *Ebony* and *Jet* magazine, and they would tell all about the conflicts going on in different parts of the South. What I was reading about in those magazines was nothing like what we saw and experienced in Port Lavaca.

"One thing that eased my transition was my English and speech teacher, Pat Ulrich. She got married to one of the coaches there, and she became Pat Fogarty. She gave me a lot of support. My senior year was when they tried to integrate Little Rock Central High School.

"We were in the library one day, and I saw a copy of *Look* magazine with a photo of Little Rock on it and the title on the cover, 'What's Happening in Little Rock?' She said to me, 'Why don't you give your speech about what's happening in Little Rock? I believe this is something that you can speak on. You could talk about the problems they're having up there that we're not having in Port Lavaca.'

"I was the only black kid in my speech class out of about twenty-five or thirty students. I ended up giving that speech, and it was well received by the other students. Giving that speech is one of the best things that could have happened to me. Mrs. Fogarty was a great supporter of us. She also taught theater, and when my younger brother came through Calhoun, he was the first black thespian.

"Myself, Moses Clay, Ray Leonard, and Floyd Robinson were all accepted on the football team. We had a great time. Let me tell you about the kind of relationships we formed back then. I live in South Carolina, and in October 2015 we had some bad weather roll through the state. I was on the golf course a couple of days later, and I get a phone call. It's from my old quarterback from Calhoun, David Denham. He said to me, 'Hey, Von, it's David Denham. I saw on CNN you guys are having some problems there. Do you need any help?' That was the type of relationship we had with most of the white players. It's sixty years later, and we're still looking out for each other.

"I guess about the only negative with integration football-wise was the black players not getting many opportunities to play ball in college. Floyd Robinson went and played at Paul Quinn College in Waco, but that was about it. We had some really good black athletes, like Ray Leonard, who never got a chance.

"Integration hurt us in that area. I guess that was true all over. The problem was that at Calhoun we didn't have our black coaches that we had at Wilkins to help us get scholarships. The white coaches at Calhoun didn't really help us or support us in regard to getting us into colleges to play ball. I think part of that stemmed from the fact that they had contacts with coaches at the white colleges like Texas A&M, where we weren't allowed to go. They really didn't know anyone at the black colleges like Prairie View. I don't think the coaches didn't not help us on purpose; they just didn't know how to.

"As far as any problems at any of our games, when we played at Cuero, who didn't have any blacks on their team, we did have an incident. There were some thoughts about Cuero not playing the game because we had blacks on our team. We ended up playing, and we beat them at their place by a point—I think it was 13-12. We had a tough time getting in the end zone that night. We were fighting the officials along with Cuero. There was some rough stuff during the game too. When the Cuero players would tackle me, they would use my head and push it into the ground to help get themselves up. I would say, 'Hey, ref! Did you see that?' The referees would say, 'Just play ball!'

"Well, after the game, the Cuero guys walked up to me and Moses Clay and Floyd Robinson, the three black players, and they shook our hands, but not the white players' hands like David Denham. They said to us, 'If it hadn't been for you guys, we would have won.'"

Although Robstown High School had their September 2 game against Yoakum cancelled because the Cotton Pickers had Willie Jones and other African Americans on their team, the following Friday they played in a historic game in Robstown against Refugio. Refugio, about forty miles northeast of Corpus Christi and Robstown, had also integrated their schools in 1955. When the two teams met, it was the first fully integrated high school football game in Texas public school history.

Refugio integrated when it closed Barefield High School after the *Brown v. Board of Education* Supreme Court decision in 1954. Four African Americans from Barefield ended up playing for Refugio in 1955: running back James Lott, lineman Kennard Rydolph, guard Murray Wills, and halfback Johnny Youngblood. The Refugio Bobcats ended up beating Robstown on that historic night 28–7, en route to a perfect 10–0 regular season.

Coach Paul Gips and some of the former players made observations about integrating Refugio and playing for the Bobcats. Gips said, "I had an idea of the caliber of players that were going to join our team from Barefield. I had watched them play the year before in a segregated game, and I was impressed. We were just delighted to have the black players, and we tried our best to make them feel at home. We had twenty-three kids from Barefield come out. After a week, though, nineteen of them had quit. I always worried about that. James Lott later told me, 'It wasn't your fault. They just weren't used to working like that.'"

Kennard Rydolph said, "There was some opposition to integration at both Refugio and Barefield. Some people were just resistant to change no matter where they were at. I didn't have a problem. Some others carried baggage with them, though."

James Lott was the star running back for the Bobcats in 1955. He had the distinction of being the first African American player to be named the *Corpus Christi Caller Times'* "Player of the Week" when he ran for 116 yards on thirteen carries and scored three touchdowns in Refugio's 27–18 win over Sinton on September 16, just a week after the Bobcats integrated the Coastal Bend when they played Robstown. Although Lott later scored six touchdowns in a game against Yoakum and five in a game against Beeville, Lott was left off of the all-state teams at the end of the season. He ended up playing college football at New Mexico Highlands University and is a member of their athletic hall of fame.

James Lott said, "Getting named 'Player of the Week' was a big deal because at Barefield we didn't get a lot of publicity. When we got to Refugio, there was a change of pace in terms of publicity. They were friendlier when we were at Refugio.

"The races did mix in Refugio before the schools integrated. We would play against each other in sandlot games when we were growing up. Some things were segregated, though. The movie theater and restaurants were segregated. There were 'colored' water fountains. I didn't get that concept when I was a kid. I thought 'colored' meant the water was colored, like there was Kool-Aid in the fountain.

"At Barefield we had good teams. We pretty much played the black schools in the area in the towns that had them: Beeville, Cuero, Kenedy, Karnes City, Gonzales, Yoakum, and Sinton. I think having those good teams at Barefield was a factor in the schools integrating in Refugio.

"Refugio High School could have been a model for integration. Everyone—kids, teachers, coaches, administrators—embraced it. I had a great senior year. We had a great team. I was treated real nice by the opposing teams. There was no racial stuff, no name calling. People were respectful. When we played Nederland in the playoffs that was the only exception. We lost to them. Bum Phillips was the coach. When we went to Nederland to play, we had to stay in a 'colored' hotel in Beaumont, about fifteen miles away."

The Bobcats rolled through the regular season undefeated. Their first playoff game was to be in Bay City against a Black Cat team that was still segregated. The Bobcats hung on for a tense 21–20 victory, but the game took its toll on Refugio's star player. James Lott was hammered constantly, and he said, "I was elbowed in the face; I got a concussion."

There were opposing views about why the Black Cats targeted Lott. Ken Rydolph said, "Everything was racially motivated. All the teams gunned for Lott. They didn't go after us because we were on defense, but they went after Lott."

Johnny Youngblood believed it was a mix between Lott's race and his star status. "It was a little of both," Youngblood said, "but I think they mainly wanted to get him out of the game."

The injuries Lott sustained against Bay City, including a likely concussion, kept him out of the following weeks' playoff game against Nederland, just fifteen miles southeast of Beaumont in deep East Texas. It was there the Refugio Bobcats got their first real taste of racism. Nederland was considered to be what was known to African Americans in the South in the mid-twentieth century as a "sundown town." It was estimated there were up to ten thousand sundown towns throughout the United States, predominately in the South, during this time period. A so-called sundown town were communities that formally or

James Lott, Refugio High School, 1955. Courtesy of Refugio ISD.

informally kept out African Americans for decades. They were so named because many of these towns had signs posted in town that would say something along the lines of, "Nigger, don't let the sun go down on you in our town."

Traveling by automobile throughout the South during this time period could be perilous for African Americans, so much so that in 1936 an African American mailman from New York City, Victor H. Green, published a book titled, *The Negro Motorist Green-Book*. The book advised African American motorists on which towns were "sundown towns," along with information on which white-owned businesses would refuse to serve them. Green published this book every year until 1966 to "give the Negro traveler information to keep him from running into difficulties and embarrassments, and to help make his trip more enjoyable."

In the days before the game, the Refugio team received threats from Nederland. Ken Rydolph remembered them well: "They told us, 'Don't bring your niggers because we won't be responsible for their safety.' They said, 'If any niggers run for a touchdown, they'll be shot.'"

With those words ringing in the Bobcats' ears, the Refugio coaches could not find accommodations for the team. There was talk the game might be cancelled. However, two assistant coaches from Barefield who made the trip found a place for the four black players to stay in Beaumont.

Rydolph said, "The game was played, and you could hear the people in the stands yelling 'Nigger!' all the time. They won, but only because James Lott was hurt."

"We were always treated nice up until the Nederland game," Lott recalled. "It was a lot different than what I was used to. You could hear things while I was standing on the sideline. It was an odd situation. That was my first time experiencing blatant racial hatred. I prayed and forgave them, though."

Eltra Youngblood, widow of Johnny Youngblood, said, "Johnny was at Barefield High School in 1954, the year before Refugio integrated, and he graduated in 1957. I graduated from Refugio in 1960. When the school integrated, the student body was integrated but there were no black teachers. Some of the black teachers went to towns in the area that still had black schools, like Goliad, Victoria, and Solomon Coles in Corpus Christi.

"Integration went fairly well for the students. However, like a lot of the black teachers, a lot of blacks left Refugio and went to towns that still had black schools. Some people weren't ready to face integration. Out of the fifty or so blacks that were in my grade at Barefield, only five of us graduated. The educational system in Refugio was good. There was nothing a student wanted or needed. Refugio County was a rich county—there was lots of oil and gas there.

"I can't remember any incidents on the Refugio football team. They all got along. Refugio was and still is a football town and people liked to win. School integration was definitely helped along by football. We had a good team that first year of integration. We were undefeated until we played Nederland in the playoffs. That was about the only place the players were treated badly. The coaches had to find a place for the team to eat and sleep since they couldn't stay in Nederland. We ended up in Beaumont. There were some other times I knew of where the coaches had to make eating arrangements for some road games so the team could eat together.

"Things could have been much worse in Refugio, considering how early we integrated. We had a close black and white community. Some things in Refugio were segregated: the theater, the water fountains, and we couldn't go to the country club. My mom worked for the district attorney cleaning his house and taking care of their kid. She later worked for the superintendent of schools."

The Corpus Christi and Coastal Bend region of Texas had one other historic integration game in the 1955 season. Although Corpus Christi ISD integrated that year, Solomon Coles High School, the black high school in Corpus Christi, remained open until the late 1960s for African American students who wanted to continue to go to an all-black school. On Friday, August 24, 1955, Corpus Christi ISD Athletic Director Chatter Allen reported that Solomon Coles had entered into a contract with Corpus Christi College Academy to play a game at Buccaneer Stadium on November 16. It would mark the first time an all-black school would play a predominately all-white school on the Texas high school football gridiron. The Corpus Christi school board had decided on August 8 that this game could take place. The school board also said that Coles was authorized to contract a game with any school willing to play them.

On that historic November 16 evening at Buccaneer Stadium, Corpus Christi College Academy trounced Solomon Coles, 20–0. Quarterback Manuel Maldonado was the star for College Academy, scoring all three touchdowns for the Cavaliers. The *Corpus Christi Caller Times* recounted in its game story, "College Academy blanked Solomon Coles, 20–0, at Buc Stadium last night in a game that marked a milestone in intracity football history. Some 4,000 fans turned out for the first 'mixed' meeting between the College Academy Cavaliers and Solomon Coles Green Hornets."

Surviving members of both teams recalled the game sixty years later. Victor Benys of College Academy said, "I remember playing Coles. We had a pretty good team in 1955. They were big. I was a 172-pound tackle, and I remember the guy that lined up across from me was about six-foot-six, 205 pounds. (Coles did have two players that size, six-foot-six Willie Floyd and six-foot-seven Johnny Walker.) We had five black players of our own on our team, guys like Freddy and William Winn. There was a decent crowd at Buc Stadium. I don't remember there being any problems with any of the fans or anything."

Willie Harper of Solomon Coles said, "We got our ass tore up. Our coach had told us before the game, 'No white school is going to beat ya'll.' He was wrong. I remember they had a bad-ass lineman who only weighed about 125 pounds. I remember one of the black players for College Academy, too—Tim Sterling. He was a bad boy! There were no problems during the game. Afterwards it was nice and we shook hands. There were no riots; everything worked out."

Lacy Garcia, another Coles player, agreed with Willie Harper. "There were no problems whatsoever at our game with College Academy. I remember Freddy Winn was one of their best players. Although we lost 20–0, it was a good contest. I remember shaking hands with them after the game. You just did that, win or lose.

"You know," Garcia continued, "that's not the first time we had played against whites. Well, officially it was. We had actually scrimmaged some other white high schools in the area, like Corpus Christi Ray High School."

In 1955 there was one more school that featured an integration pioneer in the Coastal Bend. Sophomore Sherwood Thompson integrated Kingsville King High School. Kingsville, home of Texas A&M–Kingsville University (previously known as Texas A&I, 1929–93), is about forty-five miles southwest of Corpus Christi; it was a town of about twenty thousand in the 1950s.

Thompson helped pave the way for other African Americans in Kingsville, including the legendary running back James "Preacher" Pilot, who besides leading Kingsville High School to the 1958 state Class 3A finals, led the NCAA in rushing in 1961 and 1962 while playing for New Mexico State. Thompson spoke of his days in Kingsville: "I was the first black player at Kingsville King High School in 1955 when I was a sophomore. Kingsville was a little town. Most of the blacks lived in the same neighborhood. I knew Preacher Pilot. It didn't matter the time period; he would have been great in any era. He ran a 9.8 hundred-yard dash at the state meet as a sophomore in 1957.

"We all went to Frederick Douglass High School in Kingsville. Even after integration, the school stayed open until 1969. Some of the kids came over to King High School from Douglass. Most of those kids didn't make it. There was a lot of attrition. Just about everyone dropped out and joined the military.

"Growing up in Kingsville, the races were absolutely separate. As a black, you knew your place. You knew better than to cause trouble. You didn't make demands anywhere. At restaurants we had to eat in the kitchen; at movie theaters we had to sit in the balcony. We had four soda fountains in drugstores in Kingsville. We couldn't go to any of them and sit down and have a snack. You could go in, order, pick it up, and leave.

"We had a football team at Douglass, but we would only play about five games a year. When we did integrate, there was a large number at first who went out for the team. Like I said, there was a lot of attrition. One problem was when they started trying to verify ages for the black players. A lot of them were too old. Even though a large number went out, it went well for the most part. There was some preplanning before the schools integrated, and the new changes were met with an open mind.

"One thing that really helped happened a couple of years before integration. It was a preparatory thing. In 1953 the Lions Club brought Little League baseball to Kingsville. The league was integrated right off the bat. It did more than anything to help with integration of King High School a couple of years later. We all knew each other from playing ball against each other. I think it also helped make the decision easier for the school district to integrate pretty quickly after integration came in 1954.

"In football, I started as a sophomore," Thompson continued. "I made my reputation as a defensive back. By the time I was a senior, I was a running back. In 1956 and 1957 we had good teams. I thought we had the chance to go to state both years.

"I really didn't run into too much in the way of problems from opponents and fans. There was nothing major. Some things you came to expect, though. It was manageable. The UIL handled things pretty well. I thought the officials at the games didn't let things get out of hand, either. I remember we did go into one town to play, and there was some name-calling before and after the game. All in all, it was mostly a positive experience."

While the Corpus Christi area of Texas was a trendsetter in integration in 1955, it was not the only part of Texas undergoing this transformation. About 150 miles to the northwest, formerly segregated San Antonio schools, like many Coastal Bend schools, were also opening their doors to African Americans.

6

The Alamo City Breaks Down Doors

If you want to move ahead, you have to integrate and assimilate.
—ED THOMAS, FIRST AFRICAN AMERICAN FOOTBALL PLAYER AT
SAN ANTONIO JEFFERSON HIGH SCHOOL, 1956

*Sometimes I think integration did a lot of interfering with our
progress. Our teachers, schools, and traditions were taken from us.*
—CLARENCE WHITMORE, FIRST AFRICAN AMERICAN FOOTBALL
PLAYER AT SAN ANTONIO BRACKENRIDGE HIGH SCHOOL, 1956

Besides the Coastal Bend area of Texas, the other major metropolitan
area that integrated its schools in 1955 was San Antonio, which was
more progressive than other parts of the state. For example, just eighty
miles away in Austin, the high schools there remained segregated well
into the 1960s.

Although San Antonio schools integrated in all grades for the 1955–
56 school year, no African Americans stepped forward to play football at
any all-white high schools. Wheatley High School, the black high school
in San Antonio, remained open until 1970. African Americans in San
Antonio thus had to choose whether they were going to play at their orig-
inal school, where many of their family members and friends had previously attended, or attempt to become an integration pioneer.

Two football players who decided to stay at Wheatley in 1955 were
Hensley Sapenter and Trusse Norris. After completing his Wheatley
career, Sapenter went on to play center and linebacker at Prairie View
A&M University, where he is a member of their athletic hall of fame. He
later came back to coach at Wheatley and eventually was athletic director for San Antonio ISD from 1976 until 1995. He returned to Prairie
View as their head football coach in 1995 and 1996.

Sapenter described growing up in San Antonio, the progressive
nature of the city, and when the schools integrated. "Believe it or not," he
said, "the group I grew up with in San Antonio or me personally never

experienced the segregation and hypocrisy of other parts of the nation. San Antonio was unique. Everything was available to us there: movies, groceries, businesses. I didn't experience the things I saw on TV, that I saw in other parts of the country. It wasn't until I got to college at Prairie View and I had teammates from East Texas that I realized things were bad in certain parts of Texas, too. They would tell me stories of what it was like growing up there.

"I grew up in the Denver Heights area of San Antonio, which is adjacent to the East Side. It's close to downtown San Antonio. It's around where the Alamodome is now. I lived on Dakota Street. When we first moved there, the neighborhood was kind of mixed. Tommy Nobis grew up on the East Side. He eventually went all the way across town so he could attend Jefferson High School, where he could play football. As more blacks came in, more whites moved out.

"I remember in the mid-1950s at the end of my junior year. I was going to the black high school in San Antonio, Wheatley. At the end of the school year, they called all the students together for an assembly. The administrators said that the law had changed and that schools in San Antonio were going to be integrated in the fall the next school year. We were free to attend any high school we wanted to in San Antonio ISD. The program was called 'Freedom of Choice.'

"If we wanted to go to a school on the North Side, we could. That's how Tommy Nobis got to go to later on to Jefferson High, which is the northwest part of town. So in the fall of my senior year of 1955, I could have gone to an integrated school. I actually ended up being a midyear graduate, as I graduated in December of 1955.

"Although I could have gone to any high school in San Antonio and help integrate it, I stayed at Wheatley. A lot of my friends chose to remain there too. There were a variety of reasons. First, it was the closest school to our neighborhood. Second, some just didn't want to be integration pioneers. And third, there was a lot of tradition at Wheatley. For example, my staying at Wheatley was a family thing. My father graduated from there in 1935. He and my mom were some of the first graduates from there. We heard all about the school and its traditions growing up, and that's what we locked in on."

Hensley Sapenter mentioned the legendary Tommy Nobis. At the time, Nobis had a star-studded future ahead of him. He starred as a linebacker for the University of Texas, where he won the Outland Trophy as a senior in 1965. In 1966, he was the first overall NFL draft pick by the Atlanta Falcons, and went on to play in five Pro Bowls. Nobis took advantage of "Freedom of Choice" in the San Antonio ISD, a privilege available to every student, not just African Americans. The great linebacker cited the following reason for attending Jefferson High School: "I lived on the east side of San Antonio. Jefferson, where I went to high school, was on the Northwest side. I was a good example of 'Freedom of Choice.' I actually lived close to Wheatley High School on the east side. I got to associate with all types of people, black, Mexican, and white on my side of town growing up, and that helped me because I learned how to get along with everyone.

"When it came time for high school, however, I chose Jefferson. Everyone knew I wanted to play in college, and Jefferson had one of the best football programs in the city to go along with their strong academics. My parents liked Coach Pat Shannon and the fact that he ran a disciplined program. So I rode the city bus for three years to Jefferson every morning. My dad, even though he worked on the other side of town, would drive across town every day to watch me practice and then take me home. We definitely sacrificed to go to Jefferson. It was tough times, but good times."

Trusse Norris also grew up on the East Side and was attending Wheatley in 1955 when San Antonio schools integrated. He said, "We didn't have that much interaction with whites where I grew up. I did have some contact with some Hispanics. We had our own black-owned businesses in our part of town. We would go downtown to do some shopping, too. San Antonio wasn't as mean as some cities back then. I think being a military town helped.

"My family had come from California to San Antonio. My dad actually grew up in Houston and got out of there to go to college at the University of Michigan. He hid away in a dining railcar to get out of Texas and went to Chicago and then caught a bus to Ann Arbor. He ended up going to California and went to USC to get his PhD. He then went to St. Phillips College in San Antonio to teach sociology there. That's how we ended up in San Antonio. He ended up being dean of the college.

"I decided to stay at Wheatley High School to play football and graduate. My older brother had played there. After he graduated, he went back out to California and went to Pasadena Community College and then on to UCLA where he played on their 1954 national championship team.

After high school I followed in his footsteps as I played ball at UCLA too. Things were more tolerant in California back then, and even now."

Many great African American athletes did continue to play sports at Wheatley over the next few years. They included future Houston Astros player Clifford Johnson, Kansas City Chiefs defensive back Willie Mitchell, who played in the first Super Bowl, and track and football star Clyde Glosson. Starting in 1956, however, African American high school athletes stepped forward and started to integrate the San Antonio school district in addition to other school districts in Texas.

Thus, while much of Texas remained segregated in the mid- to late 1950s, the Alamo City became a pacesetter in school desegregation. Playing for the Brackenridge High School Eagles in 1956 was Clarence Whitmore, while over at Jefferson High School, Charles Brown and Ed Thomas integrated the Mustangs' football program. Whitmore, Brown, and Thomas faced the task of attending school in a totally different environment, and each player had his own set of challenges to overcome, which they reminisced on over sixty years later.

Playing end for Brackenridge, Clarence Whitmore went on to play college football at Texas Southern University in Houston. Because San Antonio had adopted "Freedom of Choice" in 1955, where students could choose the school they wanted to attend, Whitmore chose Brackenridge, not Wheatley. He described growing up and becoming an integrating pioneer in San Antonio: "I grew up on the east side, which was one of the black areas of San Antonio. I went to a segregated elementary school and I went to Frederick Douglass Junior High. Our schools were behind with some things, like equipment and books. Things were separate but they weren't equal. We didn't venture into the white neighborhoods.

"Luckily, the teachers at our school were very concerned about us and our education. They wanted us to go on and be a success. They lived in our neighborhood and knew our parents. We and the teachers enjoyed each other. We had just about everything we needed on the east side of San Antonio. My father owned a liquor store. There were doctors, lawyers, drug stores, movie theaters. We weren't dying to integrate. Sometimes I think that integration did a lot of interfering with our progress. That's what we used to call it—'interference' instead of 'integration.' Our teachers, schools, and traditions were taken from us.

"Our parents had a different set of eyes. They were more aware of the conditions and kept us from certain unpleasant things. We were aware of some things, like integration and *Brown v Board of Education*. The neighborhood helped raise the kids back then too. You couldn't go around acting stupid like kids do today. If you did something wrong, one of the neighbors would beat your butt, and then when you got home your parents would beat your butt.

"I played football at Douglass Junior High. I had some great coaches there. Three or four of them made All-America at their black colleges. Our head coach had been an All-American at Prairie View. They really taught us fundamentals. It made the transition to go to Brackenridge easy. I was ahead of other players in that regard. I wanted to help integrate. It was my love of football that made my transition to Brackenridge easier. It could have been a lot worse. It was not like Mississippi or Alabama. I thought about going to Wheatley, the black high school, because we had a choice as to where we wanted to go to school. I ended up going straight from junior high to Brackenridge.

"I do remember my first day of practice at Brackenridge someone taped 'nigger' on my locker where my name should go. I went and said to the coach, Augie Erfurth, 'Is this what I have to put up with?' He replied, 'Boys will be boys.' Needless to say, though, stuff like that stopped. After the first few weeks, things got better.

"I was not the first black athlete at Brackenridge. In the spring of 1956, a guy by the name of Melvin Houston lettered in track. I lettered in football in the fall of 1956. There were probably twenty to twenty-two black students that first year at Brackenridge. It turns out I became friends with one white kid, Dennis Smith. I didn't have many white friends. He taught me how to throw the discus.

"I do remember the first game I played was in Austin, against Austin High School. We beat them 14–13. What I remember most, though, is that my parents traveled to Austin to watch me play, but they had to stand outside the stadium and watch the game through the fence because of segregation in Austin.

"Another thing I remember about that season was that we also traveled to Houston. We played Sam Houston High School, and we lost 13–0. I was the first black to play against an all-white team in Houston. It was mentioned in an article about the game in *The Houston Post*.

"The next year, 1957, I decided to help integrate the new high school in San Antonio, Highlands. Highlands was Class 4A, which was bigger than Brackenridge, which was Class 3A. I was interested in playing

better competition. It was all right at Highlands. I had a few white friends by then. Some
white guys at Highlands still held onto the way
things were back then."

Charles Brown integrated the San Antonio Jefferson High School football program,
along with Edward Thomas, in the fall of 1956.
Brown came to Jefferson a semester before
Thomas, enrolling in January 1956. Thomas
then came in the fall. Brown and Thomas proceeded to help the Mustangs to three straight
district titles in the years 1956, 1957, and 1958.
Brown eventually became an all-city lineman

*Charles Brown, San
Antonio Jefferson High
School, 1958. Courtesy of
San Antonio ISD.*

by 1958, his senior season, helping lead the Mustangs to a 10–2 record
and a trip to the Class 4A state quarterfinals.

Brown provided a thoughtful oral history of growing up on the west
side of San Antonio and attending Jefferson High: "I grew up on Kentucky Street on the west side of San Antonio, just north of Culebra
Street. It was a mixed neighborhood. My house was two doors from the
corner. If I turned left from my front door, it was all-white and Hispanic. If I turned right, it was black. If you crossed Culebra Street, it
was all-black. Growing up, I couldn't go to school with my best friend,
Carlos Medina. We were able to play together after school. If we went
to the movies, we couldn't sit together. I had to sit in the balcony with
the other blacks.

"I went to the black schools on the west side of San Antonio, Grant
Elementary, and then Dunbar Junior High. It was right after I finished
Dunbar that the Supreme Court decision integrating schools came along,
and since I could attend any San Antonio high school I wanted to, I made
up my mind I was going to Jefferson. My counselor recommended I go
there. I was a good student. A lot of the other black students went to Fox
Tech. That was the school you went to in order to learn a trade.

"Jefferson was considered the top high school in San Antonio at that
time. What helped me decide I wanted to go to Jeff was that I worked
at a neighborhood grocery store catty-corner from my house that was
owned by a Jewish family. I would make deliveries for them. Even though
I wasn't old enough to drive, they let me drive around and make deliveries for them. They had several clients around Jefferson High School. I

would drive around the school and admire the old Spanish architecture. It was beautiful. I decided I wanted to go there.

"Like I said, I enrolled as a freshman at Jefferson in January of 1956. I went out for football as a sophomore in the fall of 1956. I never had a problem being accepted by my teammates at Jefferson. I was never aware of any animosity from a white teammate. There was one time after the end of practice we were all in the locker room and one of the white players called out, 'I'm as sweaty as a nigger!' Coach Shannon, the head coach, called him in his office and set him straight.

"When we traveled, Coach Shannon made sure Ed Thomas and I were taken care of. We traveled to places like Abilene, San Angelo, and Austin. Coach Shannon insisted we all stay in the same hotels and eat at the same restaurants. With our trip to Austin, though, we had to stop and eat in San Marcos first, because they had integrated some restaurants.

"I never experienced any problems at games, either from opposing players or from fans. I wasn't called any names or anything like that. I'm sure things were uncomfortable for some people in the stands, but I never heard anything. I ended up having a good three years at Jefferson. I was All-City defensive end and offensive tackle. We won district three years in a row and lost to Corpus Christi Miller in the quarterfinals in 1958. They beat us 40–25. They had a great black running back by the name of Bobby Smith. There's a couple of other things I was really proud of at Jefferson. I was treasurer of the senior class, and I was the second black inducted into National Honor Society at Jefferson.

"After high school, I had a couple of opportunities to play football in college. I talked to Arizona and Colorado State. None of the black colleges in Texas talked to me. I ended up going to St. Mary's College in San Antonio. I joined the ROTC program there, and I ended up staying in the military as a career."

Ed Thomas helped integrate the Jefferson football team along with Charles Brown in 1956. Unlike Brown, who grew up in San Antonio, Thomas's early years were spent in segregated Taylor, Texas, 125 miles northeast of San Antonio, and he moved to the Alamo City in 1955 at age fifteen. Some sixty years later, Thomas talked about growing up in segregation in Taylor, and then moving to an integrated San Antonio and playing for the Jefferson Mustangs.

"I was born in 1940 in Taylor, Texas, and I lived there until I turned fifteen and we went to San Antonio. In Taylor, all the blacks lived in one community on the west end of town. It was a close-knit part of town. It took a village to raise a kid back then. You could get a butt-whipping from your neighbor for something you did wrong, and then get another one when you got home.

"We never really had any contact with other white kids, though. I had a few Hispanic friends. Taylor had about eight thousand people back then. We had a Caucasian police officer, Ned Fells, who watched over our black community there. There was no real hatred between the races in Taylor. We were conditioned to the environment. Most people in Taylor did farm work. Corn and cotton were the main crops. I remember at age seven I started going to the fields to work. There would be a trailer behind a pickup truck, and we would put the cotton in that. I decided pretty early on I wasn't going to pick cotton for a living.

"I didn't grow up being bitter. I just thought our environment was the way things were supposed to be. We were content with the way things were because we didn't know any better. Like being poor. We didn't really know we were poor. My grandma used to tell me when she disciplined me, 'I'm whipping you now so the white man won't whip you later.' I found out years later what she was talking about. In the military there were a lack of promotions and opportunities for me. Also, from 1959 through 1965, I never served with another black soldier.

"I went to a segregated elementary and junior high in Taylor. I went to the black high school, Blackshear, for a little while before I moved to San Antonio. Our educational system in Taylor was good. We had black teachers teaching black students. When I moved to San Antonio and went to integrated schools, I was far advanced academically.

"We ended up in San Antonio because my grandmother was starting to get sickly and my mom was living in San Antonio, so we went there. We lived on the west side of town close to Culebra Street. The climate of San Antonio as far as accepting and implementing integration was changing when I moved there in 1956. The city bus system required that you transfer your route downtown near Houston Street and the Alamo. There was a five-and-dime store, F. W. Woolworth, where the kids would meet up. The store had separate counters with African Americans on one side and whites on the other. One afternoon, a group of African Americans decided to sit on the white side of the soda fountain. The facility was integrated the following day.

"We lived on the west side of the city. The nearest swimming pool for

African Americans was on the east side of San Antonio on Pine Street. The nearest public pool for us was Woodlawn, which was for whites only. One afternoon, a group of African Americans from the west side decided to jump into the Woodlawn pool. All of the white people got out of the pool. The next day Woodlawn was integrated. I never thought about what or who was the driving force behind these places deciding to integrate. There must have been a plan in place to react to such spontaneous acts.

"I went to Dunbar Junior High, the black school, for a little while in ninth grade. After ninth grade I had to make a decision on which high school I wanted to go to. It was 1956 and because of integration, we had the Freedom of Choice plan in San Antonio schools, so we could choose where we wanted to go to school.

"If you want to move ahead, you have to integrate and assimilate. We had to get past the institution of racism and segregation, and by me going to Jefferson, it eased any intimidation of going against people of other races. The experience gained at Jefferson removed any physical or intellectual intimidation learned from institutional racism. High school football was the perfect starting point.

"During the initial integration of high school football in San Antonio, there was no pressure to integrate teams. You were able to get on a city bus with your bus pass and attend the school of your choice. I had to choose whether I wanted to go to Wheatley, the black high school, which was a smaller Class 2A school. Coach Carrol, the Wheatley coach, wanted me to play guard, even though I was the second fastest player on the Dunbar Junior High team. Jefferson was a larger Class 4A school, and I had the opportunity to play running back. I lined up with the running backs at tryouts, and as it turned out, I made varsity in 1956.

Edward Thomas, San Antonio Jefferson High School, 1958. Courtesy of San Antonio ISD.

"Wheatley started losing a lot of football players to other schools, so they enacted a restriction that only students from Wheatley could attend their social school functions. My girlfriend and future wife of fifty-seven years went to Wheatley. This was an issue across the board for other players. Jefferson welcomed students from other schools to attend our social functions.

"During this time, there was some concern that some African American football players would become involved with some white female students. This was something that was voiced but not preached. I was not aware of any issues with white female students and African American football players while I was at Jefferson.

"I endured two racial incidents while playing for the Jefferson Mustangs. The first incident occurred early on with the team. It may have been our first game away from San Antonio. I was the only black player on the team. We stopped in San Marcos to eat, and as I was entering the restaurant, a man at the door held out his arm and blocked my entrance. I ate my meal on the school bus. The next week, the Jefferson principal came down to our practice field and apologized for the incident. He told me that it would never happen again. Later that week, I was interviewed by Channel 5 News. They inquired about my experience in San Marcos and how I was being treated at Jefferson. After the incident in San Marcos, wherever the team went, so did I.

"I know that some places we visited were not integrated because other than the hired help, I was the only African American present. The look of astonishment on their faces upon seeing me was amazing. Then you would see them give me a subtle smile.

"The second racial incident involved a player on San Antonio Burbank's team. He used a racial slur toward me. The next play provided me the opportunity to run over him and put my cleated football shoes into his chest. Respect was gained, and I didn't hear another word out of that player the rest of the game.

"As far as my teammates, some of them called me Black Angus because of my running style, which was to run over you rather than around you. I didn't care for the name, but I tolerated it. I did have one fight with a senior teammate my first year at Jefferson. It was a part of a hazing ritual. It involved putting analgesic balm on an inappropriate place on your body. I wanted no part of it.

"Playing on the Jefferson team was sort of like working at a job. After practice and games, we went our separate ways. We attended school functions together. This was a new day, and our relationships seemed to be based on ability and respect for the game of football.

"Case in point: my exercise partner in football was Ronnie Driver. Ronnie and I spent a lot of time together doing two-man exercises. I never communicated with Ronnie outside of football practice. Ronnie just happened to be from Alabama. He was paired up with me and did what was required of him. When we graduated, though, Ronnie wrote in my yearbook, 'Edward, thanks a lot for changing my mind about a lot of things.'

"After I graduated from Jefferson in 1959, I didn't receive any scholarships to play football. I was approached by one of the coaches who asked me if I was interested in playing at UCLA. I declined because of my lack of resources for college. I ended up joining the army because jobs were difficult to obtain for African Americans. Eighty percent of the help-wanted ads in the San Antonio paper requested Anglo applicants. I applied for the San Antonio Police Department. I was told that I had 'failed the physical.' I was a high school athlete in top physical shape. When I joined the army not long afterward, I passed their physical easily.

"When I think about some of my other black teammates like Charles Brown and John Jason Wilborn, there must have been some type of divine guidance in our chosen path when it came to Freedom of Choice and deciding to attend Jefferson High School. We were not cherry-picked to participate in the Freedom of Choice program or to integrate the football team. It all just happened to work out. Someone or something was looking out for us."

In spite of progress being made in cities like San Antonio in the mid-1950s, much of the state was still mired in the same segregation patterns of the previous decades. Separation of the races was still the norm in cities in the eastern part of Texas, while black schools still received inferior supplies and equipment in the classroom and on the football field.

However, in 1956, a new glimmer of hope appeared at the college football level—two more colleges, one a two-year "juco" and the other the first four-year Texas college to integrate its football program.

Charles Brown, #38, and Edward Thomas, #26, San Antonio Jefferson High School. Courtesy of San Antonio ISD.

7

Colleges' Integration Pains and Victories

Get them niggers off the field!
—NAVARRO JUNIOR COLLEGE FANS WHEN ABNER HAYNES AND
LEON KING ARRIVED IN CORSICANA TO PLAY THE BULLDOGS IN 1956

The year 1956 was a landmark period for the integration of Texas high schools and colleges. Besides the San Antonio Independent School District's integration of its high school football programs, two Texas colleges took the desegregation plunge three years after Ben Kelly integrated college football in Texas and the former Confederate states when he suited up for San Angelo College in the 1953 season.

Cisco Junior College, in Cisco, Texas, forty-five miles east of Abilene, integrated its program en masse with five players from Abilene Woodson High School, the black school in that West Texas city. And just north of Dallas in Denton, North Texas State University became the first four-year institution in Texas to admit African Americans into their football program when Abner Haynes and Leon King joined the squad out of Dallas Lincoln High School.

Through the years since these historic events unfurled, Cisco Junior College has seen far less notoriety than the larger North Texas State. One of the five players from Abilene Woodson who enrolled and played football at Cisco was quarterback Robert Kelley, who was older than the other four players, which included younger brother, Louis, a fullback. The elder Kelley had spent his freshman season playing at Southern University in Baton Rouge. Robert Kelley decided to join Louis and the three others to attend Cisco. Those three were end E. A. Sims, tackle Ira Black, and guard Otis McLin.

Out of the five players that integrated Cisco in 1956, Louis Kelley is the only surviving member. After he left Cisco, Kelley went on to New Mexico State, where his senior year of 1959 he was captain of an 8–3 Aggie team.

In 1961, Kelley embarked on a long coaching career. He was the head football coach at Lubbock Dunbar High School from 1970 to 1974, where he fashioned a 30–19–1 record. From 1975–2000, Kelley was the head coach at Lubbock Estacado High School, where he had a 202–85–8 record. His 1983 Estacado team made it to the Class 4A state finals, the last Lubbock team to do so. Kelley was voted West Texas Coach of the Year eight times. In the year 2000, Louis Kelley was voted the Lubbock "Coach of the Century" by the *Lubbock Avalanche-Journal.*

It originally appeared that Louis Kelley would follow his brother Robert to Southern in the fall of 1956 to play football. Kelley recounted the decision-making process: "My brother Robert, who was a year older than me, was playing football at Southern University in Baton Rouge. I ended up getting a scholarship there too. I stayed about a week. I had done pretty well football-wise. I started out as the number six fullback, and by the end of my week, there I was up to second team fullback.

"There was something about it I didn't like, though. The year before when I visited my brother, there were girls on campus. This time when

Louis Kelly, circa 1955. Courtesy of Louis Kelley.

I was there in August of 1956, I noticed there weren't any girls there. I said to myself, 'This isn't good, no girls.' So I decided to call Cisco Junior College about letting me and my brother Robert play there. They were happy to have us, so we left. Little did I know the next day that the rest of the student body, including all the girls, arrived on campus for the fall semester. I said to myself again, 'What have I done?' Cisco had already sent us train tickets, though, so off Robert and I went to Cisco. My parents didn't even know we were coming back home close to Abilene. We hadn't told them. They had to read about it in the paper.

"I experienced no racial problems on campus at Cisco. The school had just integrated. I really didn't think anything about being among the first to integrate. We just did it. The coach at Cisco, Arnett Weeks, let us know up front that we would be the first black players there.

"I really don't know why the five of us were chosen to integrate the football program at the same time. It probably had something to do with Abilene only being about forty-five miles from Cisco. I think part of it also had to do with the fact that we were pretty good football players. Cisco only won one or two games before we got there. Our first year at Cisco, I think we won seven games. I do know Coach Weeks recruited us hard to come to Cisco. He had offered me a scholarship before I went off to Southern with my brother.

"The five black players kind of lucked out. Instead of staying in the dorms like everyone else, we all got to stay in some duplexes off campus, which were close to where the coaches stayed. That was good because the dorms on campus were ratty."

Split end Jerry McWilliams was a white teammate on the 1956 Wranglers. After finishing playing football and basketball at Cisco, McWilliams finished his college education at North Texas State University. He later became a high school football coach, rising to be head coach at Meadow, Trent, and Henrietta high schools. His sons Jay and Chris were also head football coaches at McCamey High School in West Texas.

Years later, Jerry McWilliams recalled that historic 1956 football season. "I don't think segregation and then integration was as big of a problem in Texas as it was in some of the other southern states. We welcomed the black players. We didn't think much about it. Even though the campus was now integrated, it was still kind of segregated. I remember the black players stayed in housing close to where the coaches were. We had to stay in Bivins Hall, one of the dorms on campus. It wasn't much then. It's still there on campus and is being used as a girls' dorm, I think. I went by campus not too long ago, and I noticed that on the front of Bivins Hall, it says it was built in 1927.

"One of the other black players I got to know was Ira Black. We actually roomed together on our first road trip to play the military team at Fort Hood in Killeen. Our coach issued the room assignments, and he put me with Ira. Ira was a big guy for back in those days. He was about six-foot-four and 240 pounds. Ira and I talked about the situation nonchalantly before we left. We agreed it was a different feeling for both of us, but in the end it was no big deal. It was the only time I roomed with one of the black players.

"Another thing I remember was that none of the black players had a car. Me and a couple of buddies of mine from my hometown of Trent, who were also going to Cisco, would give them a ride back to Abilene sometimes. Trent is about twenty-two miles west of Abilene, so it was no problem dropping them off. There was one time when we went to drop the Abilene guys off when one of them invited us into their house to have a Coke. This was the first time in my life I had ever been in a black person's house. It was a nice, well-kept house. When my friends from Trent and I left to go home, we were saying to each other, 'There's something different about that house.' We finally figured it out. All of the pictures on the walls of that house were of black people. We had never seen that before."

On the playing field, however, the Wranglers did face some problems. Two of their games that season were cancelled due to the fact Cisco had black players on its roster. Not surprisingly, the two cancelled games were from Texas junior colleges in East Texas, where segregation and Jim Crow still prevailed.

The first cancellation was when Blinn Junior College in Brenham, about sixty miles west of Houston, cancelled its October 6 home game with Cisco. Blinn administrators said the reason was that Cisco had Negro players. Blinn President Dr. Thomas M. Spencer said the school board formulated a policy that competition for the Blinn College athletic teams for the school term of 1956–57 would be limited to schools whose athletic teams are composed of all white participants. The game went into the books as a 1–0 forfeit win for the Wranglers.

Later that season, Texarkana Junior College on the far northeastern border of Texas cancelled its November 1 home game against Cisco. Once again, the reason given was that Cisco had African American players.

Because of this cancellation, Cisco Junior College rounded up a scrimmage game against the Hardin-Simmons College freshman team out of Abilene. They played the game in Cisco.

Neither Louis Kelley nor Jerry McWilliams could recall any racial tensions at any of their games. However, both remembered one postgame incident where the black players were refused service in Corsicana, home of Navarro Junior College. Kelley said, "The restaurant wouldn't let us eat with our teammates. We left and went back to Cisco. Other than that one time, I really don't remember any other times we were treated badly."

McWilliams had a slightly different version of the incident. He said, "On the road, we only ran into a problem one time. We were somewhere like Blinn or Navarro College and the team went to eat after the game. I guess we had about sixty or so on the traveling squad. We went to a local restaurant to get some chicken fried steaks. When we arrived, the owner said the white players could come through the front door and eat, but the black players had to go around to the back. Our team captain went up to the owner and said, pointing to our black players, 'If they don't come through the front door, then none of us will.' To say the least, we all got to go through the front door to get our meal."

Also in 1956, at North Texas State College (now the University of North Texas) in Denton, forty miles northwest of Dallas, the football team and school made history when the first two African American players suited up for the Eagles (now Mean Green). This marked the first time that African American football players took the field at a four-year college in Texas and, for that matter, the South: Abner Haynes and Leon King from Dallas Lincoln High School, located on the city's south side. Haynes, a running back, and King, a receiver and punter, grew up as best friends from the same neighborhood and decided they were going to attend college together.

In the summer of 1954, North Texas State had accepted their first black student in school history into the doctoral program. Tennyson Miller was principal at Port Arthur Lincoln High School in Southeast Texas. Miller had previously taught at the black high school in Denton. Although he was accepted into the graduate school program, this graduate student was not allowed to live on the North Texas campus.

When the school actually integrated, school president James C. Matthews did not want media coverage of the event, for fear it might cause unrest on campus and in Denton. The Dallas–Fort Worth area media didn't initially report that Tennyson Miller was now attending classes. Not even the black media filed a story until later on.

President Matthews knew integration was now inevitable at North Texas State with the acceptance of Miller and the passing of *Brown v. Board of Education* in the months shortly before. Matthews and the Board of Regents decided on a plan that would desegregate the school gradually: black graduate students in the summer of 1956, seniors in the fall of 1956, juniors in the fall of 1957, sophomores in the fall of 1958, and freshmen in the fall of 1959.

However, in the fall of 1955 a young African American by the name of Joe Atkins filed suit to be admitted as a transfer student. The district courts agreed with Atkins, and he and other blacks wanting to attend North Texas State were admitted. Matthews decided to obey the law to the letter and said, "The court order was not debatable." As with the admittance to North Texas State of Tennyson Miller in the summer of 1954, when black undergraduates were admitted to North Texas in February 1956, Matthews kept publicity to a minimum by forbidding television stations from carrying the event.

Meanwhile, resistance to integration was wearing down at other colleges. The courts ruled that Texas Western College in El Paso open its doors to blacks. The ruling held forth at Texarkana Junior College as well. The University of Texas at Austin also decided to admit black undergraduate students. Through intimidation and sometimes violence, colleges such as Texarkana and Lamar State College in Beaumont refused the admittance of African American students.

But North Texas had little of the racial strife found on other campuses. In the summer of 1956, two black coeds moved into the previously all-white dorms. Two years later, there were 133 blacks attending North Texas. The school and the city of Denton did not see the violence witnessed on other campuses. Besides President Matthews not drawing publicity to integration, Denton's locale seems to have been a major factor that eliminated major race-related problems. Texarkana and Beaumont are located in East Texas, which history shows was a more prejudiced section of the state. Denton formed a geographic triangle with Dallas and Fort Worth—both only about forty miles to the south. Denton more resembled racially tolerant West Texas rather than the more racially edgy East Texas. Denton also did not have a history of racial violence.

This formed the backdrop for the stage used by Abner Haynes and Leon King to integrate the North Texas State College football program in the fall of 1956. Haynes had already spent a lot of time growing up in Denton because his father, Fred Haynes, had established St. Andrew's Church of God in Christ there in 1922. After preaching in Denton for many years, Fred Haynes had earned the respect of both the black and white communities.

As a child in Denton, Abner Haynes roamed freely through town, had black and white friends, and generally experienced a happy childhood there. He later recalled, "I could run around in Denton, and I didn't have to fear the white man was going to hurt me."

However, in the seventh grade, Abner Haynes and his family moved to Dallas. His life changed from the freedom of Denton to the rigid segregation of Dallas. "Segregation," he said, "was a world in itself. You had to learn early as a black child how to avoid the traps. For example, there were things you just didn't do to stay out of trouble. The police didn't want us gathering on the street corner, just hanging around. They would yell at us, 'Don't stand on the corner!' We would avoid a trap like that by not doing it in the first place.

"When we moved to South Dallas, black kids knew they could only go so far. We weren't allowed to go past Forest Avenue. That was right where the Cotton Bowl was. It was eight blocks from South Avenue, where I lived. We weren't allowed to go to the State Fair or football games at the Cotton Bowl. Sometimes we would dodge the police and sneak into the football games."

Haynes met Leon King at Lincoln High School. They became close friends, which led to their decisions as juniors at Lincoln to attend the same college together. After they both received scholarship offers to Wiley and Prairie View, Haynes turned them down because of the lack of quality facilities at both campuses. The University of Colorado offered Haynes a scholarship, but not King. Haynes put off the decision as long as possible to avoid a potentially sticky situation.

Right about this same time, Fred Haynes became ill, and the family encouraged Abner to choose a college closer to home. Abner's older brother Sam, who Abner looked up to and admired, suggested he try North Texas State College. The two visited there, and Abner was offered a half scholarship. Eventually Leon King was also offered a half scholarship. When the offer for Abner Haynes to play football at Colorado dried up because he waited too long to give them his decision, he and Leon chose to attend North Texas.

Haynes credits his father in the decision-making process. He said, "Once Colorado wanted me to go there, that was where I wanted to be. I wanted to get out of the South. My dad, though, was the one who made me see the people of Denton were different. He said, 'Abner, can we get you interested in going to a college in the South? You can change things in the South by going to North Texas.' I said, 'No!' The message, though, was that it wasn't about just me. My dad said I could do this, and if I did, we could have blacks and whites playing together all over Texas. He also thought Denton was the perfect place to do it because our family was known there. Daddy said, 'No one's going to hurt you because you've grown up there—they know you.' I also went to North Texas to inspire younger kids. That's why I did it.

"My dad also said since the people of Denton knew me," Haynes continued, "if I went to Colorado, it might take five or six years for them to know me up there, and by that time I'd be gone. He felt I could have a bigger influence on kids in Denton and in Texas, since I was from there. Once Daddy explained that to me, it all started to make sense.

"I really did want to go to Colorado. I'd been up there on a recruiting trip. My older brother was at the University of Denver, plus I had other relatives there. I also had relatives in California. Actually, it was my cousin Sly Stone's dad who went out there. Apparently back in Denton he got caught with a white woman, and he was run out of town. Sly and his mom and dad moved to Vallejo. About half the family moved out to California with him. As I was getting out of high school, Sly started making records. He was one of the first to have an integrated band—Sly and the Family Stone.

"The point is, to escape segregation growing up, my dad would send us to visit our relatives in California and Colorado. We'd get a chance to live in an integrated society. I liked it. So when Colorado offered me that scholarship, I jumped at it. However, with the advice of my daddy and family, I decided to attend North Texas State."

When Abner Haynes and Leon King walked on to the football team at North Texas State in the fall of 1956, there was relatively little fanfare. The Associated Press ran a story on September 1, 1956, with the headline, "2 Negroes Try for NTSC Team." The article said, "For the first time in the school's history, two Negro players were among the freshmen bucking for a spot on the squad. Leon King and Abner Haynes turned out for the first workout and are shooting for an end and halfback position, respectively." Other than that short AP article, there were no other mentions of the integration of the North Texas State football team.

To prepare for the arrival of Haynes and King, head coach Odus Mitchell sought the advice of President Matthews. Matthews informed Mitchell that any African Americans who showed interest in the football team should be given a fair chance. And the college had no choice but to let them try out for the team, according to the law. Matthews added, though, that the coaching staff would decide whether Haynes and King made the team or not.

Abner Haynes remembered, "What I learned was that the president of North Texas, Dr. Matthews, was not necessarily a liberal who was trying to help blacks. He said us attending North Texas was the law, and he was going to abide by it."

For the most part, coaching Haynes and King was left to assistant coaches Ken Bahnsen and Fred McCain. Abner Haynes said, "Coach Bahnsen, he delivered. At first, I was out there struggling with the freshman team, and then he showed up. It was like night and day after he came, as to how I was treated. Fred McCain, the other coach, he was great, too. His wife Mary was a wonderful woman. They treated my mother and sisters great. Those two showed me it's not the color of the skin; it's the character—it's integrity. You know, every time I ran into a problem someone stepped up to help me—whites, blacks, men, women. I got help I didn't know existed.

"I'll give you another example of how people helped me along the way. What brought me to playing football was my family and my four older brothers. F. L. and Sam played ball at Prairie View. I used to watch them, and they put the time in with me. They developed me, and that's how I got exposed to athletics. My brothers helped me, and it set the tone for the rest of my life.

"There were some people on campus who wanted me there, and there were some who didn't want me there. But what I also saw was other people who didn't look like me tried to encourage me to go to class and things like that. I learned not to worry about the people who didn't want me there. You don't have to party with them; you can hang out with people that like you. I hadn't thought of that. I thought everyone was against me at first. I found out that's what someone wanted me to think—and they wanted me to react to it."

Reaction by the team was mixed. Some saw it as a nonevent and took it in stride, some showed some slight resentment, and others were hostile to the idea of playing alongside an African American. The most vocal freshman Eaglet to Haynes and King was Mac Reynolds, an end who hailed from the Northeast Texas town of Marshall. Reynolds said years later, "I didn't like it. This was our school, and it was white, and it had a white football team. They had theirs to go to if that's what they wanted. Hell, if they wanted to play football, they could go to Wiley or Southern. As far as I was concerned, he [Haynes] was a nigger. Not a Negro but a nigger." About Leon King, Reynolds said, "Leon was an end. Hell, I didn't want no nigger coming in and getting my position."

For the most part, however, Haynes and King were accepted by their new teammates. Charlie Cole, brother of freshman quarterback Vernon Cole, told his brother, "They're people just like we are—the only thing we need to worry about is if they can play football." When Vernon Cole first met his new African American teammates, he greeted them with a handshake. The rest of the freshman Eagles followed suit.

Vernon Cole, the quarterback from Pilot Point, just a few miles northeast of Denton, was the unquestioned leader of the freshman team, and his leadership and influence continued through to the senior season of 1959. Acceptance began with the quarterback offering that first handshake. Ken Bahnsen said, "Vernon Cole was the reason the team accepted Abner and Leon. If Vernon hadn't accepted them, it's very possible the team may have turned their back on them. Vernon had the respect of everybody on that team and every other team he played on at North Texas. Nobody questioned integration once Vernon accepted them."

Not that things were totally easy for Haynes and King. During the first contact drills, they were objects of cheap shots, many of them courtesy of Mac Reynolds. Later, in the showers, Reynolds let his animosity be known when he said to Haynes, "By God, I ain't showering with no nigger!"

Haynes and King had to gain acceptance from their new teammates with their performances on the field. Haynes was the early star of the team with his work at running back and defensive back, while King showed skill as a receiver and punter. Once their teammates realized these two fellow players would help them win games, they were accepted by their teammates within a week.

This was evidenced by the transition of the racial attitudes of Mac Reynolds. He said, "There was no question who the best running back was. [Haynes] gained our admiration and respect by being a great athlete. When [Abner] scored a touchdown, he was helping you as a team member, and you appreciated it."

Most importantly, Reynolds's overall attitude changed before the season was over. He said, "I guess I grew up more on the racial thing in a month or two months of the football season than all the other times put together. We'd been around Abner and Leon long enough that this didn't bother us. The black and white thing was gone, as far as me not liking Abner, not showering with him. Hell, he was a friend of mine by that time, not just an acquaintance. I considered him a friend."

Another problem that arose for Haynes and King was the living arrangements. Since they were not allowed to live on campus, they had to walk to and from school from the black section of Denton, some two miles away. King said, "It was a hardship not to live on-campus. We really didn't know what college life was like."

When football season was over, things worsened. Haynes recalled, "Without my teammates around, all of a sudden my life was nothing. I'd go to school, I'd go to class, and I'd walk back to the black part of town."

The much-anticipated first game for the North Texas freshman team was on September 20 against Hardin-Simmons University of Abilene. Luckily, the game was played in more racially tolerant West Texas, and other than some racial name-calling by the Hardin Simmons players across the line of scrimmage, the only other potential problem was averted when Coach Bahnsen found a restaurant in Abilene that would seat the whole team together upstairs and away from the local white clientele. The freshman Eagles defeated Hardin-Simmons 13–9, and immediately returned to Denton.

However, Haynes and King were not readily accepted when they headed to the Central Texas town of Corsicana on September 27 for their second game of their freshman season, when they played the Navarro Junior College Bulldogs. Haynes and King just wanted to play football; they weren't looking for social change.

"Get them niggers off the field!" was the chant from the bleachers when the Eagles arrived at the Navarro Junior College field. Leon King said, "It was one of the scariest moments of my life. The crowd was angry and the bleachers seemed so close that people could just reach over the fence and grab you. I was scared that day, but it didn't bother us as much as it did our white teammates. The crowd just seemed to lump them in with us as 'nigger lovers.' My teammates got angry too. They were angry that people could be so cruel to any person."

King said North Texas tackle Joe Mack Pryor went out of his way to help protect Haynes and King. "The more they picked on us, the madder Joe Pryor would get," King said. "We'd make up plays just to nail a guy who tried to do something to me and Abner."

Even before the game, Haynes and King's teammates stood up for them. Coach Bahnsen had forgotten to inform the restaurant that the team sitting down to eat had two African American teammates. When the restaurant found out, the man in charge informed Haynes and King they would have to eat in the kitchen. Several teammates rose up in defense of their black teammates. Joe Mack Pryor, one of the linemen, informed the waitress that everyone would eat together. Coach Bahnsen then called the manager over and said, "If they can't eat with us, then you've prepared a bunch of meals for nothing. We're a team, and we eat as a team." The whole team got up and left when the manager refused to back down. Haynes said, "When the whole team got up and walked out, man, that felt good. I realized these guys were my teammates and were in the process of becoming my friends."

The team members ate baloney sandwiches on the team bus for their pregame meal.

They also stuck together when the fans in Corsicana expressed their views that it was wrong for black and white players to be on the same field.

Haynes said, "I was scared to death! I had never experienced anything like that. Those angry people in the bleachers that day didn't realize how they made our team come together. If they'd left us alone, we might have ended up fighting among ourselves. But by attacking and terrorizing us, that kind of adversity brought the whole team together—black and white."

Bob Way, an Eagles linebacker on the freshman team, said, "To me, Abner and Leon were just two more players on the team, and I didn't have any feelings at all beyond that. But things changed at Navarro College. I have a real respect for them. Abner huddled us together and told us it didn't bother him and not to let it bother us."

When the freshman Eagles arrived at the game, Coach Bahnsen heard the threats they were receiving. Someone yelled, "There's the nigger-loving coach!" Then, three men met him at the gate and asked Bahnsen if he planned on putting his two black players into the game. Bahnsen did, despite the threat of violence. He then made the decision to instruct the bus driver to park the bus close by.

Early in the game, Haynes butted heads with a Navarro College player. Haynes had a slight concussion, but the other player was carried off the field on a stretcher, which angered the Navarro fans even more. They started taunting Haynes with the chant, "Get that nigger boy! Get that nigger boy!" from the stands.

At halftime, the team had to stay on the field because the crowd prevented them from going to the visitors' locker room.

Haynes recalled no one doing anything about the taunts and jeers from the crowd: "The police grinned like it was funny, and the people in the stands didn't care."

North Texas found itself down 14–0 before Haynes exploded for four second-half touchdowns. Leon King added another touchdown on a scoring pass from quarterback Vernon Cole. The freshman Eagles garnered a 39–21 victory, which only made the home teams fans angrier.

As soon as the game was over, Coach Bahnsen told his players to run for it. He said, "When that whistle blows I want to be the last one on that bus. Don't shake hands, don't do anything." The players made a tight formation around Haynes and King and headed for the bus.

"Me and Leon headed to the back of the bus, and George Herring—he used to call me Butch—came back with me and said, 'Butch, I didn't know y'all go through stuff like that,'" Haynes said. "We ended up crying together."

Leon King added, "We became blood brothers that day. What affected one of us affected all of us."

"We became a family in Corsicana that night," Haynes said. "My white teammates had no idea what they were getting into. Sixty years ago we started integration in this part of the country. We were just kids. The adults, though, didn't want us playing together. I'm proud of my teammates for what we did and how we stuck together. No other segment of society was integrated, yet here we were playing together."

The rest of the season was relatively incident-free. The third game for the freshman Eaglets was on October 11 in Oklahoma against Murray

Abner Haynes, circa 1958. Courtesy of UNT Athletics.

State Agricultural College. The team was able to eat their pregame meal together at one of the school's dormitories. The Eagles won 27–14, and there were no reports of incidents at the game.

For their fourth game they returned to Abilene on October 25 to defeat the Abilene Christian College freshman team 27–7. However, when they tried to eat at the same restaurant where they had dined together earlier in the season when they played Hardin-Simmons, they were refused service.

Their last game was the only one they played in Denton that 1956 season. On November 1, before a large crowd, the Eaglets beat Paris Junior College, 27–12. In their final freshman game, Haynes was the leading ground gainer and scored two touchdowns, and King took in a scoring pass and scored a two-point conversion. For the season, the freshman team won all five of its games, the best record in school history.

Once Haynes and King made the varsity as sophomores, they rarely encountered racial situations for the rest of their college careers. One reason was that all of the southern teams they had scheduled for future games, like Mississippi, Mississippi State, and Southern Mississippi, cancelled their games with North Texas when they found out the Eagles had two black players. Haynes said, "Once I joined the varsity team, some teams cancelled games. Ole Miss was one of them."

Only twice in his varsity career did Haynes play in segregated conditions. The last game of his junior season, the Eagles made the trek to Louisville to play the Cardinals. Although the Eagles scored a 21–10 victory, Haynes said, "Things were a little rough in Louisville, name-calling and everything."

In Haynes senior season, 1959, the Eagles traveled to still-segregated Houston to play the University of Houston Cougars on October 24. The Eagles improved their record to 6–0 with a hard-fought 7–6 win.

What upset Haynes, however, was that he was not able to stay with his teammates in Houston. "Although I had been born in Denton," he said, "I had visited Houston a lot growing up. My dad had a friend there, Bishop Galloway. I had sung in the choir at his church there. My family liked to sing, including my cousin Sly. I felt comfortable there in Houston.

"However, before we went to go play the Cougars my senior year, I was surprised when the college president and Coach Mitchell came to visit me a few days before the game and they told me I couldn't stay with the team in Houston. I was shocked. President Matthews told me, 'Abner we've been looking all week for a place where the team can stay together, but we can't find one.' Once again, I felt comfortable in Houston; it was almost like home. It was like they turned their back on me. I have to admit, it hurt a lot.

"My white teammates tripped out when they found out I couldn't stay with them. They came to my rescue. Then when the students at North Texas found out the situation, a bunch of them rode down on the train together with us to Houston to make sure we were all right."

Interestingly, there were some cases where the Cisco and North Texas players crossed paths, both during the 1956 season and then later when they were upperclassmen. North Texas and Cisco had two common opponents in 1956: Navarro Junior College and Paris Junior College from the Northeast Texas town of Paris. Both North Texas and Cisco played Paris on their home fields and defeated the Dragons. Both schools played Navarro Junior College in Corsicana, with North Texas winning their game, while Cisco suffered a defeat.

However, at Navarro, unlike Abner Haynes and Leon King at North Texas, Louis Kelley and the other Cisco Wranglers didn't encounter the racial problems during the actual game, although after the game, Cisco had problems with the segregated eating accommodations. There was really no explanation why North Texas State, with two black players, barely got out of Corsicana with their lives, where just a few weeks later Cisco, with five black players, encountered no racial problems at their game, only to face the segregation problem at the restaurant. It's possible the problems for North Texas arose because they were the first to integrate the football field at Navarro, whereas Cisco didn't face Navarro until later in the season, when racial tensions had quieted down. It may have also helped that Navarro dealt Cisco a 40–20 defeat to keep the home fans appeased.

Ironically, Haynes and Kelley faced each other in the last college football game they both played. Haynes's 9–1 North Texas team faced off against Kelley's New Mexico State Aggies in the 1959 Sun Bowl in El Paso. After his freshman season at Cisco, Kelley transferred to New Mexico State University in Las Cruces. The Aggies made it a habit of welcoming African American players by the late 1950s, thanks to Coach Warren Woodson. Kelley's Cisco and Abilene Woodson teammate, E. A. Sims, accompanied Kelley to New Mexico State and fashioned out a fine career there before playing in Canada. The aforementioned Billy Ray Locklin from Rockdale, Texas, was also a big contributor in the Aggie trenches.

New Mexico State also had a pair of African American running backs, Bob Gaiters and Pervis Atkins, who each led the nation in rushing. Atkins led in 1959 with 971 yards, and the following season, Gaiters led the nation with 1,338 yards. After their Aggie careers were over, both played professionally. Atkins played five seasons for the Rams, Redskins, and Raiders. Gaiters became the first overall pick in the 1961 AFL draft after being selected by the Denver Broncos. The quarterback on the team was future Pro Bowler Charlie Johnson.

Kelley became the starting fullback on an Aggies team that produced its first bowl win in school history. In spite of all the star power of the 1959 New Mexico State team on offense, it was Louis Kelley who was chosen by his teammates as their most valuable player when the season was over. The Aggies upset heavily favored North Texas, 28–8 to cap an 8–3 season.

Kelley described what he believed led to the Aggies' victory over North Texas: "When the teams were preparing for the Sun Bowl, we stayed on our campus in Las Cruces, which is only forty-five miles from El Paso. We had a hard week of workouts. Coach Woodson kept telling us how good North Texas was, and we had to really work hard to stay within twenty points of them. Coach said we pretty much had to play a perfect game to beat them. We ended up playing great that day, and we beat North Texas by twenty points, 28–8.

"Another factor in our win was that North Texas stayed in a hotel in

El Paso the week of the game. From what I understand, they had a good time in El Paso and also across the border in Juarez. In fact, Abner and some of his teammates drove up to Las Cruces one evening to have a little fun. I think we were much more focused and business-like than North Texas, since we were practicing and staying at home in Las Cruces."

Abner Haynes added, "Yes, we did go to Mexico and had some fun. We even got to go to a bullfight. We actually got in trouble at the bullfight. We were pulling for the bull, which we found out from other people in the crowd that's not something you did. It just didn't seem like we were into that game when we played New Mexico State. I guess we were distracted by all the fun we had."

In one last bit of irony, when Louis Kelley's Cisco teammate Jerry McWilliams transferred to a four-year college to finish his studies, he chose to attend North Texas State. McWilliams said, "Ironically, after Cisco I ended up at North Texas State and I was in the class of 1960, the same graduating class as Abner Haynes. At North Texas, it was fully integrated and there were blacks everywhere on campus. They would hang out at the student union and other places. Abner and I did have one class together, and we sat by each other. It was anatomy and physiology. I remember in one of the first classes, the professor went over and pulled a human head out of the freezer for us to study. Needless to say, Abner and I got the heck out of that class and found another."

Now that Cisco Junior College and North Texas State University joined San Angelo College by integrating their football programs in 1956, the state continued its sometimes slow but steady progress with integration of high school and college football.

8

Integration on Both Sides of the Ball

I had a teacher in eighth grade, Mrs. Garrett, who encouraged me to take the entrance test to get into Dimmitt High School. . . . She then argued with the high school administrators that I had the smarts to go to their school. They agreed, and that's how the high school integrated.
—JUNIOR COFFEY, THE FIRST AFRICAN AMERICAN PLAYER FOR THE DIMMITT BOBCATS, AND LATER A MEMBER OF THE 1965 GREEN BAY PACKERS NFL CHAMPIONSHIP TEAM

Integration continued in certain Texas school districts such as San Antonio and Corpus Christi/Coastal Bend. By the late 1950s, however, the formal end to segregated schools occurred in sections like the Rio Grande Valley, Central Texas, and up in the Panhandle. Military towns tended to be a common denominator. San Antonio had several military bases and led the state in desegregation in 1955. Coastal Bend military cities that integrated their school districts early on were Beeville, Kingsville, and Corpus Christi. Down in the valley, Harlingen and Del Rio were military towns that also integrated their school districts during this period. The Central Texas town of Killeen counted on Fort Hood as a major economic contributor and developed integrated schools. Amarillo military bases appeared to spur integration in schools in small towns surrounding Amarillo, such as Tulia and Dimmitt.

By the early to mid-1950s, Texas military bases were integrated, a factor that certainly hastened the integration of nearby public schools. Willie Paschall, who played at San Antonio Jefferson High School in the late 1950s and early 1960s and then at the University of Nebraska, was in a military family that moved to San Antonio in the late 1950s. "Blacks from all over were transferred to these military bases in San Antonio and other parts of Texas," Paschall recalled. "These blacks from northern military cities were used to integration. With four or five military bases in San Antonio, it was hard for towns to hold on to segregation with the influx of people from elsewhere."

Johnny Roland, who led the first integrated team in Texas high school history—Corpus Christi Miller—to a state title in 1960, said, "Corpus Christi was a seaport town; people came from all over. It was a melting pot. I'm guessing a lot of the places people came from were integrated. That may have helped speed up the process in Corpus Christi."

Joseph Searles helped integrate Killeen High School in 1956. "When integration came along in 1954, Killeen was one of the first school districts to integrate. I think one of the reasons Killeen had to integrate was the preponderance of federal money because of Fort Hood." After desegregating Killeen schools, Searles, a running back, went to Pratt Junior College in Kansas and from there to Kansas State. Eventually, in 1970, Searles became the first African American to be on the floor of the New York Stock Exchange.

"In Killeen," he remembered, "we had black areas and white areas of town. When we went to Fort Hood there in Killeen, it was integrated. When I was growing up, things weren't always integrated in the military. My dad was a sergeant first class in the army. I grew up on military bases: Hawaii, Japan, and Fort Hood. We were stationed in Hawaii when I was small. I remember one day I saw a bus in Hawaii, and I told my mom to hurry up so we could get on it. She had to explain to me that was not our bus. There was a bus for blacks and a bus for whites back then. In 1948 President Truman integrated the troops, and all of that ended.

"We didn't have too many problems in Killeen when we integrated. I think it was because Fort Hood was already integrated and the kids all knew each other growing up. We did face some problems outside of Killeen, though. One was in 1957 when we were going to play Cameron, which is about fifty miles east of Killeen. That area was still heavily segregated."

The problems with Cameron were not new. The previous year when the Killeen Kangaroos faced the Cameron Yeomen, there was some talk of the game being cancelled because Killeen had Joseph Searles and Cecil Anderson on its team. *The Cameron Herald* reported, "There is a possibility that the coaches of the Killeen team will run an integrated team against the Yeoman. Cameron coaches have been instructed that should such be the case, they are to leave the field of play, forfeiting the game on policy, not on ability."

Because the black players in question were on the junior varsity team that season, the 1956 Killeen game versus Cameron was played. Cameron defeated Killeen, 7–6.

In 1957, however, both Searles and Anderson were on the varsity Kangaroo team, so the issue resurfaced against Cameron, the host team. Again the talk turned toward cancelling the game. The Yoemen and the Kangaroos were scheduled to play on November 1. Cameron checked with the Texas Interscholastic League about what would happen if they refused to play the game. The TIL informed Cameron that they would have to forfeit the game. But Cameron relented, and arrangements were made to have the game moved to Killeen.

Searles described the game: "Before we went to play there in 1957, we got threatening letters that said things like, 'Don't send those black Kangaroos to Cameron!' Of course, those letters weren't signed. The game was moved to Killeen at the last minute, though, so Cecil Anderson, my black teammate, and I could play in the game. It ended up being a bad game for me. They were pissed off that the game was moved to Killeen, and that they had to play against black players.

"Before the game I remember the commanding general of Fort Hood, Gen. William Biddle, arranged for the Military Police to be stationed at the game to help keep us safe. I went to high school with General Biddle's daughter, Susan. General Biddle felt there was a need to protect us. When we did play the game, when I was tackled, I learned to get up quick. The Cameron players would roll on me, hit me in the face, and punch me in the balls. If I went out of bounds close to the Cameron sideline, I got out of there as quick as I could. They also were saying some bad racial stuff to me. The best thing about all of it was we won the game 26–6."

In the Rio Grande Valley, integration and the challenges for African Americans entering an all-white environment also came to high school football in 1957. The black population in the Valley was and still is very sparse, usually running no more than 1 percent of the total population. With numbers so small, the transition from segregated to integrated schools was mostly seamless and incident-free. The first black player in the Rio Grande Valley appeared to be Leon Jackson, a running back out of Weslaco, about sixty miles west of the Gulf of Mexico and about ten miles north of the Rio Grande. Located between Harlingen and McAllen, Weslaco had a population of about twelve thousand in 1957. A senior during the 1957–58, school year, Jackson, who passed away in 1992, played his only varsity season in 1957.

Teammate Rayford Mixon recalled, "Leon was a pretty good player, but not one of our best. We weren't much good anyways. We tied two games and lost the rest. Leon was a running back. Everybody liked him. We had no problems at school. We only had two black kids in the school, Leon and another boy by the name of Jones. His dad shined shoes in town. So naturally his nickname was 'Shoeshine Jones.' I really don't remember much about things being segregated in Weslaco. I do remember down by the railroad tracks there was a Texsun Orange Juice warehouse, and there was a Mexican restaurant next door. I do remember a little place off to the side of the restaurant that said, 'colored.'"

Gerald Madden was another teammate. "Leon was unique because there were so few blacks in the Rio Grande Valley," Madden said. "He was popular. He got recognition when either ABC or NBC came to Weslaco to interview him about being named 'Most Popular' at Weslaco High. It was a national story—a black kid in the 1950s being chosen most popular at a white school. Sometimes Leon would run around with the guys, but I never saw him out on dates or at the prom or anything like that. There were no black girls at the school back then."

Just as Madden recalls, indeed in the spring of 1958, Leon Jackson was named "Most Popular Boy" at Weslaco High School. He was chosen by his fellow classmates, about five hundred total, as the most popular senior. The story made national news, and it appeared on television and in print. The Associated Press wire service story carried a quote from math teacher Hazel Lyons, who was the senior class sponsor: "This is the highest compliment the students could pay to themselves. They have learned to look for the real person and not at his color. As long as we have students like this, we need have no fear for our future."

The AP article also quoted school superintendent Grady Hester. He said that Leon was selected, "not because he was an underdog but because the kids just like him."

Another African American football pioneer in the Rio Grande Valley was Lonnie Davis, who hailed from Harlingen, just twenty miles east of Weslaco. Harlingen had a slightly larger African American population than other cities in the Rio Grande Valley, mostly due to the post–World War II military installations. By the late 1950s, Harlingen's population had jumped to close to forty thousand, up from the prewar figure of twenty-three thousand. Davis did not make his varsity debut until 1958, the year after Leon Jackson. Davis, who still calls Harlingen home, currently owns Lonnie Davis and Associates, an insurance firm. He attended Booker T. Washington High School in Harlingen prior to the 1958 integration.

"There were a fair amount of blacks in Harlingen," Davis said. "With the military base, there were a lot of World War II babies born. The blacks lived mostly on the west side of town. All in all, though, I had a great time growing up in Harlingen.

"When I played football for Harlingen in 1958, I was the only black playing in the Rio Grande Valley. Leon Jackson had been in Weslaco the year before me, though. Growing up in Harlingen was kind of strange. We went to a segregated school, but they let us play Little League baseball with the white kids. We had some exceptional black players, so I think that was part of the reason we were able to play. One thing to emphasize—In the late 1940s and early 1950s, Jackie Robinson was our hero. That, and with baseball being so popular back then, was the reason so many of us black kids played.

"When I went to junior high and high school, I started playing football too. In Texas, that's what you do. It's kind of expected of you. A lot of the really great football players from the area were also great baseball players. There was Gene and Marvin Upshaw from Robstown. Gene was a pitcher, and Marvin was a catcher. They were such great athletes they could have played any sport. Another one was Preacher Pilot from Kingsville. I knew him well. They had a heckuva football team in 1958. They made it to the state finals.

"As far as any problems while playing football for Harlingen, there was one time we were on our way to Corpus Christi to play Ray High School. We stopped in Kingsville at a place called Nolan's Beef and Reef. When we got there, the busboy was none other than Leon Jackson from Weslaco, who was a freshman at Texas A&I. He warned us that they wouldn't serve me, and he was right. We ended up going to the local Dairy Queen to eat. Other than that incident, things went fairly well integration-wise."

About one hundred miles north from Harlingen up Highway 77, running back James "Preacher" Pilot of Kingsville made his mark in the Coastal Bend. Although Sherwood Thompson was the first African

American to play football at Kingsville in 1955, the following year the legendary Pilot suited up for the Brahmas. By his senior season of 1958, Pilot led Kingsville to the Class 3A state finals, where they lost to Breckenridge 42–14. The game against Breckenridge was significant because it was the first time African American players appeared in a state title contest. After high school, Pilot attended Kansas his freshman year before transferring to New Mexico State. Pilot led the NCAA in rushing in 1961 with 1,278 yards and in 1962 with 1,247 yards. He was drafted by the 49ers of the NFL and the Chiefs of the AFL. However, because of injuries suffered as a senior at New Mexico State, Pilot never played professional football. Pilot passed away in 1991, but many friends and former teammates never forgot him.

Jack Burchers said, "I played defensive tackle. I started playing Little League baseball with Preacher when I was twelve. He was always the stud. He pitched. Everybody liked Preacher. In football he played both ways, running back and defensive back. He was a pretty big kid, about 200 pounds. Preacher could run a 9.8 hundred-yard dash, though. He did pretty well in school too. He was no dummy. We really didn't have any problems with Preacher or any of the other black players on the team."

Doug Harvey was the all-state quarterback for Kingsville in 1958. He went on to play at Texas A&I, where he was a teammate of Sid Blanks. Harvey was inducted into the Javelina Hall of Fame in 1978. He said, "Preacher was a great guy. We really had no problems integrating. I played Little League and Pony League with Preacher, so I knew him already. What an athlete. He was about 5-foot-10 and 210 pounds, and could run about a 9.7 hundred-yard dash. We had a great time the year we went to the finals in 1958. I never heard or saw any type of problems."

Barbara Roe Herrington was a classmate of Preacher Pilot. Now retired after a long career as a school administrator, mostly in Fort Bend Independent School District, Roe married Pilot's close friend and teammate, Whit Herrington. "Preacher and my husband Whit were good friends," Mrs. Herrington recalled. "I knew Preacher. We didn't travel in the same circles. He lived on one side of town by the old cemetery, in an apartment which was kind of like the projects. I do remember graduation night we walked down the aisle together. I knew his mother; she was a maid for one of my friends. Her name was Rosetta, and she was a lovely woman. I remember there were about ten or twelve blacks that came to Kingsville High School. I really don't recall any incidents; I don't recall any issues. Preacher was a great football player. We went to state because of him."

James "Preacher" Pilot, circa 1961.
Courtesy of NMSU Athletics.

Whit Herrington moved to Kingsville from Austin his junior year of 1956–57, the year after Kingsville integrated. "I became friends with Preacher," Herrington said. "Most people don't know how he got the nickname 'Preacher.' He liked Preacher Roe, a pitcher for the Brooklyn Dodgers. Roe had an unusual windup, and James tried to copy it. We started calling him 'Preacher' because of that.

"Preacher couldn't have been any friendlier. Everyone liked him. Nobody I knew ever said anything like racial slurs behind his back. About the only problem we ever had in football was when we went to Refugio to play, and after the game they wanted to put the team in a separate room so as not to offend the white customers. At the away games I don't remember anyone yelling at him. Everything directed at Preacher seemed to be positive. And what an athlete. He ran the hundred in about 9.7 seconds. Preacher lived in the projects in the black part of town, which was the southwest corner of Kingsville by the cemetery."

In Del Rio, 150 miles west of San Antonio on US Highway 90, Sid Blanks arose to take the football world by storm. Not only did Blanks desegregate San Felipe ISD in Del Rio in 1956; he also integrated the football program at Texas A&I College (now Texas A&M–Kingsville) in 1960, when he took his talents as a running back there. The Chicago Bears drafted Blanks in the third round of the 1964 NFL draft, while the Houston Oilers took him in the fifth round of the AFL draft. Playing for the Oilers in 1964, Blanks enjoyed a Pro Bowl season, amassing more than 1,200 yards running and receiving. A severe knee injury in 1965 limited his effectiveness the rest of his career. Blanks ended up playing six seasons in the AFL and NFL before he retired after the 1970 season.

Blanks described how his family ended up in Del Rio and the resulting lifestyle. "There was a small black population in Del Rio," he said. "My grandparents, John and Tracea Blanks, came from Kerrville not long after the Civil War. The Texas Filibusterers were still trying to enslave blacks after the war. A lot of blacks, including my grandparents, went to the Mexican border, and some actually went into Mexico to live because they had abolished slavery there a few years before. My grandparents lived there, and that's where my father Roscoe was born. He met my mom Leona there.

"Eventually they came back across the Rio Grande and settled in Del Rio. My dad was an engineer with Del Rio Western Plumbing. He dug the ditches for plumbing in the city. I'm the youngest of eleven children. I was born in 1941, and I'm the youngest by four or five years. I had five brothers and five sisters.

"I went to the black school in Del Rio before we integrated. There were about 150 kids in grades one through twelve. We went to Langston Hughes Elementary. It consisted of two rooms. One room was a storeroom; the other was the classroom. All of us elementary kids were in that one room. We had an outhouse behind the school. Then we went to the Tarver School. It was also a small school.

"As far as growing up black in Del Rio, we had to sit in the balcony at the movie theater. However, we were able to shop and eat in the white part of town. If we wanted to buy clothes, though, we couldn't try them on in the store. You had to eyeball them or hold them up to you. Sometimes if we got out of sight from the sales person, we would sneak the clothes on real quick.

"We didn't mix much with the white kids growing up. We did play some sandlot ball against them. Sandlot ball was where I learned how to play tackle football. Eventually I met all of the guys that were athletes at Laughlin Air Force Base. We used to run around and play ball with them.

"There were two school districts in Del Rio back then: the Del Rio School District, which was for the whites, and the San Felipe School District, which was for the Mexicans. After *Brown v. Board of Education* in 1954, the San Felipe School District was very progressive and integrated in 1956. There were five of us black students that integrated the high school. There was no violence, and there were no problems. It was located in the barrio in the poor area of town. San Felipe Creek, which ran through town, basically divided the school districts.

"San Felipe ISD was east of the creek and Del Rio ISD was west of the creek. The two districts merged in the early 1970s. I remember when one of the coaches from Texas A&I came to recruit me; he said we were the poorest school in the state. The school was rundown. We got hand-me-downs in everything. I remember showing some of the black soldiers at the air force base some of our books, and they couldn't believe how bad they were. They said, 'How in the heck do you learn?' We just didn't know any better.

"Luckily, I was blessed because I had some teachers who taught me very well. One in particular was Whita Whiteside. I had her when I was a sophomore, and she helped me all the way through high school. I loved her, and she loved me. It was fairly easy for me to go to San Felipe High School. In fact, I embraced going there because of my background, me being from the barrio. Spanish is actually my first language.

"As far as playing sports, I played football, baseball, and ran track. I was a good baseball player. I was a catcher. The St. Louis Cardinals were interested in signing me. I did play baseball and run track against Preacher Pilot when he was at Kingsville High School. I must say I was faster than he was.

"San Felipe High School was a small school. We were Class 1A. Some of the other schools in our district were Alpine, Sanderson, Hondo, Uvalde, and Devine. I remember at Alpine they didn't want me to play. I did, and I scored four touchdowns. At Hondo they didn't want me to play, either. They were calling me names, spitting on me. I finally went into the game in the fourth quarter, and I scored three touchdowns. Joe Martinez, our coach, was sensitive about his players. An assistant coach at Hondo said they wanted to get our game with them off their records because we didn't play 'their type of football,' whatever that meant. Our coach said, 'Well, you can't stop us.'

"I scored those three touchdowns, and they called us all kinds of names. I learned, though, to block all of that stuff out. I learned not to retaliate. If Coach Martinez would see me start to get upset, he would pull me over to the side and say, 'Don't listen to that; just play ball.' That really helped because I had a temper and that helped calm me down.

"I wore number twenty-five in high school. I remember one game in high school, some big German guy said to me, 'Hey you! Number twenty-five is a shit number!' I then ran sixty-five yards for a touchdown. I proceeded to tell that guy from the end zone, 'How do I smell from here? What stinks is your team!'

"I was a hitter in high school on defense. At one game, some boy's parents told our coach to get me away from their son; they said I was hitting illegally. We started to get noticed as a football team. Eventually a Spalding sporting goods salesman told Coach Steinke at Texas A&I about me. He came and saw me play one night, and I scored three touchdowns. The parents for the other team came on the field after the game and said we were cheating, that we were using players from the air force base.

"One time we played Sam Houston High School in San Antonio. They had some blacks on their team, too. We were refused service at a restaurant that we went to. They said, 'You can't eat in here; we don't serve coloreds.'

"I do remember after we played Alpine their coach said, 'You're a great athlete; don't let all of that other stuff bother you.' He also said, 'I see you being very successful.' No other coach ever said anything like that to me. I tried to apply what he said to my everyday life."

More than three hundred miles north from Del Rio, another region of Texas that integrated at the high school level was the Texas Panhandle. In the late 1950s two cities in the Panhandle, Tulia and Dimmitt, just thirty miles from each other, integrated their football programs.

Tulia High School, about halfway between Lubbock and Amarillo, was the first to integrate in 1958 with halfback Billy Dick. Dick played on the "B" team in 1957 and sometimes as a varsity reserve in 1958. He recalled, "I was the third black to enter Tulia High School. The first two students enrolled in 1956 and stayed only a few weeks. In 1960, I was the first black student to graduate from Tulia High. My three sisters followed me in graduating from Tulia. I was voted the most popular male student in 1960."

Dick was very popular, being named Mr. Tulia High School when he graduated in 1960. His former classmates attested to his popularity. Bobby Doan recounts, "Billy was a first-class guy. He had an interesting life in Tulia. I think his family was the only black one in town. He was highly regarded and popular. He was class favorite as a senior. I don't know of a single person who didn't like him."

Larry Stewart was sheriff of Swisher County, where Tulia is located, from 1991 until 2008, and a teammate of Billy Dick. Stewart recalls, "Billy and his three sisters fit in real well in Tulia. When Billy came to Tulia, he came in and showed he wanted to go to school. He took his studies seriously. For the most part, Tulia accepted him. Some people from my parent's generation and even some from mine weren't too pleased with him. People for the most part are treated the way they act. The person sets the standard. In that respect, Billy was liked and respected because of the way he carried himself. In football, I was a lineman and mostly rode the bench. I never remember anything racial directed at Billy from the stands either at home or on the road."

James Hoggins was another teammate. "When Billy was named Mr. Tulia High School, I was the one who nominated him," he said. "I also gave a speech in front of the student body supporting my nominating him. Billy was popular and well-respected. He wouldn't have been named Mr. THS if he wasn't. By and large, Billy was accepted at school. Some of the kids who were a year or so older than us did have quite a bit of prejudice against him.

"A friend of mine, Harry Lewis, was on the track team with Billy. They were on the same relay team. One night Harry was caught on the track by some of the older students and got beat up. It had to do with Harry touching the same baton on the relay team as Billy. They told him a white guy shouldn't touch the same baton a black guy touched. I was little and slow, and I didn't start on the football team. I never heard anything from the stands directed at Billy while I was on the sideline.

"I don't remember any problems with being served at restaurants, because we always went straight home after our games."

Jerry Vandergriff was the Tulia quarterback with Billy Dick. After Tulia, Vandergriff played ball at San Angelo College, Henderson County (now Trinity Valley) Junior College, and the University of Corpus Christi. He recalls, "Billy was a really good guy. He was a pioneer for what was going on back then. If you were going to have someone break down barriers, he was the guy to do it. There were not very many black families in Tulia back then. We were not real good in football until Billy and another running back by the name of Buzzy Poage came along. They were a terrific 1–2 punch. Billy used to socialize with us. The bottom line is that someone was needed at that time period to help break down barriers, and Billy was the perfect guy to do it. He had outstanding character. He was the perfect guy to integrate."

Although Billy Dick proclaimed himself to be African American, looked African American, and newspaper articles referred to him as such, there was some question as to whether he was really African American. James Hoggins said, "Billy always claimed he was part Indian. I don't know if that was true or not."

When Tulia faced Dimmitt on November 6, 1959, the *Castro County News* reported that Tulia defeated Dimmitt 16–14 and "Billy Dick, Tulia's hot-shot Negro back, snagged a pass for the two points after touchdown," referring to Dick's two-point conversion after Jerry Vandergriff had returned an intercepted Dimmitt pass for a touchdown.

Dick's son-in-law, Jim Sparkman, when told that Dick had been referred to as a Negro, said, "Billy's not black; he's actually Choctaw Indian. Back then they may have said that when he was in school. His family is from Oklahoma, which was the Indian Territory. He may have a little Chickasaw and Creek Indian blood too."

The first African American to suit up for the Dimmitt Bobcats in 1958 was Junior Coffey, who is regarded by many as the best athlete in Texas Panhandle history. Junior Coffey played running back and defensive back. As a junior, Coffey led Dimmitt with 185 tackles on defense, and he ran for 1,294 yards on 165 carries. As a senior, he rushed for 1,562 yards in 11 games. In a bidistrict playoff game against Olton, Coffey's last high school contest, he rushed for 253 yards on 34 carries, and scored both Bobcat touchdowns in a 15–12 loss. After his senior season of 1960, Coffey was named Class 2A first team all-state.

Billy Dick, Tulia High School, 1959. Courtesy of Tulia ISD.

Coffey also was an accomplished basketball player, leading Dimmitt to the state tournament in Austin in 1960 and 1961. Coffey thus became the first African American to appear in the UIL state basketball tournament. James Hoggins said, "Junior Coffey—he was the greatest athlete I've ever seen. We played against him in football when he was at Dimmitt, but where I really remember him was in basketball. We had a great team at Tulia my senior year. We were a run-and-gun outfit, and we could have won state that year. However, we couldn't get past Dimmitt and, more specifically, Junior Coffey. He was just outstanding."

After his career at Dimmitt, Coffey chose to play football at the University of Washington, and eventually made the All-Pacific Coast Athletic Conference team at running back. Coffey then went on to play seven seasons in the NFL for the Packers, Falcons, and Giants. Coffey was a member of the Packers NFL Champion squad in 1965. After his retirement from pro football, Coffey became a trainer of racehorses in the Seattle area for many years.

Coffey talked about coming to Dimmitt and his early years there: "My uncle heard about jobs in the cotton fields of the South Plains, and so we left San Marcos when I was in the eighth grade. It was like moving to heaven. They accepted me for who I was, not the color of my skin. I went to eighth grade at the black school in Dimmitt. For high school, though, I was going to have to go to the black high school in Olton, about thirty-five miles away.

"I had a teacher in eighth grade, Mrs. Garrett, who encouraged me to take the entrance test to get into Dimmitt High School, which had just integrated in 1957, my freshman year. She then argued with the high school administrators that I had the smarts to go to Dimmitt High School. They agreed, and that's how the high school integrated.

"When I got to Dimmitt, everything changed, thanks to a couple of new white friends. Hal Ratcliff and Kent Hance encouraged me to go out for sports, even though I had never played before. I was in a high school where there had never been integration before. I lived with my aunt and uncle, and they didn't want me roaming the streets, so I started playing. I was kind of a natural for football. It required more strength and natural athletic ability rather than skill.

"In basketball, even though I was pretty good and I kind of liked it better than football, I got by on natural ability. Since I didn't start playing until high school, I was way behind in fundamentals. I didn't know anything about sports. When the quarterback first threw me the ball, I flinched because I had never tried to catch a ball before. I thought he was doing it on purpose, throwing the ball at me because he didn't like blacks.

"My new teammates had to set me straight on what he was trying to do. Fortunately, the guys didn't make fun of me. They told me to hang in there. I was six-foot-one and two hundred pounds. There weren't too many players over two hundred pounds back then. When I first went out, the coaches put me at defensive tackle. After I recovered a fumble, though, and knocked people over returning it for a touchdown; that's when they made me a running back.

"Winning helped in Dimmitt. They had never won much before I got there, so I think winning made integration easier. When I would go into town to buy groceries for my aunt and uncle, people knew me and would complement me. That was pretty cool. However, even though things opened up a bit in Dimmitt, we still had to get our shopping done before the sun went down.

"Even though I was accepted by my classmates, some of their parents weren't too thrilled about their kid going to school and playing sports with a black kid. One of my friends, Stanley, cried the day he told me his parents wouldn't let him play football because of me. I told him, 'It's not your fault. You don't feel that way.'

"As far as playing games in the Panhandle, when we played on the road in Muleshoe, that was the worst experience I had. There was a lot of name-calling. Coach called the team over and asked if I wanted to continue playing. If I didn't, the whole team was going to walk off the field and forfeit. We ended up playing, and we won 44–0.

"We weren't always allowed in restaurants on the road, and we had to stay in subpar hotels on road trips. At the state basketball tournament in Austin in 1960, we stayed in the State Hotel on the outskirts of the city. There were prostitutes and drugs there. It was a place so bad the criminals wouldn't even want to get a room there. But you know what? My teammates subjected themselves to all of that so we could stay together as a team.

"We left a barbeque place in Amarillo because they wanted me to eat in the kitchen but my teammates would have none of it."

One of Coffey's teammates, Hal Ratcliff, said, "He had some experiences that were unbelievable. Junior couldn't get a haircut in Dimmitt; he had to go to Plainview, over forty miles away, to get one. When we went to state in basketball, we drove through Brownwood and practiced at Howard Payne University. There wasn't a single place between there and Austin that we could stop as a team and eat. We ended up getting some hamburgers and eating in our hotel rooms in Austin."

Another helpful Coffey teammate was Kent Hance, who later would defeat George W. Bush in a race for the Nineteenth Congressional District in 1979, and went on to serve as chancellor of Texas Tech University from 2006 to 2014. Hance would always go in and check restaurants to see if they would serve Coffey. If they wouldn't, Hance would make up an excuse so as not to hurt Coffey's feelings. He would say the place was too expensive or a dump. One time he told Coffey one restaurant was just too crowded. "Well," Coffey retorted, "there's only two cars in the parking lot, so how could that be?"

Years later, Coffey said, "I now realize Kent Hance and my teammates were covering for me. I could never imagine a group of people, my teammates, being the way they were for me. I've carried that with me my whole life."

It seemed fitting that in the last regular season game in the Texas Panhandle in 1959 and, for that matter, the last game of the integration decade of the 1950s, on November 6, Junior Coffey of Dimmitt and Billy Dick of Tulia faced off against each other. This marked the first fully integrated game in Panhandle history, where each team had an African American player on its roster. Tulia beat Dimmitt that night, 16–14. In the waning seconds, Tulia quarterback Jerry Vandergriff tossed a pass to Billy Dick after a botched point after touchdown attempt for a two-point conversion to provide the Hornets with the margin of victory.

Junior Coffey recalled, "I didn't realize that when Billy Dick and I played against each other, we fully integrated the Panhandle. I knew Billy Dick a little, but I really didn't know him very well. We ran against each other in track. He was one of the better track guys. Football was my forte but not his."

The historic Tulia-versus-Dimmitt game on the last regular season Friday of the decade—although people did not realize the significance of it at the time—helped set the stage for integration events to come in the new decade of the 1960s.

9

The Bucs Bring in the New Decade

We were the first team in UIL history to win with blacks on our roster and also the first team to win a state title with three ethnic groups on the team. We were pioneers.
—Pete Ragus, Head Coach of the 1960 Corpus Christi Miller State Champs

After the integration of Cisco Junior College and North Texas State in 1956, integration of high school football continued throughout Texas, with the exception of East Texas and the Houston and Dallas metropolitan areas. Following the lead of Coastal Bend school districts like Robstown, Kingsville, and Refugio, Corpus Christi Independent School District saw its football teams integrated in the late 1950s.

The Corpus Christi school that led the way was Roy Miller High School. Miller had achieved a measure of football success in the mid-1950s under Head Coach Tom Pruett, as he guided the Buccaneers to a 35–7–1 record in the four seasons from 1953 until 1956. Pruett was the head coach when Miller integrated its football team in 1957 with LeeFord Fant and Bobby Smith. The Bucs' record in 1957 was 7–3, and after the season, Pruett took an assistant's job at Baylor University.

In 1958 Miller handed the football coaching reins to thirty-one-year-old Pete Ragus, a California native who played his college football at Abilene Christian College. He spent one season coaching in the West Texas town of Stamford as an assistant under Texas coaching immortal Gordon Wood in 1951. The following season, he went to Miller as an assistant under Tom Pruett. With Pruett gone, the school administration—according to Ragus—"looked around at some other coaches first and couldn't get the guy they wanted, so they ended up hiring me."

Ragus led the Buccaneers to a 58–13–1 record over the next six seasons, including a trip to the state semifinals in 1958, the 1960 state title, and the state finals in his last season in 1963. From there, Ragus accepted the job as athletic director of the Lubbock school district, where he led

Pete Ragus, Corpus Christi Miller Head Football Coach, circa 1960. Courtesy of Pete Ragus.

them down the path of integration of the district's athletic programs. The Class 4A state title that Ragus and the Bucs captured in 1960 was significant because Corpus Christi Miller became the first integrated team in Texas scholastic history to claim a state title.

The groundwork to that title was laid three years earlier when the program was integrated with junior tight end LeeFord Fant and sophomore running back Bobby Smith. Fant, after his senior year, integrated the Texas Western football program in 1959.

In Coach Ragus's words, "LeeFord was a tall and lean player, a good athlete. He played mostly tight end, but every so often we would have him split out wide if we needed him to. LeeFord was a quiet type of guy, but he had a beautiful spirit and was a great asset to our team. He led mostly by example. In 1957, when he and Bobby Smith were the first two blacks to play on varsity, I was still an assistant coach. I was the line coach, so I got to coach LeeFord since he was a tight end. He was our first black letterman, since he was a junior in 1957 and Bobby Smith was a sophomore."

Homer Mascorro was a teammate of Fant and Smith in 1957 and 1958. "My first year on varsity I played for Coach Pruett," Mascorro recalled, "and my senior year in 1958 I played for Coach Ragus. Those were two outstanding coaches to play for. I learned so much from those two. They changed my life. After two years in the marines after high school, I was able to play in college at Santa Rosa Junior College and then at Sacramento State College for my last two years. I then taught for thirty-five years and was a football coach for twenty-three years. The things I learned about life I learned at Miller playing for Coach Pruett and Coach Ragus. Everyone at Miller owes Coach Ragus a lot. He's one helluva guy.

"As far as playing with the first blacks at Miller, LeeFord Fant and Bobby Smith, it wasn't a big deal. It was a good experience, and there were no problems within the team. We did run into a couple of problems when we traveled. LeeFord and Bobby couldn't stay at the hotel with us when we went to play in Houston, and the same thing happened in Odessa and Wichita Falls. They also couldn't eat with us at some restaurant, so they had to eat in the kitchen.

"LeeFord was the class clown of the team. He was pretty funny. Although he was our tight end and had pretty good hands, I thought he was a little overrated as a player. He tended not to block very well. Now Bobby Smith, there was a player. He was much more serious. Bobby actually took my job when I was a senior. I ended up being all-district on defense, but I lost the running back spot to Bobby. He was faster and quicker than me. It was not a problem because Coach Ragus explained how it was the best thing for the team, and it was. I was still a good running back, though. That's what I played in college, not defensive back."

Marcos Perez was the quarterback on the 1958 Miller semifinal team. In addition, Perez was named senior class favorite by his peers in the 1959 Miller graduating class. He recalled, "I split time at quarterback in 1958 with Freddy Cuevas. When we integrated in 1957, we noticed a slight change, but it wasn't much. LeeFord and Bobby were good players and good guys. If you're good and can carry your own weight, it didn't matter what color you were. LeeFord was a jolly, happy-go-lucky guy. He, like Bobby Smith, got along with everyone. I think LeeFord's personality helped carry him through the integration thing. I played against LeeFord in junior high. He went to Cunningham, and I went to Northside Junior High.

"The only time I remember running into a problem in Corpus Christi was one time we went to eat after one of our games in Corpus at a place called the Chat and Chew Restaurant. I remember they wouldn't let the black players in. On the road, when we played in Midland, Bobby Smith ran back the opening kickoff one hundred yards for a touchdown. As I was standing on the sidelines afterwards, I heard a fan yell, 'Look at all those niggers and Mexicans!' Bobby also ran for an eighty-one-yard touchdown on the first play of the second half, and we ended up winning

18–8. After the game, I remember Coach Ragus huddled us together and told us to put on our helmets, don't look at anyone, and put the windows of the bus up!

"I also remember when we went into Wichita Falls to play. I think there may have been a problem with the housing there as far as letting the team stay together. Also, after we got off the plane and headed into town, there was a big sign that said, 'Nigger, don't let the sun set on you in this town.' That was a little scary.

"Coach Ragus was all business. He didn't say that much; he let his assistants do a lot of the talking. When he spoke, though, you sure as heck listened. He expected you to behave and to compete. He never really got too upset, and I only heard him yell once. I had finished a spring training workout and I decided to run the steps in the stadium to work on my conditioning. Coach Ragus was out there coaching track. He was the head track coach before he was the head football coach, and he was good. I heard him yell at one of his track guys. Coach Ragus said, 'Don't tell me what you're going to do, just do it!' I sure paid attention to that! Coach Ragus's mannerisms, the way he carried himself, and the way he treated us made us want to compete for him."

Ragus had good words about Bobby Smith. He said, "Bobby Smith was the greatest game player I've ever seen. Bobby hated practice. When the game started, he was something else. You couldn't let his laid-back personality fool you. He was a great back, though. Every time he got the ball, he was a threat to make something happen. It was electric when he had the ball."

Smith's senior year of 1959, the Bucs finished with a 7–3 record, losing the district title to Corpus Christi Ray, which went on to win the state Class 4A title that season. That year also saw Bobby Smith became the first African American in Texas high school football history to make first team all-state. After receiving eighty-one scholarship offers from all over the country, Smith played his college football at North Texas State. He then played for the Buffalo Bills in the AFL and made the Pro Bowl in 1965 after helping the Bills win the AFL title the same season.

In 2017 Smith still resided in Corpus Christi, where he owns a food-catering business. He survives Fant as the only integration pioneer left from Corpus Christi Miller. He spoke of the trials of being an integration trailblazer and helping pave the way for future African American Buccaneers. "I loved Corpus Christi," Smith said. "I was born and raised there, and I still live here. My roots are here. If fact, my grandfather has a street named after him in Corpus Christi.

"I started out at the black school, Coles Junior High, in 1954. I just wanted to play football. I was small, though. The coach, John Thomas, told me, 'You'll never be a football player.' I remember crying and crying after he told me that. My grandmother told me, 'Don't you worry.' Well, the next year we integrated, and I went to Cunningham Junior High as an eighth grader. I couldn't make the team there, either. I kept working, but they amazingly ran out of uniforms every week and I would put on a white practice uniform and sit on the bench.

"For ninth grade, I went to a new school, Ella Barnes Junior High. Ninth graders were still in junior high back then. That summer between going from Cunningham to Barnes, I finally started growing and I found out I could run like the wind. I stuck it out. I was told I would never be a football player. I didn't accept that.

"Pete Ragus took over as coach my junior year in 1958. He was a heckuva coach, a disciplinarian. We had a great year in 1958. We made it to the semifinals and lost a 7–6 game to Pasadena High School. I got along with everyone. My senior year I was named class favorite. I do remember at a school dance I was not allowed to dance with the Hispanic girl who was named class favorite. It didn't bother me, though. On the team my senior year people like Willie Adams and Johnny Roland would defer to me because everyone came to me for leadership. Miller was a special place. I was fortunate to be associated with some great classmates, teammates, and coaches. Those days were really the best time of my life.

"Not that things were always easy. We did pay the price. There were six blacks on the team in 1958 and 1959. We were the first black high schoolers to play at Rice Stadium in Houston in 1958, when we played Pasadena High School in the semifinals. When I ran track at the Border Olympics in Laredo, I couldn't stay in a hotel. I had to sleep on the floor in the gym. When we went to Midland to play in 1958, things were a little rough. Before the game, while we were warming up, the Midland fans surrounded the field and started chanting, 'Let's beat the nigger team! Let's beat the nigger team!'

"Coach Ragus had to send us to the locker room it got so bad. We ended up winning the game 18–8, and I returned the opening kickoff one hundred yards. That was satisfying. I guess I was running so fast because I was so scared. What's really weird is, after the game, some of the Midland

Bobby Smith and teammates celebrate a Miller victory, 1959. Courtesy of Ray Gonzales.

fans came up to me and started touching me, like they'd never encountered a black person before. I was glad to get out of that place."

When 1960 rolled around, six years after *Brown v. Board of Education*, the Civil Rights movement was in full swing. On February 1 in Greensboro, North Carolina, black students from North Carolina A&T College began a sit-in at a segregated counter at a Woolworth's store lunch counter. Although they were refused service, the students were allowed to stay seated at the counter. This event inspired similar sit-ins in cities throughout the South, including Houston, Galveston, and San Antonio.

It was under this backdrop of progress to start the 1960s that Corpus Christi Miller made football and integration history. The Bucs rolled to a 13–1 record and captured the state Class 4A title with a 13–6 upset win over heavily favored Wichita Falls High School. Miller lost only to Galveston 14–7 in nondistrict play. The Bucs scored 290 points on the season and gave up but 83 points in fourteen games. In the playoffs, the Bucs only surrendered eighteen points in four games. Wichita Falls, which was making its third of four straight appearances in the state finals, was heavily favored to defeat Miller. They were averaging more than thirty-two points a game. Miller held them to six points.

"We had eighteen whites, seventeen Hispanics, and six blacks on our 1960 state championship team," Coach Ragus said. "We were the first team in UIL history to win with blacks on our roster, and also the first team to win a state title with three ethnic groups on the team. We were pioneers. It was a completely different time and era. When you put it into context, considering the time and circumstances, it was quite an accomplishment by an exceptional group of kids that came together at the same time. I couldn't find a problem with integration at Miller. I credit the school, the administrators, and the members of the team for the smooth transition.

"We were fortunate to get the black players we got. After *Brown v. Board of Education* in 1954, schools in Corpus Christi started integrating but the black school, Solomon Coles High School, stayed open until the late 1960s. Blacks in Corpus could choose to stay at Coles or come and play at one of the white high schools. Coles had some really good teams back then. In fact, the year we won state in 1960, they won state in the PVIL. Now, I didn't recruit some of those guys over at Coles to come play for us at Miller, but I must say I encouraged them.

"Not that things didn't go our way too. All of our playoff games, with the exception of the finals against Wichita Falls, were played at Buc Stadium, our home field. I remember when we played Port Arthur in the playoffs. Jimmy Johnson, the Dallas Cowboys head coach, was a guard on that team. We flipped a coin as to where we were going to play the game. I prayed that we would win that toss, and we did. We played them in our home stadium. Can you picture trying to go to Port Arthur with black players in 1960? I don't think we could have won in Port Arthur. We ended up beating them 6–0 to go to the state finals."

"Why did integration at Miller go so smoothly? I think part of the reason was the black guys were good players and good people. Bobby Smith was class favorite when he was a senior. I also think Miller was easier to integrate instead of a school that was 100 percent Anglo. There were a lot of Hispanics at Miller. I'm most proud of integrating Miller without problems. I also think what helped is how I dealt with players individually. I would discipline all of our players, white, black, Hispanic, the same.

"I think our players sensed there was absolute love and respect for them. I honestly believe what a person's color was wasn't part of my makeup or made any difference to me. Part of that may have had to do with my being from California, where racial attitudes were a little better as opposed to Texas, but maybe not. I think one thing that helped me being from California, though, was dealing with the Hispanic players. In Texas, the attitude was that Hispanics couldn't play football very well. I never believed that. It never dawned on me that they were different. We came along ten years before the team in the movie *Remember the Titans*.

"There were some people we talked to about making a show about our team, but we didn't have the conflict on our team as they had in *Remember the Titans*. We were told our story was too boring; there was not enough conflict within our school or team. I guess that's a good thing. One great story in the whole integration thing is how athletics helped integration move forward."

Buddy Neubauer was an Anglo player on the Miller championship team. An offensive guard and defensive end, Neubauer moved to Corpus Christi from rural Arkansas in the seventh grade. He said, "I guess I haven't really thought about it, but I never really had any contact with blacks until I moved to Corpus Christi between sixth and seventh grade. When I went to Driscoll Junior High in Corpus, that's when I met Henry Williams. He was the first black kid I ever really knew. When I went to Miller, we were fully integrated. We were all from the west side of Corpus Christi, where Miller is located. The west side was mostly a working-class, blue-collar place. It's where the oil refineries are. The wealthier schools in town, like Ray High School, were on the south side of town.

"Nineteen sixty was a great year. It was a unique mix of guys, and we had no real problems on the team. I don't recall any incidents or bad blood between anyone. It's fifty-five years later and I still communicate with a bunch of the guys on the team. Coach Ragus was the leader and our catalyst. He set the tone. He believed in character. He had that strong work ethic, and he got that across to us.

"We worked hard and we practiced hard. I remember when I played I thought he was an old guy. It turns out I found out later he was only thirty-three years old when we won the state title. I don't remember much in the way of problems at away games. I do remember in Midland we couldn't stay in the hotel there because we had black players, so we had to stay in San Angelo and take a bus to the game with Midland High School. I don't ever remember any name-calling or anything like that.

That's not to say it didn't happen; I just don't recall seeing or hearing anything along those lines."

Victor Gonzalez played defensive back. He got to the point in his recollections: "Coach Ragus was the number one reason for our success. He was very enthusiastic. He got the best out of us. Most of us that went to Miller came from poor homes, and we didn't have much parental guidance. I didn't grow up with a father, nor did a lot of us, and he filled that role for a bunch of us. He had very high standards for us, and we always wanted to please him. He was kind and mild compared to other coaches, but he wouldn't settle for second-best from you. He wouldn't harp on us and criticize us. He would point out our mistakes, made sure we corrected them, and then that was it; it was on to the next thing.

"We were willing to sacrifice for Coach Ragus. We also never heard a discouraging word from him. He also had such a great reputation at Miller. Kids wanted to play for him. At Miller, the year we won state we didn't have exceptional speed or size, but we gave it our all. He made you want to go out there.

"I was the starting free safety. That meant I got to go up against Johnny Roland, Bobby Smith, and Philip Gonzales every day, since our first team offense would go against our first team defense every day at practice. It was no-holds-barred, and our practices would run three or four hours.

"I didn't go to school with any blacks until fifth or sixth grade, when Corpus Christi schools integrated. I found out that bigotry is taught, and it is pushed on you. I felt all my teammates in junior high and at Miller were great individuals. It's amazing that we never had an argument or fight among the three races. It was really three different worlds coming together on the practice field.

"Like I said, I was poor growing up. My mom was a maid and was paid $1.50 a day, and that was on days she found work. I was hungry a lot. That's where Coach Ragus came through again. Since a lot of his players were poor, Coach Ragus in his office would keep sandwiches and fruit there for us, and we could go by there if we were hungry. It was great. I ate many a meal in Coach Ragus's office.

"In the end, we were Coach Ragus's fans and followers. I loved it and lived it that year in 1960. I wouldn't change a thing. The whole experience of playing football at Miller made me a better person. I had a chance to play football in college, but I didn't have a penny to my name, so I had to go to work."

Lineman Willie Adams, one of the African American stars on the Miller team, was named to the all-state team after the 1960 championship season. Adams received eighty-seven scholarship offers from around the country, including every Big Ten school but Northwestern. Adams played his college football at New Mexico State and played two seasons for the Washington Redskins before going to play in Canada. Adams said, "I went to Miller instead of Solomon Coles because it was closer to my house. There were some problems with integration, to be sure. You had to be on your best behavior at all times. Things were not easy, not by a long shot. We did have good teamwork on our Miller team, though. Johnny Roland and I were sort of neighbors."

After the 13–6 win over Wichita Falls for the state championship, Adams said, "You know we've got three races of people on this team, and we've all been working to accomplish something in winning the state football championship. It shows you what can be done by people of three races who work together."

Art Delgado played defensive end and linebacker for the Bucs and tight end on offense. Voted a senior class favorite at Miller, he was named second team all-state after the 1960 season, and then went on to play at Baylor, where he earned three varsity letters. He said, "Coach Ragus was the key. He did an outstanding job talking to and communicating with us. We in turn had a tremendous amount of respect for him. Right off the bat, he found leaders from the three groups: white, Hispanic, and black, and any time there were any concerns or problems, he would meet with them and the problems would be solved before they ever escalated. He was proactive. Coach Ragus had a saying, 'We have to stay ahead of the hounds,' which meant head off any problems before they ever started.

"On the road, we did run into a couple of problems. When we went to Waco to play Waco High, we couldn't stay in town because of our black teammates. We had to stay in a hotel in Temple, a few miles away. We didn't find out why we had to stay there until later. The coaches did a good job shielding us from that kind of stuff. Back in Corpus, we were a typical football team; we hung out together and stuff. One incident I do recall in Corpus Christi was that a bunch of us went to an all-you-can-eat buffet at this one restaurant, and they tried to turn away our black teammates. All of us got up and walked out of the restaurant."

Ray Gonzales was the quarterback on Miller's state championship team. "When I was growing up I watched Miller as a kid," he recalled.

"They had some good teams of mostly Hispanic players. They played all the big boys of Texas high schools. When the black players came to Miller starting in 1957 or '58, that's what put them over the top. My sophomore year of 1958 I was on JV, and the varsity made it to the semifinals. Bobby Smith was on that team.

"It all started when we were in junior high. We had a large group of players from the different junior highs that came into Miller as sophomores. Ninth graders were still part of junior high back then. That spring between eighth and ninth grade they sent all of us through our own spring training. The coaches eventually chose about twelve of us to work out with the older players in the fall. I came from mostly white Driscoll Junior High. Art Delgado, who ended up at Baylor, Willie Adams, and Johnny Roland all came from Cunningham Junior High.

"Coach Ragus knew he was getting some great players. He instilled in us from day one that we could win the state title as seniors. He was right. We had a good year as juniors in 1959, but Ray beat us and went on to win state. I had hurt my knee as a sophomore, and I didn't play much my junior year while it healed. Johnny Roland started coming into his own that year. The summer before his junior year, he really filled out. He put on like fifty pounds. Speaking of size, I was pretty small. I was only about 125 pounds my senior year.

"We got along great in Corpus Christi in general, as far as race relations, compared to other cities. Corpus even got some nationwide attention as far as race relations. In 1959, when I was a junior, we were on the bus going somewhere to play, and Bobby Smith was showing me a black magazine (I believe it was Jet) that had an article about Corpus Christi and how racially friendly it was to 'Negros.' It mentioned Roy Miller High School, and how it had black players on the football team as well as in other sports.

"Then, in 1960, we had about the same number of whites and Hispanics, around seventeen or eighteen of each, and about six blacks on the squad. We just all got along. We would tell little ethnic jokes amongst ourselves, just giving each other a hard time. Going to Miller sometimes didn't seem like the outside world. When you walked on campus, you didn't feel or see any prejudice. Playing sports helped too. Sports levels the playing field. It doesn't matter your color, as long as you can play.

"We ran into a few problems here and there on the road. Coach Ragus usually had to check out restaurants ahead of time to make sure we could eat at them. When we went to play at Galveston Ball High School, we had to look around and find a little motel that would take all of the players. Before I forget, there was another incident when we went to Galveston that bears mentioning. When our team bus rolled into Galveston, we stopped by the stadium, which is still there today and, as it was then, right in the middle of an all-black neighborhood. As we were getting off the bus, we were surrounded by at least a hundred blacks, both kids and adults. The kids helped us with our equipment and everyone wished us luck in beating Ball, then an all-white school. They all wanted to see our black players together with the rest of the team. Unfortunately, we lost that game, the only game we lost all season.

"The biggest problem we had, though, was when we went to play at Midland out there in West Texas. When you were standing on the sidelines, you could hear the Midland fans behind us in the stands hollering, 'Black crows!' to our black players. Their fans didn't just get on the black players case, either. There was one play where I got hit in the stomach, and it knocked the wind out of me. As I was going to the bench, someone from up in the stands yelled, 'Kill that fucking Mexican!' Then at the end of every game, Coach Ragus, who was pretty religious, would always have the team gather on the field after the game to say the Lord's Prayer. Not in Midland, though. I heard Coach Ragus cuss for the first time when we skipped the prayer and went to go get on the bus. Coach Ragus said, 'C'mon, let's get the hell out of here!'"

Philip Gonzalez was a backfield mate of Ray Gonzales. After his career at Miller, he went to play college football at North Texas State, rejoining former Bucs teammate Bobby Smith, who had gone there the year before. Gonzalez said, "I grew up poor across the tracks on Morris Street. There were some bad sections, poverty-wise, around Miller, and some were not so bad. Now at Ray, our crosstown rivals, they were a little better off than we were.

"We got along really well as a team. We just wanted to win and contribute to the history of the Miller football program. There was a lot of competition among the team, and you had to work hard just to be a starter. It was challenging because a lot of the guys on the bench could easily take our place.

"We had some great leadership among the players. Guys like Willie Adams, Ramsey Muniz, and Art Delgado. Ramon, or Ray, Gonzales, our quarterback, was also a great leader. He was just a little guy, though, about 129 pounds. These guys would bring something to your attention if it was hurting the team. For example, if your grades were slipping, they would let you know about it.

"Then, of course, there was Coach Ragus and the coaching staff. He was a motivator. Sometimes he wouldn't have to say a word to you; he'd just give you a certain look. He treated you with respect and fairness. We didn't want to let him down. The whole coaching staff was dedicated. Coach Neely was great; he coached me in track too. Coach Herrera and Coach Simmons were really good also. It was just like a big family. I thank God that Coach Ragus was my coach.

"As far as problems when we went on the road because we black players, there was the time we went to Ball High in Galveston. The restaurant didn't want to accommodate the team. This was new to us. We didn't look at the skin color of our teammates; other parts of the state did. We looked at competitiveness, toughness, and whether you had the talent. That's all that mattered to us.

Johnny Roland, along with Willie Adams, were the stars of the 1960 Bucs. Roland, six-foot-two and 185 pounds, ran for 1,224 yards and scored 90 points to lead Miller in scoring. In the Bucs' state finals win over Wichita Falls, Roland scored the first Miller touchdown on a 37-yard run in the 13–6 Miller victory. Roland led all rushers in the title game with 103 yards. Roland, along with Adams, was named first team all-state in Class 4A, the state's largest division for schools. After his Miller career, Roland played his college football at Missouri under Coach Dan Devine and was named all–Big Eight running back his sophomore year in 1962. After having to sit out the 1963 season after a suspension for what Roland termed "a college prank gone wrong," his last two seasons he switched to defensive back. In 1965, Roland was consensus all-America and became the fourth round draft pick of the St. Louis Cardinals. In 1966, he was switched back to running back and was named the NFL Offensive Rookie of the Year. He also played in two consecutive Pro Bowls. A 1968 knee injury limited his effectiveness after that, but he ended up playing eight NFL seasons. After his playing career, he was a long-time running back coach for several NFL teams. Roland was elected to the College Football Hall of Fame in 1998.

Pete Ragus said about his star go-to player, "I only played Johnny Roland on offense because he took a beating every week. We had to slow Johnny down in practice or he would hurt someone. I used to ask

Johnny Roland, circa early 1960s. Courtesy of Mizzou Athletics.

Mrs. Roland, 'Why did you have only one child?' I had to talk Johnny into coming out for football. He started out as an end. As a sophomore, though, my first year as head coach in 1958, Johnny wasn't even playing at the start of the season. Our coaches couldn't talk him into playing. We finally put a uniform in a locker for him. We even put his name on the locker. Then, one day, I caught him on campus in between the school and the gym. I said to him, 'Johnny, I demand that you show up and start playing ball for us!' To my surprise, he did! His first game on junior varsity, the coaches decided to play him at running back. His first carry he scored a touchdown, and the rest is history!"

Roland reminisced, "Growing up in Corpus Christi was for the most part great. It's a seaport town and a more elderly community. You also have the military there. It's kind of a melting-pot town. There was a black part of town in Corpus that was called the Cuts. There were black businesses, theaters, ice cream parlors. It was a thriving area. I actually lived crosstown in the Hillcrests addition, which was another area where blacks stayed in Corpus. We were able to shop freely at the white businesses in town. We did have to sit in the balcony at the white movie theater, though. I had contact with white kids growing up. We used to play sandlot ball against each other.

"When Corpus Christi integrated its schools in 1955, they did it totally, not grade-by-grade. They did it all at once. Before *Brown v. Board of Education*, I would have gone to Coles High School. I could have still gone to Coles, but I chose to attend Cunningham Junior High, which was being integrated. We had a real good team there. We won the city championship. Coach Ragus at Miller was fortunate. He was getting a ready-made team. We played together constantly outside of school. All Coach Ragus had to do when we got to Miller was put the finishing touches on the team. Seriously, though, our success started at the top. Coach Ragus was the one who molded us together. He knew he was getting himself a team. We were a good mix of players. The Mexican kids were small, but they were tough. We did have some good size amongst the white and black players, though. I think our story is better than Remember the Titans because we had three ethnic groups mixing together, and for the most part we got along great.

"Coach Ragus pretty much kept any problems away from us. For example, when we played Wichita Falls in Waco for the state title, we couldn't stay together as a team, so we stayed in Temple, just a few miles away. I swear there were fifty thousand fans there that day. You know, we were young and we didn't realize at the time the full impact of our integrated team winning the state championship. Whenever we did face any problems with discrimination, we rallied around each other, and it made us really close as a team.

"I was on the B, or sophomore, team when I first started playing at Miller in 1958. We were cannon fodder for the varsity. They were really good that year; they went all the way to the semifinals. I didn't go out for the team right away at Miller. I hadn't cut my teeth yet. I remember Coach Ragus telling me, 'We'll have a uniform in your locker for you.' We had a good team in 1959, my junior year. I was mostly a blocking back for Bobby Smith. Ray High School beat us and ended up winning state that year. They were better than us. They had a veteran club. Nineteen sixty was our year, though. It was also a year in football for a lot of Corpus teams. Besides us winning state, Coles High School won the PVIL, and one of the private schools won a state title too. Then Del Mar College went to the Junior Rose Bowl. It was a great year for Corpus in football."

In the end, however, there were some doubts cast by Wichita Falls about whether the Buccaneers' state crown was legitimate. In a 2006 Texas Monthly magazine article, Terry Worrell of Wichita Falls, a guard and defensive end on the 1960 squad, was among some people who questioned the ages of some of the Bucs. He said, "None of us could tackle Johnny Roland. We were just a bunch of kids. They may not have been thirty-five, but they damn sure had been shaving longer than we had. We were helping each other on the bus after that one."

Ray Gonzales said, "I remember the 'age' issue being discussed at one point during the season. I know that there were three of us—myself included—that turned nineteen during the season. The UIL rule was that a student had to be eighteen or younger at the start of the school year to be eligible to participate in sports. I believe the other two were Victor Gonzalez and Art Delgado. In my case, I was born in Kingsville, Texas, in November 1941, and the school district rule at that time was that all Hispanic kids had to be six before the school year started. The belief was that Hispanics couldn't speak English (or were too dumb, I guess) at five years old. English was mostly spoken at our house, so I didn't have that problem, but I still was not allowed to register. So when I started kindergarten, I was six but turned seven in November. I turned nineteen in November of my senior year. I believe Art's birthday is in December. In the case of Roland, he was born in 1943 and was seventeen years old throughout the whole season.

"That's the first time I've heard about the Texas Monthly article, and yes it had to have been sour grapes, plus the fact that we had blacks and a lot of Hispanics on the team. Our team was also a bunch of kids, but the coaching staff brainwashed us, as we came into high school as sophomores, to believe that we could win state as seniors. Wichita Falls had a great team. I believe they were the top-ranked high school in the country, but they were still running a single wing offense. Coach Simmons, our line coach and an old timer, said he knew how to stop that offense, and our defense did."

And, as expected, Coach Ragus had his opinion: "Absolutely it was sour grapes, saying we had players that were too old. When someone's knocking your head off, you have to have a reason why or an excuse. I also absolutely feel some of that may have come from the fact that we had the Hispanic and black players, that there was a little prejudice there. Wichita Falls was a heavy favorite to beat us. In fact, one of the newspapers said they would beat us 40–0. We didn't have any illegal kids. No one was over age—they were all within the legalities of playing."

Sour grapes aside, what the 1960 Corpus Christi Miller Buccaneers accomplished in their run to the state title was historic. By being the first integrated team in Texas history to win a title, they dealt with the challenges that had been presented to them, and the Bucs opened the door wider after it had been cracked by earlier African Americans playing high school football for the first time, creating more opportunities in the future.

10

Texas' White Schools Challenge the HBCUs

I don't give a shit if they're from Mars if the kid can play football!
—WEST TEXAS STATE FOOTBALL COACH JOE KERBEL
ON RECRUITING BLACK PLAYERS

Prior to 1960, any African American wanting to play football at a four-year institution of higher learning in Texas was limited to one of the historically black colleges and universities, or HBCUs. During this era there was only one exception: North Texas State College.

If a black player went to a segregated high school, he was limited to a HBCU for two primary reasons—mainstream Texas colleges were segregated and the limited coverage of African American teams severely hampered the exposure necessary to attract the attention of recruiters. Talented 1940s and 1950s players such as Ralph Allen, Joe Washington, John Payton, Percy Hines, and Charles Brown had only one opportunity to play college ball—for a historically black school.

This custom changed somewhat in the mid-1950s due to the growing number of integrated high schools. A few black players received scholarship offers from northern colleges. Ben Kelly of Abilene Woodson attended Illinois, Garland Boyette of Orange Wallace High School went to Northwestern, and Anthony Guillory of Beaumont Hebert chose Nebraska. But they were the exception, not the rule. It became obvious that the exposure that came from playing for an integrated high school well served talented players who wanted to go north or west to attend college. Examples were Willie Jones of Robstown, Rudy Johnson of Aransas Pass, and Preacher Pilot of Kingsville. Each benefited from playing on integrated teams in the late 1950s.

Although these teams had inferior football and training facilities, the HBCUs had extraordinary talent. Prairie View A&M and Texas Southern regularly sent players to pro football in the 1950s and 1960s. During those decades, Texas Southern sent twenty-eight players and Prairie View sent seventeen to the NFL and AFL.

The coaching at both schools was first-rate. Alex Durley led the Texas Southern Tigers from 1949 until 1964, compiling a record of 101–55–8 and earning the 1952 Black College National co-title. Billy Nicks, the head coach of the Prairie View Panthers, took coaching to another level. After a stint at his alma mater, Morris Brown College, winners of the black national championship in 1941, Nicks spent seventeen years at Prairie View, from 1945 to 1947 and then from 1952 to 1965, racking up a record of 126–40–8. More importantly, during Nick's tenure the Panthers won Black College National Championships in 1953, 1954, 1958, 1963, and 1964.

Inferior conditions, lack of facilities, and less exposure to pro scouts led to less opportunity and sometimes injury for players that went to HBCUs from up through most of the 1960s. Such was the case with John Payton, Prairie View's star running back of the mid-1950s. Payton set the single-season school record for rushing yards, with 1,546 yards in 1954. He also still holds the career mark for rushing yards, with 3,703. In 1956, Payton was a rarity in that he came from a HBCU and was drafted by an NFL team, the Chicago Bears, in the eighteenth round. In the thirty-round 1956 draft, out of 360 players chosen, only 4 were from HBCUs. Two of the draftees, future Pro Football Hall of Fame defensive end Willie Davis of Grambling and Sherman Plunkett, were drafted by the Cleveland Browns. The Browns and Paul Brown had in the past proven to be progressive when it came to putting black players on the roster. The Chicago Bears chose the other two players from HBCUs, Payton along with Willie Galimore of Florida A&M.

The NFL virtually ignored players from HBCUs up until the 1960s, when the AFL came into existence. The AFL actively scouted and drafted HBCU players, including in 1963 when the Kansas City Chiefs made defensive tackle and future Hall of Famer Buck Buchanan of Grambling the first overall pick in the draft. But then John Payton was not able to play for the Bears because of an injury he suffered in college. Quite possibly if Payton had access to the same quality medical care offered at white colleges, his fate would have been different. As mentioned previously, Prairie View, as well as other HBCUs, lacked facilities, including those needed for medical treatment for injuries.

"Prairie View had very little in the way of facilities compared to other schools, white or black," Payton said in reflection. "We didn't have much and that may have contributed to my demise. We were playing Texas Southern one week, and I was late getting to practice. I put on some old thigh pads; they were the last pair. I ended up using those pads in the game that Saturday.

"During the game, I got hit hard in the thigh. It was a good clean hit, but the old thigh pad just didn't protect me. It didn't bother me at first. The next week we were playing a school we knew we could beat easily, but I played anyways. No one had taken an x-ray of my thigh or anything.

"My thigh kept getting worse, and a couple of weeks later, the trainer at Prairie View took me up the road to Texas A&M to have me checked out. They asked me, 'What's your problem?' I explained that I got hit in the thigh. They checked it out, and it turns out I had a calcium deposit on my thigh. The problem was I had taken too long to get it treated. They could have operated on it, but the doctors couldn't guarantee success.

"The doctor at A&M said, 'If you were playing here you never would have missed a game.' Had I gone earlier, they would have sent me to Houston to have my thigh operated on. I was scared, but they said it'd be OK as long as I didn't play football anymore. I decided to go teach and coach, even though I was drafted by the Bears.

"We won two national championships when I was at Prairie View. We got the best blacks in Texas. We were *the* school for blacks to play football at when Coach Nicks was there. He was a great motivator. I guarantee that if we had integrated back then, we could have beaten a lot of the white schools."

Starting in 1960 the level of talent at the HBCUs, while still strong, was beginning to be depleted. That's because more four-year colleges in Texas started integrating, leading to more opportunities for African American high school football players in the Lone Star State. This influx of desegregation at these traditionally all-white colleges eventually led to a talent drain from the HBCUs by the end of the 1960s and early 1970s, and they have never retained the level of talent they had before integration.

Like the other Texas African American football players that preceded them, Ben Kelly, Abner Haynes, Leon King, and Louis Kelley, it took a special kind of courage from the young men who integrated several Texas colleges in the early 1960s to press on in the face of discrimination. Sometimes the players experienced this intolerance on their own campus, on occasion from their teammates, and at times when they traveled to opposing schools. Several players from the early 1960s told their uplifting stories of integrating their prospective schools.

The college that opened the decade of integration was Texas A&I College (now Texas A&M–Kingsville), some thirty miles south of Corpus Christi. Besides integrating the football program at San Felipe High School in Del Rio in 1957, Sid Blanks became an integration trailblazer again when he went to Texas A&I in 1960.

Blanks had a choice of several colleges he could have attended. "I had been talking to Washington State and Oklahoma. I got an offer from TSU. I even got a letter from Dartmouth," he said. "How I got to Texas A&I was that there was a local Spalding sporting equipment salesman who saw me play. He was friends with Gil Steinke, the Texas A&I coach. The salesman told Gil Steinke, 'Come see this kid—he's good. He's a black kid, though.' Coach Steinke came to see me play, and I scored three touchdowns. He wanted me to go to Texas A&I. Then, later that fall, I was in Del Rio watching Texas A&I win the 1959 NAIA national championship on TV. That convinced me I wanted to go there."

Steinke integrated A&I football. A native of Ganado, Texas, he played four years at A&I at running back and rushed for more than a thousand yards as a senior in 1941, which was second in the nation. He then served

Sid Blanks, Texas A&I College, circa 1963. Courtesy of Javelina Sports Information.

in the US Navy during World War II. Starting in 1947, Steinke played five seasons in the NFL with the Philadelphia Eagles. He then returned to his alma mater to become head coach in 1954. In twenty-three seasons, Steinke compiled a 182–61–4 record, which included six NAIA national championships. His last three teams from 1974 to 1976 won forty-two consecutive games. He was inducted into the College Football Hall of Fame in 1996, one year after his death.

When Blanks arrived in Kingsville, though, Coach Steinke did not tell him one small detail—that as soon as he took the field as a player, he would be integrating the football program at Texas A&I. "I found out after I got to A&I that I was the only black on the football team," Steinke's star recruit recalled. "I also found out that I had grown up pretty poor in Del Rio. I wasn't privileged to other things the other college students had growing up, like the proper books for school, or just life experiences in general. Some of the coaches at A&I worked with me. They taught me how to study and do schoolwork. They also taught me social things so I could adjust to things. When I first got to A&I, I stayed with a coach. Eventually I got to stay on campus."

At first, Blanks was not allowed to live on campus. He eventually lived with a Kingsville family, as he was told by the college he would be more comfortable in a home environment. Only in a speech class presentation made by a classmate did he learn that he could not stay in the football players' dorm because of a Board of Regents ruling. Out of respect for Coach Steinke, he did not "push the issue."

Eventually, because of Sid Blanks helping to break down these difficult racial barriers, on December 20, 1962, all facilities at Texas A&I were open to people of all races and creeds. This included dining halls and dormitories.

Blanks was accepted by the people of Kingsville fairly quickly. Clarice Blanks, who was dating him at the time, said, "Sid ran Kingsville back then. He was like the black mayor. Sid got to go places in town that other blacks couldn't go. He helped break down barriers."

"It made me feel good that I could help people by breaking down some of those walls," Sid Blanks said, "not just in Kingsville, but in places like Commerce where East Texas State was. I helped break down the housing barrier there by staying in the hotel there and being able to dine with my teammates. I helped them move toward integration.

"When I got to Texas A&I, Coach Steinke took care of me. I was a small-town country boy. I had to learn about the real world, and he was there to help me. I was blessed to have a coach like him. He kept dangerous stuff away from me. I remember we had a meeting. Coach Steinke told all the players to 'protect me like a brother, because that's what Sid is, a brother.'"

There was one incident that stuck in Blank's memory: As a freshman in 1960 when the team traveled to East Texas State College in Commerce, the players encountered serious problems, still vivid in Blanks's memory. "The teams stayed in a small town by the name of Greenville, Texas, because there was no hotel to house a team in Commerce," he said. "As we drove into the city limits of Commerce, there was a large billboard which read, 'Welcome to Commerce, Texas—The Blackest Land and the Whitest People.' Upon arrival at the hotel, there were several people who wanted to see, I suppose, if I would be not only the first black to participate in a game in East Texas, but also the first black to sleep in the only hotel within a one-hundred-mile radius. . . . The hotel manager had made arrangements for me to stay with a nice black family who would house me overnight.

"The black family walked up and introduced themselves, and assured me that I would be welcome and safe in their home, and they would be pleased to have me. Before I could react in any way, Coach Steinke had retrieved all of the keys and promptly ushered us out. The manager wanted to know what the problem was. Coach Steinke answered him by saying, 'If we all can't stay here, then we all leave.'

"Seeing that this was probably the bulk of the hotel's business during football season, the manager felt like it would be more profitable if the whole team stayed at his hotel. Not only did I get a room in the hotel, but my roommate and I slept in the bridal suite!"

During the game, there was a great deal of name-calling. "But my teammates backed me up by opening big holes in the line so I could run for long yardage." As a result, "the name-calling only made my teammates block harder and me run faster." Soon the opposition realized "that their little nasty ignorant remarks worked against them instead of for them."

Blanks remembered that prejudice "was much more of a problem off the field than on the field," and "I could see that I had won a big victory for blacks everywhere against people who were small-minded and afraid of something they knew nothing about." Blanks believed that people who were in a position at Texas A&I "to make changes that should have been made long before I came to school" did not have the courage or insight "to allow something in this capacity until they saw the result of the efforts of a man who, to me, is a great man—Coach Steinke."

The following year, 1961, some 640 miles from Kingsville, there was a college coach at West Texas State College (now West Texas A&M) in Canyon, up in the Texas Panhandle just fifteen miles south of Amarillo, who integrated his football program in a fashion different from Gil Steinke and the other Texas colleges that had previously integrated their football programs.

Joe Kerbel came up through the high school ranks in Texas to become the head coach at West Texas State in 1960. He had won two state titles at Breckenridge High School in 1952 and 1954. In 1958 he became offensive coordinator at Texas Tech under Head Coach DeWitt Weaver. When Weaver stepped down after the 1959 season, Kerbel was passed over for the Red Raiders head coaching job. Instead, Tech chose its defensive coordinator, J. T. King. West Texas State had just fired Coach Clark Jernigan after two seasons and a 2–18 record, setting the stage for athletic director John Kimbrough to hire Kerbel for the job of bringing the Buffaloes out of the doldrums.

Finding the team he inherited almost barren of talent, Kerbel hit the recruiting trail in search of better players. He decided to use a nationwide search. If there was a local Texas Panhandle player talented enough to play for the Buffaloes, Kerbel and his assistant coaches would try to recruit them. He also made it clear that they would recruit black athletes as long as they qualified academically. Kerbel went against the grain. When other Texas college football teams were integrating, they exclusively used Texas high school players. Kerbel brought in black players from outside Texas—such as Ollie Ross from Harrisburg, Pennsylvania, and Bobby Drake from California. Along with Pete Pedro, they were the first African Americans recruited to play football at West Texas State. Kerbel pointedly got players, white and black, from Pennsylvania and the California junior colleges. Some other early black players Kerbel brought to Canyon were Russell Mundy and Willie Thompson from Pennsylvania, Ted Wheeler from Detroit, and Hank Washington from Los Angeles. Some key out-of-state Anglos were Larry Patterson from Beaver Falls, Pennsylvania (where he was the center at Beaver Falls High School for Pro Football Hall of Fame quarterback Joe Namath), and Steve Oakley and Bob Petrich from California.

Ollie Ross was part of the trio of African American football players Joe Kerbel brought to Canyon in 1961. He was originally from Harrisburg, Pennsylvania, and Kerbel recruited him out of Palo Verde Junior College in California. Ross was a fullback, and although he spent much of his time as a blocker for Pete Pedro, he still rushed for 950 yards on 182 carries in his West Texas State career, averaging 5.2 yards per carry. Ross also scored thirteen career touchdowns for the Buffs. When Pedro was injured as a senior in 1963, Ross led West Texas State in rushing. For his career, he also kicked four field goals and eight extra points. Ross also handled the kickoff chores for the Buffs. He also was a fine defensive back, recording six interceptions and one touchdown for his career.

An Anglo teammate, Jerry Behrens, called Ross "an outstanding individual and a close friend. He went through some tough times back in those days, but he never complained about the rejections he experienced on campus or in Canyon or Amarillo."

Although Ross was a standout on offense, defense, and specialty teams, the player that turned the corner for the West Texas State program was "Pistol Pete" Pedro, out of Lynn, Massachusetts, via Trinidad Junior College in Trinidad, Colorado.

When Kerbel's first season at West Texas State ended with a 3–7 record in the fall of 1960, Kerbel proclaimed, "I'm not going to sit around here forever and wait for this football team to develop into a winner. There's not much we can do about it this year, but, dammit, next season we're going to win. And the way we're going to do it is with a running back who can put some punch into our offense!"

Jack "Sleepy" Harris, Joe Kerbel's assistant coach at the time, was told by Kerbel, "I want the best damn junior college running back in the country. I don't care where you have to go to find him. Just find him and bring him back here!"

After Harris scoured the country looking for a running back with no luck, he stumbled onto his savior, out in California, by accident. Harris was visiting with Bakersfield Junior College Head Coach Ray Newman, who told him, "There's a kid at Trinidad Junior College who's really fast. He played on the football team and ran a leg on the 440 relay team that won the junior college national championship last year."

Harris asked, "Can he play? What's his name?"

Newman replied, "I really don't know the answer to either question." Harris then proceeded to call the Trinidad coach a couple of days later, and he said that Pete Pedro had a chance to be one of the best running backs in the country. Harris then informed Kerbel about his potential diamond-in-the-rough and how he was back at his parents' house in Lynn, Massachusetts. There was a potential roadblock. "Joe, there's something you ought to know," Harris said cautiously. "Pete's daddy is black and his mom's Puerto Rican."

Kerbel replied, "I don't give a shit if they're from Mars if the kid can play football!"

Before Pedro decided to come to West Texas State to play football, his mother had some concerns about the racial situation. She argued, "If my boy comes to Texas, they will make him sit in the back of the bus." Joe Kerbel replied, "Ma'am, if your boy is as fast as everyone says he is, he can sit in my lap in the front of the bus." Kerbel didn't mention to Mrs. Pedro that Canyon, Texas, had a reputation as a sundown town. Kerbel figured he would cross that bridge when he came to it.

"Pistol Pete" Pedro was the player that put West Texas State football back on the map. In his sophomore season of 1961, Pedro finished second nationally in rushing with 966 yards, averaging 7.1 yards per carry, and led the country in scoring with twenty-two touchdowns. In one game, a 56–27 victory over Texas Western College in El Paso, Pedro ran for 235 yards and six touchdowns. That performance earned him the Associated Press Back of the Week award. The Buffaloes went from a 3–7 record in 1960 to a 6–4 record in 1961. The next season, despite some minor injuries, Pedro again led West Texas State in rushing, with 831 yards. The Buffs finished with a 9–2 record, with upset wins over Texas Tech and Arizona State, and a 15–14 Sun Bowl win over Ohio University.

Injuries hampered Pedro his senior year, as he only rushed for 360 yards, and West Texas State stumbled to a 4–5–1 record. Those injuries hampered his shot at a pro career. He spent one season in 1964 on the Boston Patriots taxi squad before being cut. He finished his career at West Texas with 2,157 rushing yards and averaged 6.8 yards per carry.

Pistol Pete recalled his days at Trinidad Junior College and West Texas State. He said, "Our athletic director at Lynn High School had contacts with a lot of junior colleges. I went with five or six guys from Lynn to Trinidad Junior College. We took the bus to Denver and then south to Trinidad. I really didn't like Trinidad or the coach. I didn't think he was fair to me, so I didn't go back after my first year.

"Some of the guys on the team transferred to junior colleges in California. I couldn't afford to do that, so I went home to Lynn. Apparently when West Texas State was recruiting in California, my name came up and the next thing I knew, Coach Kerbel called me at home. He talked to me about coming to Canyon. I didn't know much about segregation at the time. I asked Coach Kerbel, 'Is it prejudiced there?' Coach Kerbel replied, 'Prejudiced? We're going to change things here! I promise you there will be no prejudice against you if you come here.'

Joe Kerbel and "Pistol" Pete Pedro, West Texas State, 1962. Courtesy of WTAMU Athletics.

"I had some doubts. I had actually gone through Canyon when our Trinidad track team was on its way to Big Spring, Texas, for a meet. I remember passing by that sunken stadium in the ground. We stopped in Canyon at a restaurant. We walked in, and the owner made the whole team sit in the back of the restaurant because we had several blacks on the team. In the back of my mind, I said to myself, 'I can't wait to get the heck out of here.'

"I finally decided to come to West Texas State. I asked Coach Kerbel if one of my football playing friends from Lynn, Bobby DeLuca, could come with me. Coach Kerbel agreed to give him a scholarship too, and we were on our way. When we arrived in Texas in February of 1961, we ran into a big blizzard and got to Canyon late. We were met by Coach Harris, and he took us to meet Coach Kerbel. You know, if I had to do it again, I would still do it.

"Coach Kerbel opened up doors for me and my black teammates. We never had a problem with our other teammates. Coach Kerbel called a meeting and sat the team down and explained things to everybody. Me and my white teammates still get together after all of these years. They watched out for us at school. Guys like Larry Patterson, Jerry Behrens, Bob Petrich, Kyle Campbell, John David Bryant—they were right with us through everything.

"Sometimes some of the cowboys in town there in Canyon would drive by in their pickup trucks and holler 'nigger!' at us. Or they might yell 'nigger lover!' if our white teammates were with us. For example, Jerry Behrens's parents were like a mother and father to all of us. We used to go over to their house all of the time. Jerry's parents would also make us all go over there so we could study for finals.

"Larry Patterson was from Beaver Falls, Pennsylvania, and grew up with Joe Namath. One time, a bunch of us—Larry, myself, Ollie Ross, Willie Thompson—took the train back east to visit our homes. Who should meet Larry at the train station but Joe Namath. I found out that Joe knew who I was because Larry had been sending Joe my newspaper articles while he was down at Alabama playing for Bear Bryant."

Pedro thought highly of Coach Kerbel: "He was a character, he certainly was. He was a great guy, though. He knew how to motivate you. He didn't miss any tricks. At practice if you messed up, he would come right up to you and tell you the way it was. He let nothing get past him.

"Coach Kerbel could be tough. He was a captain in the marines during World War II. I learned that if I came out of the game after I messed up to not get anywhere near him on the sidelines. One time early on I was standing too close to him on the sidelines, and he yelled, 'Come over here!' and when I did he grabbed me by the facemask. He told me the play to send in, 'Black left 89!' and then told me to repeat it. He then shoved me into the game. I never got close to him again on the sidelines.

"I'm not sure why Coach Kerbel integrated the West Texas State program with me and Ollie Ross. There have been so many stories and versions of stories why through the years. I personally think part of the reason was he was losing to schools his first season at West Texas State, like Arizona State, Arizona, and New Mexico State, who had already integrated, and he decided he needed the best players possible—it didn't matter what color we were. He often told us that without us black players, he couldn't win."

Jerry Don Bryant played backup quarterback on offense and safety on defense for the Buffs during these pivotal years. He said, "I probably knew Coach Kerbel as well as anybody. I played for him at Texas Tech for two years when he was the offensive coordinator there. When he got the head job at West Texas State, I played for him three years there. I then went into the service, and when I came back from Vietnam, I worked on Coach Kerbel's staff for a couple of years while I earned my master's degree. Coach Kerbel recruited the country, not just Texas, for players, white and black. He just wanted the best player he could get. He would go into schools that other coaches wouldn't be caught dead going into to get a player. I'm talking 'Blackboard Jungle' types of schools.

"Pete, Ollie Ross, and Bobby Drake were the first three black players at West Texas State. I never knew of an incident on campus or with the team involving those three. For one thing, Coach Kerbel wouldn't allow it. They were like brothers to us. I used to take them home with me to Hereford, about thirty miles from Canyon, on the weekends sometimes. They would spend the night at my parents' house, and then on Sunday morning they would all go to church with us and we would all sit in the front row.

"Bobby Drake was the other black player besides Pedro and Ross who came in 1961. He was from California, and he was smooth. He tragically died on his way going back to California in the spring, so he never got to play for us. Some people tend not to remember him because of that. None of the black guys had cars, so I would take them around sometimes. One night Bobby says, 'JD, you're gonna go with us to the 77 Club in the Flats in Amarillo.' Basically, it was an all-black nightclub. I was the only honky in the place. I stayed close to Ollie Ross because he was a big guy. Well, Bobby gets out on the dance floor, and he starts doing a popular dance at the time, the pony. Back then, it was a somewhat suggestive dance. Today it'd be nothing. I tell you what, his moves were something else. He was embarrassing the ladies out on the dance floor with some of those moves."

Joe Granato was another teammate. A graduate of San Antonio Edison, Granato played a year of junior college football at Del Mar College in Corpus Christi before transferring to West Texas State in 1960, the same year Joe Kerbel took over the Buffalo program. After his playing days were over, Granato was a high school and college coach for forty-two years, with a stint with the University of Oklahoma under Chuck Fairbanks from 1971 to 1973. "I went to Edison High School in San Antonio," he said. "When we integrated, there were about twenty-five or so blacks that came over to Edison. It really didn't bother me. I had known blacks all of my life. Also, at home, my father wouldn't let us use the n-word or anything like that. We're full-blooded Italian, and Italians back then had gone through a lot of the same crap the blacks had gone through.

"A couple of black kids came out for sports at Edison, and they didn't last very long, maybe a couple or three weeks. They weren't the greatest players, and they had to be bused across town. Most of the better black players went to some of the better football programs in the city.

"When I got to West Texas State, I didn't think anything about blacks being on the team. Guys like Pete Pedro and Ollie Ross were my teammates, and it didn't matter what color they were. Not everyone on the team felt that way, though. Some of the players I'm sure left because of integration—well, that and Coach Kerbel coming to take over the program. Our first year under Coach Kerbel, 135 players tried out, and we only ended up with 33 players. Like I said, some of those guys left because we now had blacks in the program, but many of them left because Coach Kerbel was so tough.

"One incident sticks out in my mind at West Texas State. We would have an alumni game in the spring as one of our scrimmages. Ollie Ross was a senior, and as I was going into the dressing room, one of the alumni players from a few years back told Ollie to 'get your black ass out of the locker room!' That guy was a lot bigger than me, but I told him a thing or two. You know, twenty years later, we were at a team reunion and Ollie said to me, 'Joltin Joe, thank you, you had my back on that day. "

Larry Patterson of Beaver Falls, Pennsylvania, was one of the out-of-state Anglo players Joe Kerbel brought to West Texas in 1961. Patterson was the center and linebacker for the Joe Namath–led Beaver Falls team that won the Western Pennsylvania Interscholastic Athletic League AA title, with a 9–0 record, in 1960. Patterson said, "I looked at a few colleges fairly close to Beaver Falls. I really had no intention of going to college, but we were the state champs, so we got some attention. I think ten or so guys on our team got scholarships. Of course, Joe Namath was our quarterback. There was a college coach in the area, a black guy, who was recruiting for Coach Dick Mansberger for I think Arizona or Arizona State. He got Coach Kerbel down at West Texas State to get with me. Coach Kerbel called me and convinced me to come to West Texas State.

"Going to Canyon was like going to a different culture in a sense. The people at West Texas State and Canyon dressed different and talked different. I guess I dressed different and talked different to them. I was more like the black guys that were brought in to play, so I hung around them at first. Eventually, though, I was accepted by everyone. At first, the guys from the east stuck together and the guys from the west stuck together, and the West Texas guys stuck together. We ended up mixing together after a while, and it all worked out. It took me a while to feel at home, but in the end the people treated me well and it was a good experience. It took some adjusting. I would talk to Joe by phone fairly often. Since he was at Alabama, that was like a whole different world for him too. We were both in a strange land. We would talk about what our new, different cultures were like. But neither one of us was a quitter, so we stuck it out.

"Playing with the black players wasn't that big of a deal with me. We had quite a few on our team at Beaver Falls. Even when I played youth football when I was around ten, I played with and against blacks. My team only had a couple, but the team from the lower end of town—the team Joe Namath was on—had a lot of blacks. When I went to West Texas State, there were six of us that came from Pennsylvania. Five of the players were black, like Willie Thompson, and most were running backs. I had played against several of them in high school.

"I think the black players were treated pretty well in Canyon. Most of the people there didn't treat them any different. There were some that did, though. Even talking to Pete Pedro years later, he felt he wasn't treated any different. If they were good people, which those first black players were, they were going to be treated well. Now, if they had arrived at West Texas State with a chip on their shoulder, then it would have been different.

"As far as Coach Kerbel, he treated me well. I was not a great player. When my family came down to visit, though, he really bragged on me to them. That was off the field. On the field, that was a different story. He was tough on us. Sometimes we would scrimmage three times a week during the season. He had to be tough on us, though. He had brought in players from all over the country and different backgrounds, and he had to get everyone working together. There wasn't much love for him while we were playing for him. After we were done playing for Coach Kerbel was when we realized what he had done for us."

After Kerbel recruited his initial group of African American players, he continued to bring in out-of-state blacks. The most well-known of these later players was another player from Pennsylvania that Kerbel personally recruited in 1965. Running back Eugene "Mercury" Morris was recruited out of Pittsburgh. Morris eventually became the NCAA's all-time leading rusher by the time he finished his college career. Morris then went on to play eight seasons in the NFL, including a stint on the Miami Dolphins' undefeated 1972 Super Bowl Championship squad. "Coach Kerbel came to my high school and got me out of English class, and I thought he ruled the world," Morris said. "I remember him selling my grandparents and my mom and dad on how good he was going to treat me. Once I got to Canyon, though, it was like he said, 'I got you now!'"

By the late 1960s, Kerbel turned to African American players from Texas. The most notable was future Dallas Cowboys and Super Bowl Champion star Duane Thomas, a running back who came out of Dallas Lincoln High School in 1966. Kerbel told Thomas one time, "Duane, we can't win with players from up here in the Panhandle. I recruit black players because you guys will make us a winner, and as long as I keep winning, those SOBs can't say anything to me."

Unfortunately, Kerbel's belief didn't hold up, because after eleven seasons and a 68–42–1 record, including two bowl victories, the West Texas State Board of Regents, tiring of Kerbel's maverick ways, his rough treatment of players, and his recruiting blacks from both coasts in favor of white players from the Panhandle, Kerbel was let go in 1970 after eleven seasons. He is still the top winning coach in the history of the school. He died of a heart attack in 1973 at age fifty-one.

Lamar State College of Technology (now Lamar University), in Beaumont, just thirty miles from the Louisiana border, was the next Texas college to integrate its football program. That happened in 1962. Just six years earlier, Lamar College was the site of protests against the integration of the school, when US District Judge Lamar Cecil ordered desegregation on July 30, 1956. Two days later a twelve-foot wooden cross was burned on campus.

In spite of the cross-burning incident, twenty-six black students enrolled amid violent protests for a few weeks until the Texas Rangers were brought in to restore order. On September 25, the first day of classes, protestors were stationed at all eleven entrances to the college. The protestors insulted and jeered white and black students alike. History professor Ralph Wooster said the protestors "seemed by their appearance to be white lower-middle class . . . these were real hillbilly types." The Lamar campus, with the aid of the Rangers, was eventually able to continue classes, and the college was integrated.

The young African American who desegregated the Lamar football program six years after these protests was Beaumont native Anthony "Tony" Guillory. Guillory had been a star guard, tackle, and middle guard at Beaumont Hebert High School. He played on the 1959 state champion Hebert team that defeated Dallas Lincoln 37–0. He was teammates with future All-Pros Miller Farr and Warren Wells. Guillory was named to the all-time PVIL defensive team in 1992, joining other team members that included Pro Football Hall of Famers Joe Greene, Emmitt Thomas, and Dick "Night Train" Lane. After he finished at Lamar, Guillory was a seventh round draft pick of the Los Angeles Rams.

Because of his 10.3 speed in the hundred-yard dash, Guillory started at outside linebacker his rookie year of 1965. However, in 1966, he suffered a serious knee injury in training camp and missed the whole season. Guillory was never quite the same player after his injury, but lasted three more seasons in the NFL.

After Guillory graduated from Hebert in 1961, he spent his freshman fall semester at the University of Nebraska. "In January 1962 when I came back to Beaumont and Lamar," he recalled, "things started changing. I was the lone ranger for a while. Gradually Lamar got more black players. The basketball team didn't integrate until around 1965, though. I originally signed with Wichita State. Miller Farr, my high school teammate at Hebert, agreed to go there. I stayed up there that summer, but Nebraska kept after me, and at the last minute I decided to go there. I was there my freshman year and played in two freshman games, against Iowa State and Kansas State. There were only twenty-seven blacks on campus in Lincoln, and twenty-five of them were in the athletic program. To throw a southern kid into that situation was tough.

"When I went home after the 1961 fall semester, Lamar Head Coach J. B. Higgins had talked to my parents about me integrating their football program. They wanted to get into the process of recruiting black players. Lamar also talked to Miller Farr about transferring there too, but he turned them down. Willie Ray Smith Jr., who was finishing up his senior year playing running back for his daddy over at Charlton-Pollard High School, turned down Lamar too and eventually went to Iowa. So it was just me who integrated the football program. I actually registered for class for the spring semester of 1962, and I promptly integrated the track program before I integrated football. I threw the shot and discus. I later that spring went to spring training with the football team. It was a bit of a surprise to some people that I came out there. The black community in Beaumont was excited that I was out there playing football for Lamar. There was some dissension in the white community."

Coach Higgins said about getting Guillory to attend Lamar, "I had to go to the board to get permission, but once I got the OK, things went smoothly. We had good individuals to break the color barrier and we never had any problems. Tony Guillory gained the respect of his teammates and his opponents with his great play his first year here, and he kept it up the entire time he was at Lamar. He was the second fastest player we had at Lamar, and he was a lineman."

"About the only real racial problem I encountered at Lamar was after my first day of spring training, I went into the showers and the majority of the white players left," Guillory recalled. "That was kind of hurtful. I never had a problem with the players at practice. There was a little bit of name-calling, but that went away pretty quickly too.

"When I started playing on varsity, I had problems in places like Stephen F. Austin in Nacogdoches and Sam Houston State in Huntsville. There was some pretty bad name-calling at those two places. Later, when I had another black teammate by the name of Eugene Washington, we weren't allowed to stay with the rest of the team in Nacogdoches. We stayed with a black family in the area. The only thing that bothered me was when we got back to the hotel. They wouldn't let us stay there, but the hotel let us eat with the team for our pregame meal."

The two people involved in the integration of the McMurry College football program, Kenneth Deckard and Grant Teaff, spoke of that experience. Deckard said, "I moved around a lot as a kid. I went to Palestine's Elkhart School in East Texas for a bit, but then we moved to West Texas. I lived in San Angelo and McCamey. My parents got divorced, and that's how I ended up in Kermit with my mom and sister. Kermit was an oil town of about ten thousand people in the early 1960s. I went to segregated Dunbar Junior High in Kermit.

"In ninth grade, though, I was able to go to Kermit High School. There was not much interaction with whites. Kermit was pretty much segregated before that. We had our area of town called the Flats. We had our own businesses in the Flats, like a grocery store and a café. I remember we couldn't go to the white theater downtown, but we could go to the drive-in theater. In a lot of cases, the blacks had to work for whites, like being a domestic.

"As far as sports, we didn't have enough kids at Dunbar to have a football team. We did have a basketball team, and we played the other black schools out there in West Texas: Monahans, Crane, Odessa, and Midland. I also played baseball, but not for the school. We had a Negro league, and we once again played teams from those West Texas towns. When Kermit High School was integrated my freshman year of 1959–60, we had one black senior, two sophomores, and three freshman. By the time I graduated in the spring of 1963, I was the only black senior who graduated, and there were two juniors, one sophomore, and eight freshmen. I only played varsity sports my senior year at Kermit. One of the coaches saw me in an intramural class one day and convinced me to come out. I ended up playing football, basketball, baseball, and track.

"When I got out of high school, I got offers from Sul Ross, Texas Western, Texas A&I, and McMurry. My dad decided I was going to go to McMurry. I had no problems with my teammates at McMurry; they were great. In Abilene, though, I couldn't go to the movies, and there were some restaurants I couldn't go in. I also ran track at McMurry. I did get to run against John Carlos in the hundred-yard dash in a meet at East Texas State University. I ran a 9.5 and I was beating Carlos until the eighty-five-yard mark, when he blew by me and ran a 9.3."

Grant Teaff said, "Ken was our first minority on the football team. It never crossed my mind about asking anyone if we could integrate the football program. The thought never occurred to me. No one said I could or couldn't do it, so I did it. It was a no-brainer recruiting Ken. What we all went through was extraordinary. For someone like me who grew up in Snyder in West Texas in a segregated world, it was something else. In Snyder the minority school was on the outskirts of town. Luckily the home I grew up in was not mentally segregated. A lot of Hispanics would come up to Snyder to pick vegetables for us. My dad owned a service station, and he had a black man by the name of Rufus who worked there. Rufus befriended me when I was a kid.

"I had no idea what we would go through. Our first game was against Austin College in Sherman. We stopped in a little bit north of Fort Worth on our way there, and I ordered some chicken fried steak dinners for the team so that they would be ready when we got there in Sherman. I was pretty naïve. When we got to the restaurant, which had opened just to feed our team, I was walking in with Kenneth Deckard when the owner said, 'Is that nigger with you? He can't eat in the dining room. He has to eat in the kitchen. That nigger can't eat here.' By then, the players were gathering around. The steaks were already on the tables waiting to be eaten. I said, 'You mean we can't eat together? If my player can't eat with his teammates, then we're going back to Abilene. So we went back to Abilene without dinner."

"There was one other event from Kenneth's first season in 1963. We didn't take Kenneth with us to Monroe, Louisiana, to play Northeast Louisiana State College (now University of Louisiana–Monroe). We had to let him take the weekend off. Back then, you just didn't go into Louisiana with a black player on your roster. Kenneth was lucky—he wasn't there for the plane crash."

The plane crash happened on the way home from Monroe on September 28, 1963, following an 8–7 loss on the last play of the game. Upon take-off, the pilot realized the plane's elevator controls had locked up and he could not gain altitude. The pilot got the plane in the air, and twice tried landing back at the Monroe airport. After the two failed attempts and blowing out the landing gear, the pilot decided to land at Barksdale Air Force Base in Shreveport, forty-five minutes away, because the base had a longer runway. To weigh down the tail end of the plane so they could land, Coach Teaff and assistants Hershel Kimbrell and Buddy Fornes stood in the back of the plane without regard for their lives. The plane ended up belly landing at Barksdale, and no one was seriously injured.

After the integration of Texas A&I, West Texas State, Lamar, and McMurry in the early 1960s, those colleges set the stage for the next two milestones in college football integration: Warren McVea joining the University of Houston Cougars in 1964, and John Westbrook at Baylor and Jerry Levias at Southern Methodist University, integrating the Southwest Conference in 1965. At the same time some colleges in Texas were starting to include African Americans, Texas high schools were slowly continuing the desegregation process, both in the classroom and on athletic fields.

11

The Eagles Fly High

You know, we didn't have much, but we loved and cared for each other.
—Star running back Warren McVea about the 1962 state
champion San Antonio Brackenridge Eagles

Another high school team that broke down barriers in the new decade was the 1962 San Antonio Brackenridge Eagles. The Eagles capped off an improbable run to the Texas Class 4A title with a 30–26 win over Borger in Abilene on December 22—the first inner-city minority team to achieve this mighty feat. The team had twenty-three African Americans, twelve Hispanics, and one racially mixed player, David Hardin, whose father was white and mother Hispanic. History shows that the only two other minority teams from the inner city to win state championships in the state's University Interscholastic League were Houston's Yates High School in 1985 and Dallas's Carter High School in 1988—a title they later had to forfeit. Also historically significant was that when Breckenridge defeated Borger, it marked the first championship game in Texas that pitted one fully integrated team against another.

Brackenridge started off this sterling season slowly, winning just four of its first seven games. The Eagles didn't even score against Kingsville, a 27–0 setback to Kingsville in which star running back Warren McVea and several of his teammates were suspended. McVea also was one of several players who battled early-season injuries. A 42–30 loss to Corpus Christi Miller dropped the team to a 4–3 record, usually far from championship consideration.

Then the improbable happened. Injured players regained their health, McVea displayed the star power everyone knew he had, and Coach Weldon Forren decided to open up the offense. Senior quarterback Vic Castillo adjusted to his new role as starter and threw more passes than any other offensive signal caller up until that point in Texas high school football history. The Eagles proceeded to win their final seven games. Brackenridge beat San Antonio Highlands 21–3 in the bi-district round of the playoffs and Brownsville 38–13 in the quarterfinals a week later, setting up a showdown in Houston's Rice Stadium against the hometown Spring Branch Bears, who were ranked the number one team in Texas. Brackenridge pulled off a stunning 30–23 win, which set up the state finals game against Borger, the pride of the Texas Panhandle and new number one team—and the ultimate victim of the unpredictable Breckenridge streak.

Thanks to the Freedom of Choice practice in San Antonio during this era, students could choose the high school they wanted to attend. The Brackenridge players hailed from all over the Alamo City. Vic Castillo, the star quarterback, came from a poor background in another part of the city. Castillo started that season as a third stringer. McVea said, "My sophomore year we lost to Jefferson 41–6. Luckily in 1962 we had an influx of talent. The group that ended up at Brackenridge had some great players. We were lucky we had Vic Castillo. He started the season on the scout team. He was an afterthought. He had that sidearm throwing motion. Once he got in the lineup and we started throwing the ball, our season really took off. You know, we didn't have much, but we loved and cared for each other."

Vic Castillo, San Antonio Bracken-ridge, 1962. Courtesy of Vic Castillo.

When he eventually got the starting role, Castillo had a record-setting season throwing the football. He ended up the fourteen-game season with 2,147 passing yards, thus becoming the first player in Texas history to pass for more than 2,000 yards in a season. Castillo also threw for twenty-five touchdowns, another state record. The former scout team standout saved his best performances for the last two games of his high school career. Against Spring Branch in the semifinals, he completed 14 of 25 passes for 368 yards and 5 touchdowns. Against Borger in the state finals, Castillo connected on 14 of 28 passes for 256 yards and 3 touchdowns. He earned a scholarship to Kansas State and wound up playing at what became Emporia State before returning to his hometown as a coach and school administrator.

Castillo spoke of how he, just like most of his Brackenridge teammates, overcame a life of inner-city poverty to become a state champion. "We came from all over the city to attend Brackenridge," the one-time record setter recalled. "We came from ten different middle schools. Remember there were no attendance zones in San Antonio. I would have gone to Jefferson, but I got on the bus every day and rode fifteen to twenty miles to Brackenridge. I was also really small. I was only about one hundred pounds when I entered high school. Jefferson had a good football program, and I never would have gotten a second look there. A bunch of us were pretty poor growing up, too. My house on the west side of town didn't have indoor plumbing, and I used to deliver papers, shine shoes, and deliver milk as a kid to help out. Ten of our players ended up getting college football scholarships, so we did have some talent.

What brought many of the players together was their tough upbringing. Johnny Pesina, who grew up on the east side, had to get up every morning to help his sister Stella put on her leg braces since she had been stricken with polio at birth. "That was another reason for our success," Pesina said. "We were used to discipline."

Tackle Isidro Villalobos became a father and husband at age fourteen. After school, he would go to football practice and then work the night shift at a local gas station. Villalobos said, "I used to fall asleep in class. The teachers took it easy on me. But it was football that kept me motivated."

Herbert Lacy said, "When I was growing up, poor was the norm. It was just me, my sister, and my mom growing up. My dad died one month before I was born. My mom got a little money from the government because my dad was in the army, and she worked as a server at these white people's home. She worked for the aunt of Kyle and Tobin Rote, two football stars who came out of San Antonio. On Christmas they would send food and gifts over to us. We lived in the housing projects on the west side. If you were in a single-parent household, you pretty much lived in the projects. If you had both parents, like Warren McVea did, then you might have a house. Most of us on the Brackenridge team were poor."

Lineman Roy Cantu recalled, "I grew up around Burbank High School, but I went to Brackenridge because my cousins did. I didn't intend to play football. I had never played any sports. I just went out there and got after it. When I left high school, most of my friends were black. My cousins would ask, 'Why do you hang around them?'"

David Hardin's mother was Hispanic, his father French, making him the only player on the team with Anglo blood. "I'm a half-breed," Hardin said up front. "My father was from Fort Worth, and he met my mom at Fort Sam Houston during World War II. I grew up on the east side of San Antonio, close to downtown. It's mostly Hispanic there. The blacks lived a little farther east from us. I went to Emerson Junior High. It was about half-black, half-Hispanic. Charles Eanes, Robert Wade, William Hines, and myself came from Emerson and played on the 1962 Brackenridge championship team. I was a safety and backup quarterback to Vic Castillo. My hands were kind of small, so gripping the ball to throw it was a challenge. I also played on all of the special teams, so I got to play quite a bit. I guess it helped that I was pretty fast.

"I chose Brackenridge over the other San Antonio high schools because my girlfriend, who is now my wife, was a year ahead of me and was already going there. Coach Forren at Brackenridge kept bugging my girlfriend to try and get me to come there. I was going to go there anyways. He had already come down to our school when we were in the ninth grade to recruit some of us. Pretty much all of us who played at Brackenridge were poor. We were all from the ghetto—the south side, the east side, the west side.

"I have to say, though, I probably never would have gotten into sports and made it to Brackenridge without the help of my junior high coach at Emerson, Howard Johnson. There were gangs at Emerson and I was being drawn into them, but Coach Johnson kept me out of trouble. He always talked to me and encouraged me. To this day I thank him. He got me going in the right direction."

Robert Wade was a defensive catalyst for the Eagles in their run to the 1962 state 4A title. In addition to being a force on defense, Wade played fullback and took charge as the punter and placekicker. When his career at Brackenridge was over, he played football at the University of Corpus Christi and then for the semipro San Antonio Toros. Wade came to Brackenridge from Emerson Junior High on the east side and lived just three blocks from all-black Wheatley High School. "My oldest brother went to Fox Tech High School," Wade explained, "and my second oldest brother and I went to Emerson together. He decided to go to Highlands

High School. This was back when you had 'freedom of choice' to go to any San Antonio school you wanted to. You had to fill out a 'choice slip' as to where you wanted to go. My dad informed me I wasn't going to Wheatley. Coach Johnson, our coach at Emerson, was great. He used to load us up in the back of his pickup truck and take us to the different spring trainings at the various high schools. I'm glad I didn't go to Wheatley. I didn't like their offense. They just went up the middle most of the time. They didn't utilize their speed. We went and saw Highlands practice, and I decided I didn't want to go there, even though Coach Johnson was going to coach there. When I told him I was going to Brackenridge, he was very surprised. He assumed I was going to Highlands with him."

Claudis Minor said, "I ended up at Brackenridge. I had gone there for summer school, and I found it to be so diverse and dynamic. We got together from all over the city, our team at Brack. San Antonio was segregated when I started school. When I got to middle school, we had integrated. The east side where I came from was mostly black, with some Mexicans and Germans mixed in. The magic potion was football. You could go all over the city and play pickup football games on the weekends. The great Tommy Nobis would play in sandlot games all over town. Segregation was no big deal or didn't mean anything at those sandlot games. It was all whether you could play ball or not."

Receiver and tight end Herbert Lacy, along with William Hines and Albert Davis, was just one of three sophomores on the Brackenridge

Claudis Minor, San Antonio Brackenridge, 1962. Courtesy of Vic Castillo.

team to see any significant playing time. After his sophomore season, Lacy gave up football for basketball when an automobile accident left him with a concussion. Lacy recalled, "I grew up close to Warren McVea, about a half mile or so. My middle school coach, Frank Evans, was the one that got us going. He took us right out of sixth grade and started preparing us. We would go over to the middle school the spring of our sixth grade year, and Coach Evans would run us through plays and give us some pads to work out in.

"When it came time to choose a high school, I could've gone to Jefferson, which was the closest high school to us. That's where a lot of my middle school teammates went. My sister was at Fox Tech High School, which was also pretty close to where we lived. Warren and I thought about going to Wheatley, the black high school on the east side, but we felt that Coach Carroll, the football coach, favored kids from the east side. So Warren and Floyd Boone, who was our fullback, decided to give Brackenridge a try. They were a year older than me, so I just followed them there.

"At first, it was a learning experience at Brackenridge. I was a skinny kid but I ended up playing in about half of the games. About midway through the season, I caught on right about the time our team caught fire. One thing that made us successful was our senior leadership, led by Pete Bautista and Vic Castillo. They took the younger players like myself under their wings. There was none of this 'I'm a senior, so just do what I tell you to do!' They made you learn. You went out there and hustled and played hard, just like they did. They were very inspirational. We eventually became one big family. We just pulled together."

The Brackenridge players also spoke of the improbability of them winning the state title. Roy Cantu said, "1962 was the last year of football most of us would play. For a lot of us, football was all we had. We came from all different areas, but we turned out to be a close-knit family. Coach Forren instilled that closeness and taught us to play with a lot of pride. As a team, we practiced hard and we played hard. We always gave 100 percent. We always heard from the coaches 'Give 100 percent and you'll see the rewards.' They were right.

"We didn't know how good we were until we reached the playoffs. We didn't have a great regular season. We lost some early games we probably shouldn't have. By the playoffs, though, our team of two minorities was working together like a well-tuned machine. Nobody ever told us we couldn't win state. We just worked hard. Now we became a Cinderella story. The media didn't think we could win state, especially in our home-town. We were the underdog in every playoff game we played. We weren't a big team, but we had speed. And a lot of heart."

David Hardin said, "We won the state title, but just barely. Those last two games against Spring Branch and Borger were tough. They were so much bigger than we were. It was like men against boys. What saved us was our speed. Those were two games that afterwards I came out hurt-ing. We were taking our licks. I was in pain. But, in the end, we were state champs!"

Herbert Lacy said, "The whole run to the state title was a big sur-prise. We didn't think we were going to go as far as we did. We jelled at the right time. Coach Forren also let us know that we were just as good as the other teams. We put our pants on one leg at a time just like they did. We were always outweighed, but we had other things going for us, like our speed and quickness. Coach Forren was a good coach. You better know your assignments, though. Every game we scripted the first three plays, and then we settled into our regular offense. Sometimes Coach Forren would draw up the craziest plays, but we almost always scored at the start of every game using the plays we had scripted. You better not mess up your assignment on one of those plays. Coach Forren was a hard coach. He instilled discipline in me. I needed it, because I was a rebel-lious kid. I didn't like him back when I played for him. He was white, and I didn't like taking orders from a white man. I realized later in life what he did for me."

Robert Wade said, "My daddy said I made a good choice going to Brackenridge. He was right. I had a great time. We had guys from all over San Antonio on the team. Coach Forren got us all together and said we were a team. He was right—we eventually became one. Peo-ple wondered, 'How did this coach get all of these blacks and Hispan-ics together and have them play as a team?' I look back, and somehow Coach Forren got us to do that. We were a family. It was a miracle what we accomplished."

The Brackenridge players also faced and overcame racial discrimina-tion in that 1962 season. "When we used to go out of town to play," Har-din said, "I remember we had to go around back to eat a lot. I was very naïve and didn't know any better. I thought the restaurants were doing that special for the team. I didn't realize until years later why we had to go eat in the back. Every once in a while we would run into problems in

San Antonio too. One time, Robert Wade, myself, and two other blacks and Hispanics went to eat at the Pig Stand, a popular drive-in restaurant. I remember we ordered, and when the carhop brought us our order, they refused to serve us when they saw who we were. That kind of bothered me."

Many of the Brackenridge players specifically remembered their quarterfinals playoff win over Brownsville in a game that was played in that border-town city. The Eagles pulled off a 38–13 upset that night as Warren McVea ran for 140 yards on 14 carries and scored 4 touchdowns. Castillo was 9 of 18 through the air for 183 yards and 2 touchdowns.

The team won but still encountered prejudice. Vic Castillo said, "When we played in Brownsville, we had to stop in San Benito to change for the game. Coach Forren was actually from there. Then when we got there, their fans were counting us as we got off of the bus. They were seeing how many blacks and Mexicans we had on our team."

On that same trip, Claudis Minor said, "The highway patrol stopped us and wanted us to turn around. Apparently there had been a death threat against us. We also had to stop in San Benito to change into our uniforms, so we showed up to the stadium already dressed. When we got to the stadium and were getting off the bus, we noticed that they were counting us as we got off the bus. One kid shouted, 'They're all niggers!' Robert Wade turned to me and said, 'Did you hear that?' I said, 'I sure did!'

"Robert got back at them during the game. Robert was a defensive back and a heckuva hitter. Brownsville had this all-state receiver, and Robert knocked the hell out of him. I heard later that the receiver had to give up football. After Robert had hit this kid, he was laying there on the ground, and I said to Robert, 'Wade, you killed him.' Robert looked at me and said, 'Fuck him!'"

Robert Wade also recalls the "counting" incident: "When we went to Brownsville, I remember pulling up in the buses, and as we were getting off the bus, their fans were counting us. There was one guy who said, 'twenty-three and twelve!' I went up to him and said, 'You were counting how many blacks and Mexicans we have on the team, weren't you?' He denied it. He said, 'No, no, no, I wasn't doing that.' I knew he was, though.

"Brownsville had this all-state wide receiver. He was like six-foot-two, and they would throw alley-oop passes to him all of the time. I was known as a hitter, and Coach Forren would always put me on the other team's best receiver. Well, that receiver went after one of those alley-oop passes, and I hit him so hard I knocked him out of the game. Someone told me he didn't play any more football after that." (Not true. The Brownsville receiver, John Poss, went on to play at Texas A&M.)

Roy Cantu recalls, "You would think being a border town there wouldn't be many racists in that part of the state. We were wrong! We had just assumed that we would go into Brownsville before the game, eat, and then get dressed. Along the way there, we were pulled over by a cigar-smoking cop who informed us that a bunch of 'niggers and Mexicans' could not come into Brownsville and eat, change clothes, or spend the night. We ended up stopping in San Benito, something like twenty miles from Brownsville, and that's where we changed and ate. After the game, we stopped back in San Benito and changed clothes, and ended up eating and spending the night in Alice, Texas. That's about halfway between Brownsville and San Antonio. We beat Brownsville, so we weren't too upset that we weren't welcomed in their city."

David Hardin says, "I remember after the game down there their fans started throwing rocks at us. We had to keep our helmets on until we got on the bus. Even after we got on the bus, their fans kept hitting the side of the bus with their rocks. After we won that game, though, we started thinking, 'Hey, we have a chance to win the whole thing.' We knew we could do it if we put our minds to it."

The unheralded, underdog Eagles traveled to Houston to play the unbeaten and number-one-ranked team in Texas, the Spring Branch Bears. It was in this game where Vic Castillo unleashed an aerial attack that yielded 368 passing yards and five touchdown passes, including two each to Warren McVea and Pete Bautista. Brackenridge held on for the improbable 30–23 win that sent them to the state 4A finals. After the game, Spring Branch coach Darrell Tully said of Castillo, "His performance was one of the finest I've ever seen. . . . I've never seen a more explosive team than Brackenridge."

"In the semifinals against Spring Branch," Robert Wade said, "they were so much bigger than us. I remember playing a big role in our playoff wins. I wasn't considered fast, but there was one play where I chased down their great running back Chris Gilbert at the ten-yard line after a long gain. Not letting him score turned the game around because they turned the ball over to us four plays later on downs at our eleven-yard line. Our first play on offense, Vic Castillo hits Warren McVea for an eighty-nine-yard touchdown pass. I guess my tackle was huge momentum-wise."

Brackenridge also faced inequity and racism when they traveled to Houston for their semifinal playoff game against Spring Branch.

Roy Cantu recalled, "We played at Rice Stadium, and their players seemed as big as the Rice University football players. They outweighed us by about fifty pounds per man in the trenches. Nobody gave us a chance to win, but we had superior speed. Once again, because of the black players on our team, we weren't allowed to eat or spend the night in Houston. We ended up eating in LaGrange, about halfway between Houston and San Antonio, on our way home."

Herbert Lacy added, "As far as facing discrimination, sometimes it was pretty bad. When we played Edgewood High School in San Antonio, we had to keep our helmets on at all times so we wouldn't get hurt by bottles and other things that were thrown at us. In San Antonio, sometimes we would get in fights. When we went to play Brownsville in the playoffs, we had to get a police escort. In Houston, however, when we went to Rice Stadium to play Spring Branch in the semifinals, I had never seen or heard anything back in San Antonio even close to what I experienced there.

"As we were going into Rice Stadium, the fans there were hollering racial slurs at us, calling us things like 'monkeys,' or saying things like, 'Your momma's got a tail!' As a fifteen-year-old, it was shocking. I had never been exposed to anything like that back in San Antonio. It was bad enough that we couldn't even eat in Houston before the game; we stopped on the way there. Then, we had to fully dress on the bus since we didn't have access to the locker room. Then we had to enter the stadium through this maze of people cussing and throwing things. I said to myself, 'What is going on here?'"

Their chins up after two wins in two discriminating cities, the Eagles prepared for their state final showdown with Texas' new number one team, the Borger Bulldogs. In racking up a perfect 13–0 mark, Borger had outscored their opponents 332–69 for the season.

In the state championship game that was played in Abilene, Borger got off to an 8–0 lead after the first quarter. In the second quarter, with the wind at their backs, the Eagles rolled up twenty-four points before the half. Castillo threw for three touchdowns—one to Johnny Pesina and two to Warren McVea. Borger cut the lead to 24–14 in the third quarter, but the Eagles responded with a two-yard McVea touchdown run to make it 30–14. The three touchdowns McVea scored against Borger gave him ten touchdowns in his last three games of the season. Borger added two late touchdowns, but it wasn't enough.

After the game, in which they held Brackenridge to just twenty-two yards rushing, Borger Coach Gene Mayfield said, "It's hard to say anything after getting beat in a ball game like this. They didn't run too well against our defense, but they throw like a bunch of pros, don't they?"

"Now that was one game we really weren't expected to win," Herbert Lacy said. "Once again, Coach Forren convinced us we could compete with them. Those were some big guys that played for Borger. We could hit and we had speed, though. Robert Wade was one of our big hitters. He and Douglass Coffee would bet each other on the sidelines every week that they could crack an opposing player's helmet. I think we took Borger by surprise. One of our players, Edward Coleman, was one of the fastest linemen in Texas. I remember one play he chased down one of their fastest players. Borger was good. They had some great players, like John LaGrone."

Roy Cantu added, "They were unbeaten, and they had a really good running back. He didn't last the first half; we knocked him out of the game. However, we had Warren McVea, and he was faster and quicker than anyone else on the field. It was pretty neat because we looked up in the stands before the game and a bunch of the Spring Branch players had come to Abilene to cheer us on. They wore their blue team blazers and everything. Vic had a great game, and we scored most of our points in the second quarter when we had the wind at our backs. Vic had a lot of intelligence. He could change plays at the line, and he was a great field general. He really applied himself to the game. We had some good runners on the team, like Warren McVea and Pete Bautista, but if a team shut down our running game, Vic would take to the air.

"We were not like most teams back then, just stubbornly trying to always run the ball. We didn't mind passing it. We ended up beating Borger, and we were the state champs of Texas! We were able to eat as a team in Abilene, and then we went back to San Antonio. When we got back to San Antonio in the wee hours of the morning, the Brackenridge campus was full of cars and people. The buses could barely get into the parking lot, there were so many people. In the end, the city of San Antonio said there was going to be a Brackenridge Day, but it never happened."

Warren McVea shared his reflections: "Their running back, A. C.

Tillmon, was a helluva player. He got hurt early in the game. If he had played the whole game, we probably wouldn't have won. Once he was out of there as a defensive back too, that opened up our passing game."

Not surprisingly, it was Robert Wade who knocked Tillmon out of the game. Wade said, "I think his nickname was Alternating Current. In fact, he was the only Borger player we had even heard of before we played them. We knew we couldn't let him turn the corner against us. He had hurt his leg the week before, and he was favoring it. I hit him hard, and he was through. After that, they couldn't run wide, just up the middle, and they really didn't throw the ball really well. He was bigger than I thought he was. He had big legs. The first time he carried the ball, he got about eleven or twelve yards. I said to myself, 'I'm gonna get him out of there.' I hit him the next time he carried the ball, and I knocked him out of the game. They were a completely different team after that."

David Hardin said, "We were underdogs in all four of our playoff games. While we ran the ball quite a bit, if the other team started defensing it, we would start passing the ball. We especially did this in the playoffs. We were a loose team; there was no pressure on us since we were not expected to win. Heck, up in Abilene the night before we played Borger for the championship, we snuck out after curfew and went bowling. I remember Borger had some black players on their team. A. C. Tillmon was one, and another was a wide receiver named Robinson."

Indeed, it was the first state championship game in Texas high school football history that saw both teams take the field with African Americans on their rosters.

Robert Wade, San Antonio Brackenridge, 1962. Courtesy of Vic Castillo.

Borger High School integrated in the late 1950s, and their 1962 squad had four African Americans: running backs Joe Coffer, A. C. Tillmon, and Melvin Bunn, and wide receiver Joe Robinson. Coffer was a starting defensive tackle, and Tillmon doubled as a defensive back. Robinson scored the last Borger touchdown on a fourth quarter thirty-two-yard pass reception. Robinson, a pitcher on the baseball team, signed with the Los Angeles Dodgers organization after he graduated. Coffer also was Robinson's catcher on the Borger baseball team. After Borger, Coffer followed Kenneth Deckard at McMurry College and was the second African American to play football there. After Coffer graduated from McMurry, he taught briefly and then spent a long career in the military.

According to Joe Coffer, "Borger was the way things were back then. Like in basketball, you know the rules ahead of time. The schools in Borger integrated around 1957 or 1958. I was kind of in the second wave of blacks who came to the high school. For some of the early ones who integrated, the change was too much. A lot of them dropped out and went into the military. I wasn't there at the high school yet, but the change was tough.

"At Borger, I played fullback on offense and nose guard and linebacker on defense. We had a few problems, but it was something we had to cope with. Once again, the black guys that came before me had it rougher on things like road trips. At certain places, they were told the blacks couldn't play. Things weren't violent or anything; it was an understanding. The school district and the coaches accepted it. With my coaches, there was a time we went to Amarillo to play baseball. We stopped at a place called Underwood's; it was a barbeque place. The owners wouldn't let me eat there. We were near some black businesses, so I got some money to go get something to eat. I knew the situation, and I didn't want to get our school or the coaches in trouble by me making a scene.

"The coaches were trying to help us the best they could. I also had to be careful because I could have jeopardized my dad's job. He was a plumber and worked all over Borger, and if I rebelled, it could cost him a lot of work. I was limited as to what I could do. I also didn't want to jeopardize the progress that had been made for blacks. There were no written laws, but you knew not to rock the boat.

"There were other unwritten rules, like my parents not being allowed to be in the football booster club. The black parents had no say in any matters. In basketball there were only so many blacks on the court at one time. There was another observation I made in football: the coaches would 'stack' blacks at certain positions, like running back. Three of the four blacks on the team, myself, A. C. Tillmon, and Melvin Bunn, played the same position. It was frustrating to us. It might be a tight ballgame, and we felt one of the black athletes who was on the bench was a better player than a white player on the field.

"It was strictly an observation, and we didn't make a big deal about it because we respected our coaches. We also didn't want to jeopardize the next group of blacks to play at Borger by complaining about it. Also, we knew we had been given an opportunity, and we had to make the most of it. Football got me into college and paid for it, so I had to put up with a few things. Melvin Bunn knew what I knew too. The opportunity was there, and you had to put up with a little crap to get what you want."

Coffer expressed opinions about San Antonio Brackenridge: "As far as Brackenridge, I really didn't see them as a minority team. It was not a big deal. I did happen to notice that Brackenridge had a Hispanic quarterback. He was the first quarterback I had ever seen who wasn't white. You just didn't see that in the Panhandle. It was understood that minorities just didn't play certain positions.

"Also, watching the film, I noticed that Warren McVea stood out from all the others. He would be the one to inflict pain on us, and he did. He scored three touchdowns. Brackenridge had other good players, but our focus was to contain him. They had a good team; we just came up a little short."

In the end, the Brackenridge Eagles, like their integration predecessors, dealt with a variety of challenges, like growing up in poverty and enduring harsh conditions at away games during the playoffs, yet they overcame these obstacles on the route to their state title.

Although the 1962 state title run of Brackenridge, and the fact that they played in the first fully integrated state title game against Borger, showed that progress had been made with integrated high school football in much of the state, there was still much work to be done to integrate football in East Texas, which had no African Americans yet on the field. The road to equality still appeared to be steep east of Dallas and south of Texarkana. For many of those players in that part of the Lone Star State, their opportunities lay elsewhere when they decided where they were going to play college football.

12

Leaving Texas

I took my studies seriously. I didn't want to go back to Texas.
—GENE WASHINGTON, MICHIGAN STATE ALL-AMERICA
RECEIVER FROM TEXAS

Before four-year colleges like Houston, Baylor, and SMU integrated and enabled a growing number of African American high school football players to play in their home state, most of them played major college football outside Texas.

These talented players started leaving the state known for its excellent football talent for better opportunities as far back as the 1930s. One such individual was Ozzie Simmons, who was born in the North Texas town of Gainesville but went seventy miles south to Fort Worth to play high school football. In 1933, Simmons went to the University of Iowa. Simmons and his brother Don were discovered by an Iowa alumnus who suggested they go there. Iowa had a history of having black players on its roster going all the way back to 1895.

The Simmons brothers hopped on a train to head north. It was a fruitful rail trip—Don ended up lettering at end for the Hawkeyes in 1935 and 1936, but it was Ozzie who became a star. Despite enduring abuse from opposing teams, Simmons was All Big Ten in 1934 and 1935 from his halfback position, and was a first team All-America pick in 1935. When Simmons finished at Iowa in 1936, there was not an NFL career waiting for him. From 1933 to 1945, no African Americans played in the NFL due to an informal lockout of black players by NFL owners, most specifically led by Washington Redskins owner George Preston Marshall, who would not allow black players on his team and pressured the other NFL owners to follow suit.

By the 1950s, African American Texans started heading up north and out west more frequently to continue their football careers. Some did not last long in a new environment. Recall that Ben Kelly spent just a semester at Illinois before joining the army. He left because it was cold, and it was too far from home. Anthony Guillory left Nebraska because of the long distance from Beaumont and the fact there were few blacks on campus.

Garland Boyette is another example of a player who went north but came home to Texas shortly thereafter. Boyette hailed from Orange, thirty miles east of Beaumont in deep East Texas on the Sabine River, which forms the Texas/Louisiana border. Boyette played linebacker at Orange Wallace High School from 1955 to 1957, which at the time was coached by PVIL coaching legend Willie Ray Smith Sr., father of Willie Ray (Beaver) Jr., Bubba, and Tody Smith, who played at Charlton Pollard High School in Beaumont. From Wallace, Boyette spent a short period of time at Northwestern before transferring to Grambling University and playing for the famous Eddie Robinson. Boyette eventually became the first African American middle linebacker in pro football history, with the St. Louis Cardinals in 1962. He later became a Pro Bowl linebacker with the Houston Oilers.

Garland Boyette went from Orange, Texas, to Northwestern University for just a couple of weeks because "I worked at a hotel bar in Orange. I was a bartender and barkeep. There was a naval officer by the name of John Harden who came in there. He got me hooked up with the people at Northwestern. I went there sight unseen. When I got there, there were maybe ten blacks on campus, and maybe five in the athletic department. I left after two weeks and ended up at Grambling, thanks to my nephew Ernie Ladd, who was already there. The best way to put it is that I never felt comfortable. I was a transplanted southern guy up there, and I wanted to come home."

Many African American players, however, chose a Northern or Western college to play football at and stayed there for the whole four years. Their experiences at their respective schools were unique and varied. Some faced bias; others faced being just one of just a handful of African Americans on their respective campuses. Many of the players faced prejudice when they played away games. They all have a story to tell about keeping going in the face of inequity.

When he graduated from Robstown High School in 1957, Willie Jones was one of the first black players from Texas to go north and stay there when he went to Purdue. His connection to the Big Ten was Paul "Bear" Bryant, who at the time was the head coach at Texas A&M. "Coach Bryant knew Purdue coach Jack Mollenkopf," Jones remembered, "and tipped him off to me. Bryant told him, 'I can't take him, but you can.' Purdue offered me a scholarship sight unseen. Purdue was the only visit I took; it was so far away. I took Coach Culwell, my high school coach, with me. It was the first college I visited. Michigan State, Iowa, Minnesota, and Ohio State all showed interest in me, though. I wasn't invited to any of the Texas colleges. If I would have had the opportunity to integrate a Texas college, I probably would have. I grew up in Texas, and that was home.

"After I committed to Purdue, Coach Steinke at Texas A&I in Kingsville tried to recruit me, but it was too late. They didn't really have scholarship money, and I had a full ride to Purdue, so that's where I went. My mom and I were poor, so we had to go where the money was. The University of Colorado made an offer to me when I was a junior. Darrell Royal, who was coaching up at Washington State, wanted me to come there, but it was only a partial scholarship. TSU and Prairie View also made offers. North Texas tried to get me. I ended up making a good choice. I liked Purdue, so I cancelled all my other visits."

Purdue wanted to make sure Jones would not change his mind or be persuaded to switch colleges by another recruiter, so they had him head north just ten days after he graduated from high school in order to hide him out. Jones stayed in Evansville, Indiana, at the home of a Purdue alum, Ferris Traylor. Traylor, who owned a construction company in Evansville, welcomed Jones into his home, and Jones and the Traylor family became very close.

When University of Illinois athletic officials learned of this arrangement, they threatened a lawsuit based on a rule against sequestering a recruit. Ultimately, no suit was filed. As Jones remembered, "I was instructed not to talk to anyone. I really didn't know what was going on. I worked for Mr. Traylor that summer at one of his construction sites. One day, this man came there and started asking me questions. He was from the Big Ten, and Illinois had sent him there to investigate me. Mr. Traylor spotted this guy, and he ran up to him and threw him off the property. He then turned and said to me, 'Never talk to anybody! Ever!' I was seventeen. I didn't know what was going on.

"When I got to Purdue, there were about one hundred blacks on campus. Purdue had about fourteen thousand students back then. I was used to not having many other blacks around living in South Texas. It was different at Purdue, though. I pretty much hung around the athletic guys. My social life was poor. Trying to adjust academically was tough too. I just didn't have the background. I wasn't prepared for college work. I had tutors, though. My life consisted of practice, dining hall, and tutors. I ended up staying up there to work on my studies. I think I came home for one week one summer. I did end up graduating, though."

Willie Ray Smith Jr. was an almost mythical figure in Beaumont football by the time his senior season of 1960 came around. Bubba Smith said about his older brother, "He was the best player I've ever seen in my life. He's the only person I've ever idolized."

Another Beaumont native, Jerry LeVias, who later in 1965 became the first African American scholarship football player in the now defunct Southwest Conference, added, "Willie Ray was my personal hero."

Tony Guillory said, "Willie was the best athlete out of all of his brothers. He could do all of the sports, and he could run. He was a great athlete. His brothers Bubba and Tody were just average athletes compared to Willie Ray."

John Payton was an assistant at Charlton-Pollard when Willie Ray Smith Jr. was playing there. He said, "Willie Ray was a legend in his own time. He was one of the best backs I'd ever seen."

Miller Farr, from rival Hebert, said about Smith, "If Willie Ray hadn't have hurt his knees, he could have been a great one."

When he graduated from Beaumont Charlton-Pollard High School in 1961, Willie Ray "Beaver" Smith was another player who escaped segregation to play in the Big Ten. While Anthony Guillory, who played at crosstown rival Hebert against Smith, went to Nebraska for a short period, Smith chose the University of Iowa. Willie Ray Jr. recalled, "At the time, the Big Ten was one of the formidable powers in college football. Forrest Evashevski recruited me, and then Jerry Burns took over. I liked the state and the university. I decided on Iowa because they ran the Wing-T. They ran a lot of traps, and I saw myself fitting in with the team. It was the same kind of offense that my dad ran. It wasn't 'three yards and a cloud of dust.' There weren't that many blacks around, but Willie Fleming and Bob Jeter had been there and helped Iowa win the 1959 Rose Bowl, just a couple of years before I got there.

"At the time, there weren't too many black athletes at white schools, so they were an influence as to why I went to Iowa too. I enjoyed Iowa, but I had to leave there because I got caught plagiarizing some work. As a black athlete I was trying to adjust to college work, and I went about it the wrong way. From there I went to Kansas, where I played with Gale Sayers. I liked it there too. Gale came to Beaumont with me one time. My first summer at Kansas, he came down with me and we hung out."

When Junior Coffey graduated from Dimmitt High School in the Texas Panhandle, he too had to make his college choice, but like the other African Americans, his choices were limited because of segregation. "When I graduated in 1961," Coffey said, "Texas was on the verge on integrating. I talked to my coaches, J. D. Covington in football and John Ethridge in basketball. We talked about me possibly going to West Texas State because they had heard that new coach Joe Kerbel wanted to integrate their program. My coaches thought the timing wasn't right, that maybe I should go to a different environment. Texas Tech showed some interest in me too. I would have liked to have gone there. I wanted to stay close to home. Coach Covington and Coach Ethridge felt the Southwest Conference wasn't ready to integrate for a few more years, so that eliminated Texas Tech.

"I always rooted for Tech. One reason I wanted to go there was I could help them beat the University of Texas and bring the Red Raiders some notoriety. I ended up visiting Minnesota, Illinois, Oklahoma, Kansas, and several other schools. I then took a trip to the University of Washington. When I got there, Seattle seemed to be pretty well integrated. On my visit, I stayed at the Olympic Hotel. Everyone there was Caucasian—the car people, the maître d', and the waiters. I was able to go into the restaurant at the hotel without being asked to leave.

"That's when I decided to go to the University of Washington. Another reason I went was that one of their assistant coaches was Chesty Walker, who had coached high school ball in Phillips, Texas. He remembered me from a scrimmage Phillips had with Dimmitt while he was still coaching there. He saw some film and convinced me to go there."

Sometimes African American players ended up at their respective colleges through a chance meeting or a fluke. Bill Gregory from LaMarque was one of those players. He ended up a Wisconsin Badger. Gregory was born in Galveston but grew up in LaMarque and played for Lincoln High School. Gregory, a defensive tackle, eventually played his college football at Wisconsin and was All Big Ten his senior year of 1970. Gregory became a 1971 third-round draft pick of the Dallas Cowboys. Gregory played seven years for the Cowboys and three for the Seattle Seahawks. Gregory was a member of the Cowboys Super Bowl winning teams of 1971 and 1977. "I wasn't heavily recruited," he said. "I was 6-foot-5 by the ninth grade, however, so I was pretty big. Being that tall, my mom took me to a men's store in Galveston the summer before my senior year. When we got there, the salesperson asked me, 'Do you play football?' I told him I did, and he replied, 'I'm gonna get you a scholarship to the University of Wisconsin!'

"Now this guy didn't know if I could walk and chew gum at the same time. The salesman inquired a little bit about my background, and then he took me back to his office. It was a shrine to the University of Wisconsin. Turns out he was some kind of de facto scout for them.

"I promptly forgot about the whole thing until months later when we played Galveston Central, our big rivalry game. All of a sudden, before the game, the locker room door opens up and here comes that salesperson through the door with my coaches, and he was wearing this red Wisconsin jacket. The whole thing was unreal. During the game, however, in an attempt to impress this man, I got kicked out of the game before halftime. I figured, 'Well, that's that. There goes my shot at my scholarship.' Turns out, they still wanted me, and that's how I ended up at the University of Wisconsin.

"Some other factors that helped me choose Wisconsin? Well, for one, I went to visit; that was my first airplane ride when I went to Madison. I went in the winter and stayed in a nice hotel. I look out the window, and I see cars driving on the lake close by. They were ice fishing. I had never seen that before. That made an impression on me. Madison was more than a thousand miles away from home, so that was another reason I went there. I wanted to get away.

"There were also some Texas connections already there. Lewis Ritcherson was an assistant coach there. He had been a very successful high school coach at the black high school in Waco, and he took his son Lewis Jr., a quarterback, with him. A couple of other black players from Texas were there too—Leonard Fields from Galveston, who I knew, and James Johnson from Lubbock.

"I was a good student, so it was important for me to get a good education. I have no regrets going to Wisconsin. My other choices were some place like TSU or Grambling, or Vietnam. We weren't very good in football. Other than our losses, it was a good experience. There were not many African Americans on campus. There were maybe two or three hundred out of about forty to fifty thousand students. It was culture shock. Pretty much everybody was white. I had never really been around white people before.

"Classmates, coaches, players, with but a few exceptions, were white. I know it's a cliché, but some of my best friends ended up being white. My best friend was a fellow defensive lineman, a white guy. I really didn't have much in the way of problems—a few issues, but nothing major. I was a senior and had graduated before I ever heard the 'N' word used up there. Would I do it again, now knowing what I was getting in to? I would have to say yes. I had no qualms about going to Wisconsin."

Although it is more in Central Texas than East Texas, Waco schools remained segregated until the late 1960s. Eddie Bell graduated from Waco Carver High School in 1965 and eventually ended up at Idaho State, where he achieved All-America honors in 1969 after recording 96 catches for 1,522 yards and 20 touchdowns. From there, Bell was a 1970 ninth-round draft choice of the New York Jets, where he spent six seasons, followed by one season with the San Diego Chargers. In 2016, Eddie Bell was nominated for the College Football Hall of Fame.

For Bell, it was a fluke that he got to play college football in the first place, much less end up at Idaho State University in 1967. Bell told his story: "I wasn't even recruited by the black colleges in Texas coming out of high school, much less the white ones. I was small, only 160 pounds. I just happened to be invited to the PVIL all-star football game in Houston in July 1965. I had a decent game, and I was approached by the football coach at Navarro Junior College, who asked me if I wanted to play there. He offered me a half scholarship. So I started off playing football at Navarro in Corsicana. I played the one season there, and I stayed six months. Turns out, a guy named Willie Brown and I integrated Navarro that fall. I decided I wasn't Jackie Robinson, and the integration thing was for someone else.

"After the fall semester, I went to California to stay with my aunt and attended Compton Junior College. That's how I got my nickname 'The Flea.' Walter 'The Flea' Roberts played at Compton a few years before I did, and I kind of idolized him and ended up with his nickname. I ran track at Compton. I didn't play football. I ran against O. J. Simpson when he was at City College of San Francisco. The track coach at Idaho State was a guy by the name of Milton Holt, or 'Dubby.' He had run with Jessie Owens in the 1936 Olympics and eventually became the Idaho State athletic director for many years. Well, Coach Holt saw me run in some track meets and wanted me to go to Idaho State. I did run track at Idaho State. In fact, I was the Big Sky Conference champ in the 220-yard dash. I was set on going to USC and maybe playing some receiver there. When I found out O. J. was going to play for USC, that's when I knew they weren't going to throw the ball much, so that's why I chose Idaho State. I would have ended up blocking for Simpson and watching him run. It worked out well because as a senior I was an All-American and I got to play in the NFL."

Bob Pollard from Beaumont Hebert ended up not too far from where Eddie Bell played his college football. Like Bell, Pollard started off at a college in Texas and ended up out west to finish out his college career. He said, "I started off in 1966 at Texas Southern University in Houston. I left after a year and a half. I did well there. I started, but the coaches there were manipulative. They wanted to take my scholarship money away from me and give it to some out-of-state players they had coming in. Our coaches came to TSU from Florida, and they were trying to give our scholarships to Florida guys. They took scholarship money away from some of the other players too. I didn't want to go back there, and my dad took me with him to TSU to try and find out what the deal was. He wanted to see if I had done anything wrong. When he found out I hadn't, and what the coaches were trying to do, my dad said that we wouldn't accept the situation, and we left and went back to Beaumont.

"I got a job in the shipyards in Beaumont, and my dad gave me his old car for me to get to work. When my high school coach at Hebert, Coach Ozen, found out, he knew I really needed to be in college somewhere playing football. He started making phone calls to colleges, and so did the principal at Hebert, Mr. Jackson. Somehow Weber State in Montana had contacted a scout down here in Texas, and the scout knew about me and that I was looking for a place to play. I got a call from Weber State, and they asked me if I wanted a scholarship there. I said, 'Sure, I'll come there.'

"In reality, once I realized what I had done, I was scared to death. Louisiana was the farthest I'd ever been from Beaumont. They shipped me up there on a Greyhound Bus, and it was culture shock. It was scary at first, but in the long run it was a good thing. The only other blacks up there were the athletes at Weber State. There were only a couple of black girls up there, and they were on the track team. One thing I found was there was not the prejudice up there that there was back in Texas. I ended up having all kinds of white friends at school, not just my football teammates. In the long run I was happy to be in that situation, even though I missed my family. My whole experience at Weber State changed my perception of whites from bad to a good thing."

Rudy Johnson and Willie Paschall became teammates at the University of Nebraska through chance encounters each one had in his hometown. Johnson, who integrated Aransas Pass High School in the Coastal Bend in 1958 and became an all-state running back, chose to be a Cornhusker in 1960. After he and Paschall helped lead the Cornhuskers to a 1964 Orange Bowl victory over Auburn, he played in the NFL for the San Francisco 49ers and the Atlanta Falcons.

He said, "I had about twenty schools looking at me. I was set on going to the University of Texas, but it was too soon for blacks to play there, so it didn't work out. Texas Southern and Prairie View made me offers, but I didn't want to go there. I heard from Notre Dame, Iowa, Minnesota, and Syracuse, among others. Colleges were looking for running backs.

"There was a lady and her husband that lived in Aransas Pass, and they were from Nebraska. I went and talked to them down at the local Whataburger, and I guess they liked me because a guy from Nebraska eventually came down and once he saw I had no medical problems, everything was OK and he offered me a scholarship. I figured Nebraska wouldn't be as cold as Iowa or Syracuse, so I chose to go to Lincoln.

"It was plenty cold in Nebraska. The first time I crossed campus in the winter, it was so cold my teeth were popping they were hurting so much. As I was heading to class, I kept wondering where all of the other students were. It was like the campus was deserted. I found out there was a tunnel system on campus for cold days like that, and I should have been down there with the rest of the students. In spite of that, going to Nebraska was the best thing that ever happened to me. It was great. I did want to go to dental school there, but it was closed to blacks. I did get my education, though, and I've been self-employed for many years."

When Paschall graduated from Jefferson High School in San Antonio in 1961, he had to decide where he wanted to play college football. He said, 'I had offers from Texas Southern and Texas Lutheran College, which at the time I had no idea where it was. It was an all-white college just outside San Antonio in Seguin. My parents said I would be the only black there and I would be all alone. I really wanted to go to New Mexico State. They ran the same offense I had in high school.

"I ended up at Nebraska kind of by accident. There was a colonel in the army stationed in San Antonio, and he was a Nebraska fan. He sent some films and articles about me to the coaches at Nebraska. They must have liked what they saw because one of the Nebraska coaches came to San Antonio to visit with my parents, and they invited me up for a visit in the spring of 1961. I went there and I liked it. I met a lot of the players on my trip there. I was ready for something different, so I decided to go to Nebraska. I later got to meet this colonel who helped me my junior or senior year. When I met him, he stuck his hand out to shake mine but I gave him the biggest hug in the world. I was grateful for what he did for me.

"Going to the University of Nebraska changed my life. Bob Devaney came in as coach, and I got to play in three bowl games. I met my wife there. I joined the ROTC when I was there, and I served my military commitment after that. I then went on to have a nice career as a physical therapist. I would have given anything to have been able to play at the University of Texas, but we knew that wasn't going to happen in the early 1960s. It all worked out with my going to Nebraska."

Johnny Roland, from Class 4A state champion Corpus Christi Miller High School, also came out of Texas in the spring of 1961. Roland was sought after by almost every college in America but the white colleges in Texas and the South. He said, "I was contacted by the black colleges in Texas like Prairie View and Texas Southern, but I never really considered them. I could have gone and played at Texas A&I in Kingsville. I knew Coach Steinke; we were good friends, and they had integrated the year before with Sid Blanks, but I decided against going there.

"North Texas State gave me a courtesy call because Bobby Smith from Miller had gone there the previous year. I figured we didn't need a running back controversy there, so I said no to them. I didn't want to go far away from home. I was an only child. I was actually a better baseball player than football player. I wanted to play both sports in college, and going to the University of Texas would have been nice. I did get a phone call from Darrell Royal, though. He tried to steer me toward the University of Oklahoma, his alma matter. He said, 'I can't recruit you, but you could go play for Bud Wilkinson at Oklahoma.'

"I ended up going on my recruiting visits late. Back then, you couldn't take recruiting trips until the spring sports seasons were over. That meant I couldn't go on any trips until after baseball season. I went to Nebraska, Indiana, Arizona, California, Oklahoma, and Missouri. I met with Bud

Wilkinson of Oklahoma, and he had those steel blue eyes and was a snake charmer. Once again, I didn't want to go too far from home, so I gave Oklahoma a verbal commitment. I would have been the second black to play there after Prentice Gautt was there in the mid- to late 1950s.

"I ended up going to Missouri, however. I went to work for a contractor in Kansas City for the summer. Another thing that led me to choose Missouri was I tried to look over the hill instead of looking to the hill. In other words, I tried to look at what my opportunities would be after college. There was only one major city in Oklahoma, Oklahoma City. In Missouri you had two major cities, St. Louis and Kansas City, and they were on opposite sides of the state. I figured I was going to work my ass off to get a degree, and it made sense to settle in the state that I played my college football in. That led me to Missouri. I just felt there were more opportunities for me.

"Also, Coach Dan Devine soft sold me on the attributes of Missouri. One of them was that they had integrated and had several black players on their roster previously. Two of the big African American stars were still there, and I met them while I was being recruited—Mel West and Morris Stevenson. They were juniors then, so they were seniors when I was a freshman there. It made a difference meeting those guys who helped pave the way for blacks to play there. Later, after I had been at Missouri for a while, I tried to get Jerry LeVias from Beaumont Hebert to come here, but he chose to integrate the Southwest Conference when he picked to go to SMU.

"I would go to Missouri again if I had to do it all over again. Coach Devine was a great coach, and we were on good terms. We had a good team when I was a senior. We went to the 1966 Sugar Bowl. Having the black guys there before me did help me in a sense when I went to Missouri. Now, once I got to Missouri, I found out there weren't too many blacks there—maybe one hundred. It really wasn't a big deal, however, and I was accepted by the student body. We didn't have a player's dorm, but on road trips we roomed alphabetically. My roommate was a guy from Augusta Georgia, Bob Ritter. Growing up, he didn't have much in the way of contact with blacks, but we ended up getting along fine."

When wide receiver Cliff Branch graduated from Houston's Worthing High School in 1967, he still had limited options about going on to play college football. An All Big Eight performer, Branch was a fourth round choice of the Oakland Raiders in the 1972 NFL draft. Branch became an

Cliff Branch, University of Colorado, circa 1969. Courtesy of the University of Colorado.

All-Pro receiver for the Raiders, essentially the dependable deep threat that's a key to winning. Branch played from 1972 to 1985 and ranks as the only Raiders receiver to play on all three of their Super Bowl Champion squads. Branch was a Pro Football Hall of Fame semifinalist in 2004 and 2010.

In 1967 the Southwest Conference was only partially integrated, while the Southeastern Conference had barely begun the process. "Out of high school, I left to go to Cal-Berkeley to run track and play football," Branch recounted. "I stayed for a week. I wasn't ready for college. I then went over to the University of Houston, and I practiced with them for a week. I was running second team. I was a flanker, and Elmo Wright was the split end.

"Coach Yeoman at UH recommended I go to Wharton County Junior College for a year to get some seasoning, and then I could come back to Houston. Coach Yeoman called Gene Bahnsen at Wharton, so I went down there to play. I was comfortable there. I loved it in Wharton. My old teammate from Worthing, Johnny Mays, was there. We had some good teams there. We had a good track program too. I have no regrets about going to Wharton.

"After a couple of years at Wharton, I had to decide what college I wanted to finish at. I talked to Oklahoma State, UTEP, Tulsa, New Mexico, and New Mexico State. Texas Southern, Grambling, and Southern University also talked to me. I actually had more offers in track than I had in football. The Southwest Conference and Southeastern Conference still were recruiting very limited numbers of blacks, so I decided to look at the University of Colorado. It felt good going to a school that had been integrated for a while.

"I got my first taste of playing with whites when I went to Wharton, so it felt good to be playing with whites at Colorado. I had a fun recruiting trip, and they had great academics and athletics. I would also be playing in the prestigious Big Eight Conference. Remember, I was supposed to go back to the University of Houston after my stint at Wharton. Coach Yeoman was disappointed that I chose Colorado, but he wished me well. Ironically, my last college football game was in Houston against the Cougars at the 1971 Bluebonnet Bowl in the Astrodome. We won, 29–17, and Colorado finished number three in the country."

Michigan State had the first real orchestrated effort to bring black players from Texas and throughout the South to East Lansing. Head Coach Duffy Daugherty had recruited black players in the mid-1950s, such as Pro Football Hall of Fame member Herb Adderley. But players like Adderley hailed from northern cities. Daugherty's predecessor, Biggie Munn, later Michigan State's athletic director, began recruiting blacks out of the Michigan factory towns beginning in the late 1940s. Daugherty just continued the practice. He made Earl Latimer of Dallas Lincoln the first African American Texan to play for the Spartans. The year was 1960.

The atmosphere at Michigan State was one of racial tolerance and equality. The one person more than any other who was instrumental in the acceptance of African Americans was Dr. John Hannah, the school president for the quarter century between 1941 and 1967. Dr. Hannah was committed to integration and started the process with campus housing in the mid-1940s. Eventually, Hannah had the city of East Lansing integrate their housing so African American faculty and staff members could choose where they wanted to live. The school president also encouraged the recruitment of black athletes. Munn undertook the process, but Coach Daugherty, his successor, took the practice even further—miles further! He started bringing in players from the South in a sort of Underground Railroad for football players. President Dwight Eisenhower realized the Civil Rights accomplishments and progressivism of Hannah when he named him to be the first chairman of the Civil Rights Commission in 1957.

John Hannah extended his commitment to blacks during these early days of the Civil Rights movement beyond public events such as the "Little Rock Nine" integration of Little Rock Central High School in the state of Arkansas in 1957. The event entailed black students from predominately black Horace Mann High School attempting to integrate Central High across town. President Eisenhower eventually brought in federal troops to enforce the desegregation order.

Among the seniors in the group was Ernest Green, who graduated from Central in May 1958 and proceeded to enroll in Michigan State, where this esteemed member of the Civil Rights Commission was still president. As a matter of fact, Dr. Hannah played a prominent role in Green's decision to attend MSU. "Actually," Green would explain decades later, "I had a scholarship from a smaller school when I found out I got the one from Michigan State. Dr. Hannah and I ran into each other occasionally, but we never really spent any real time together. I found out later he was watching over me from a distance. I was told by President Lou Ann Simon that Dr. Hannah underwrote other scholarships for black students besides me.

"I had a couple of incidents at Michigan State. One was when the campus barber shop refused to cut my hair. Dr. Hannah intervened. I did get into the middle of some protests at MSU. I chaired the NAACP there my junior and senior year. I picketed Dr. Hannah's house as a member of the Student Nonviolent Coordinating Committee (SNCC), as well as East Lansing stores. Luckily, Dr. Hannah didn't call me up in the middle of the night demanding his scholarship money back. He was a reasonably fair guy.

"My experience at Michigan State was very good. I got my bachelors degree and then my masters in sociology from there. The university worked very hard to make sure the whole thing worked. I had an Anglo roommate, and Dr. Hannah intervened to make sure that we were compatible. We got along pretty well. Once again, Dr. Hannah wasn't close by, but he made sure I was OK. I enjoyed going to the football games when I was there. I followed the team closely. I knew Herb Adderley really well."

Bill Yeoman was one of Duffy Daugherty's assistants. He also had good things to say about John Hannah: "He was the boss. Dr. Hannah was the perfect person to oversee the integration at Michigan State. He had the personality to get it done. If and when he committed to something, he went at it full steam. He believed in equality, and he got that message across to everyone he came in contact with.

"It took his strong personality to get Michigan State into the Big Ten after World War II. He was a tough mother goose. He was demanding, and he wanted things done correctly. He used all means necessary to get MSU into the Big Ten. He talked to politicians, university presidents, athletic directors, and anyone else who would listen. There was one time he was at a meeting with President Harlan Hatcher of Michigan, and the two ended up at separate ends of the table screaming at each other.

"Dr. Hannah was as close to the football program as any university president ever was. One thing you learned pretty quickly was you just didn't dare lose to the University of Michigan. Duffy was smart. He beat Michigan six years in a row early in his tenure at MSU. If you did anything to give Michigan an advantage, you could get fired. You better recruit your area under Duffy. If a player slipped through your fingers and ended up on another team's roster, especially Michigan's, you were in trouble."

As one might expect, Yeoman was clear about Daugherty's role in bringing African American players to Michigan State. He said, "Duffy Daugherty was the perfect guy to bring in the black players. He didn't care what color they were, and he gave them a chance to escape the South and play. He was a super human being. He could tell jokes to diffuse just about any situation. I learned how to deal with people from Duffy. He was the greatest at the social side of things. Duffy handled bad situations and resolved them better than anyone I had ever seen. I learned so much from him."

Indeed, many leaders in the Houston community used almost these same words to describe Yeoman's years at the University of Houston, where he made history with the recruitment of Warren McVea in 1964.

Gene Washington was raised in LaPorte, Texas, in the early 1960s. Washington was forced to attend high school at Baytown Carver, about eight miles away, since the African American schools in LaPorte only went through eighth grade. Washington helped Carver win a PVIL state title in football in 1961, his junior year. A world-class high hurdler, he also helped Carver win state track championships in 1961 and 1962.

The fleet-footed star went on to play his college football at Michigan State, where he achieved All-America status as a wide receiver. Washington was chosen eighth overall in the 1967 NFL draft by the Minnesota Vikings. He was a first-team all-pro in 1969 for the Vikings, and was selected for the 1969 and 1970 Pro Bowls. He played in Super Bowl IV with the Vikings. A foot injury forced Washington into retirement in 1973. He spent many years with the 3M Corporation after he left the NFL.

Washington shared his own reflections about Michigan State: "Dr. Hannah integrated campus housing first. He later integrated housing in the city of East Lansing for black Michigan State faculty and staff. He was very committed to it. It spoke volumes as to the type of person he was. Dr. King even came to our campus to visit not long before he went to Selma. I had a great time at Michigan State, much of it thanks to Dr. Hannah.

"Duffy Daugherty was great too. He was always fair with me. Duffy started getting black players from the South because he went down there and held clinics for the black coaches who had been banned from white clinics. The black coaches were always welcome to come up to MSU to get help too. Duffy didn't do this just so he could get black recruits. He did it because he cared about those coaches.

Daugherty did not totally plan this "Underground Railroad." He built up a good relationship with Willie Ray Smith Sr. at Beaumont Charlton-Pollard through his coaching clinics for black coaches. Smith, in turn, recommended players to Daugherty, who, in 1963, hit the jackpot in Texas when he recruited Bubba Smith from Charlton-Pollard High School and Gene Washington from Baytown Carver. Both became All-Americans their senior seasons in 1966, and Smith became the

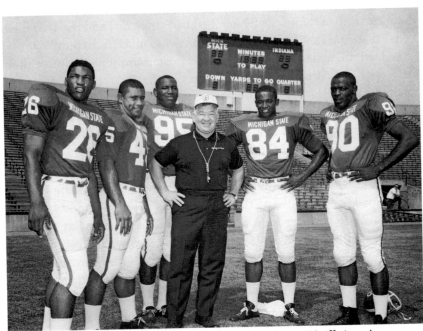

Michigan State Head Coach Duffy Daugherty with his 1966 All-Americans, including Texans Bubba Smith, #95, and Gene Washington, #84. Courtesy of Michigan State Athletics.

number one overall pick in the 1967 NFL draft by the Baltimore Colts, while Washington was chosen by the Minnesota Vikings, with the eighth pick in the first round.

Daugherty did not stop with just recruiting Texas in 1963. He recruited six other African American southerners, including another All-American, linebacker George Webster from Anderson, South Carolina, another first-round draft pick—number five overall by the Houston Oilers. Webster became a three-time All-Pro his first three seasons with the Oilers, before injuries derailed his career. He was voted as a first team linebacker on the all-time AFL team.

Daugherty continued recruiting African American players from Texas and the South until his retirement after the 1972 season. In 1964 he recruited Jess Phillips out of Charlton-Pollard, and in 1967 he snatched up Bubba Smith's younger brother Tody as well.

Bubba Smith and Gene Washington recounted their experiences at Michigan State. Smith said, "When I got out of school in 1963, the University of Texas hadn't integrated yet, but they wanted me to come there. The coach said they could give me a scholarship, but I couldn't play right away. I also wouldn't be able to live on campus. I turned that down. I knew Coach Yeoman at Houston really well. I would have considered going to Houston, but I wanted to get away from Texas.

"Getting away from the segregation in Beaumont and in Texas was my goal. In the end, I didn't have a choice where I was going to play in college. My daddy made the deal for me to go to Michigan State. He wanted to break down barriers. Overall, it ended up being a good decision. There was just so much more freedom at Michigan State. The football early on wasn't so great sometimes, but from a social standpoint, I had a good time in East Lansing. Now Gene Washington, who came up to Michigan State with me from Texas, wasn't like myself or Jess Phillips. We wouldn't see him around on campus at social events. Gene was always the corporate type. He wanted to get that education. We never had to worry about Gene getting into trouble."

"I took my studies seriously," Washington explained. "I didn't want to go back to Texas. Michigan State knew nothing about my background in athletics. I got to East Lansing solely on Bubba's recommendation. His dad may have had something to do with it too. They knew nothing about my athletic background in Houston either. I was a track man. I ran the hurdles.

"About a week before I graduated my track coach at Carver, Roy Hutchins, got me a special entry in a pre-meet before the NCAAs at Jeppesen Stadium over at UH. Myself and Randy Matson, the great shot putter from Pampa, were the only high school athletes invited. I only had a couple of days to prepare, and high school hurdles were only thirty-nine inches high—college ones were forty-two inches high.

"Conference champions from all over the country were at this meet. I didn't realize how big of a meet this was; I didn't even know what NCAA meant. I had also never competed against a white person before. Coach Hutchins told me, 'You can do it.' I was just worried about finishing the race. As I was lining up with all of these college guys, I said to myself, 'This is my chance.' Well, I almost won the race. It turns out my time was in the top five in the country.

"Afterwards, people and reporters were coming up to me and asking things like, 'Gene, where are you from? Where are you going to college? Because of segregation, no one had ever heard of me. The black newspapers in Houston like the *Forward Times* might run something, but the white papers hardly ever mentioned us. Even the paper in Baytown barely mentioned us. It was things like this that made me glad to get out of Texas.

"I was recruited by Dan Boisture, who was one of Coach Daugherty's assistants. What happened was that Bubba told me that he and his dad were going to put in a good word for me with Duffy. About ten days later, Coach Boisture called me and said he wanted to come to Texas to meet me. He was the only coach recruiting me who actually came to LaPorte. He came to my house, and my parents thought that was unusual. You see, a white person had never come to our home before. Me and my parents were not even sure where Michigan State was. Danny was good about talking about MSU and its traditions.

"Once I got to Michigan State, I felt comfortable and accepted, as opposed to in Texas. The color of my skin was never an issue. Another person who helped with my transition to college was Athletic Director Biggie Munn. I had looked into his background. It was Coach Munn, the football coach at MSU before Duffy, who started bringing in black players. He was very unique in what he was doing. Coach Munn was always very kind to me. He would always send me a personal note after I won a track meet.

"The races didn't mix in Houston, so I had barely interacted with any whites. I get to Michigan State and all of a sudden I'm sharing a room with two white swimmers. Everything was segregated in Texas, both on the field and in everyday life, but now all of a sudden, I'm in an open, friendly, atmosphere. It was great.

"About the only thing different I ran into at Michigan State was I never had white teachers before. The chemistry was different. I was used to black teachers and the small classes where we were given a lot of individual attention. The teachers in LaPorte and Baytown were a godsend to me. They did prepare me. I had these huge

Gene Washington, Michigan State, 1966. Courtesy of Michigan State Athletics.

classes at Michigan State and very little interaction and personal attention from the white professors. I eventually adjusted, though.

"Education was very important to me. After coming out of that segregated situation in Texas, I was driven to get my education so I would never have to go back to Texas. I made sure I kept my grades up so I could have a career.

"Not playing varsity as a freshman helped me get a leg up on my academics. It helped me get more acclimated as a student. I was quite busy. I was playing three sports and taking my classes. I was playing football in the fall, indoor track in the winter, and outdoor track in the spring. I stayed up at MSU in the summers to keep up with my classes. I pretty much didn't go back home to LaPorte for four years.

"When I looked back, Texas was still segregated, and I didn't have a lot of enthusiasm to return. Under segregation, it was disgraceful the way we were treated. We weren't recognized or reported on. There was no one in your corner. Your main goal in Texas was to stay out of trouble. You could get your family in trouble if you didn't. If I messed up, I could cost one of my parents their job in retaliation.

"MSU gave me an opportunity, and I took advantage of it. I didn't have anything else to fall back on. I had to be a good student. My choice if I failed was to join the military and go to Vietnam, or return to Texas. I was fearful; I didn't want to blow it. I had heard about other black players who had gone north to college, and they ended up back home with no degree and no future. Bubba was right. I was serious about my schoolwork. I just couldn't go back to Texas without my college degree. I didn't want to let my family down or disappoint them. I especially didn't want to disappoint teachers like Mrs. Evans in the one-room school-house in LaPorte, or my four high school coaches who meant the world to me: Johnny Peoples in football, Robert Strayhan in basketball, Richard Lewis in baseball, and especially Roy Hutchins in track."

Washington summed up what many of the black players from Texas who pursued college football in the North and West must have felt: "All of the black players from the South that went to Michigan State weren't wanted by the white colleges," the plain-spoken Washington said. "We had players from the Carolinas, Louisiana, Virginia, and of course, Texas. We had something to prove."

However, some other talented African American players from Texas met a different fate when they left their home state with the dream of greater recognition and an escape from segregation and discrimination. For them, it wasn't a dream but a nightmare.

13

Be Careful What You Wish For

Get out of here, nigger!
—Oklahoma State Head Football Coach Phil Cutchin
to Earl "Bud" Jones

While Michigan State served as the model for assimilating African American athletes into college football culture, other four-year institutions struggled to accept black players from Texas and other southern states. Typically a player from Texas believed he was going to a better environment, leaving maltreatment behind in the South and Southwest. Often this more promising environment proved to be real, but sometimes it wasn't much different from home. There were moments when a young black athlete found that his overall cultural challenges were far more complex and difficult to handle than they would have been at colleges back in his home state.

One such player who left Texas in hopes of better football opportunities was running back Wardell Hollis, who arrived at Oklahoma State University in the fall of 1961, after he graduated from Brackenridge High School in San Antonio. He was part of an influx of black talent recruited by the coaching regime headed by Cliff Speegle. However, Speegle and his staff were fired after a 4–6 record in 1962 after compiling an overall eight-year record of 36–42–3. The new Cowboys staff was headed by Phil Cutchin, who had played for Bear Bryant at the University of Kentucky.

Hollis told it like it was: "I went to Brackenridge because that's where Clarence Whitmore decided to go to school. He lived in my neighborhood on the east side of San Antonio. He was a little older, and so where he went, that's where I wanted to go. I was lucky. I started at receiver, and my senior year Coach Forren moved me to fullback and I did well there. It put me in a position to get a scholarship.

"When it became time to choose a college to play at, I visited TSU and Grambling. When I was at Grambling, there was a load of talent there. There were linemen who could outrun backs, like three-hundred-pound

Ernie Ladd. I decided that wasn't for me. I was offered scholarships from all of the Big Eight schools and Northwestern in the Big Ten. Coach Forren said that Baylor and UT inquired about me. But I wasn't ready to possibly integrate those schools. I was in ROTC at Brackenridge, and West Point came and looked at me. There were very few blacks at the Military Academy, and there was no one to talk to about what it would be like to be black at West Point. Then I noticed there were no girls there, so that was the end of that.

"I decided to go to Oklahoma State. Out of all the schools I visited, they had different tactics to try and recruit me. A lot of schools offered me money. At Oklahoma State I ran into a group of athletes and they told me, 'Don't come here and embarrass us if you're not going to study like some of the others that have come here.' It was important they said that. I was a good student and was serious about my studies. A lot of the other schools I visited just wanted to get me drunk and set me up on a date.

"Oklahoma State was fine at first. My first coach there was Cliff Speegle. He brought in several blacks around the time I got there to hopefully improve the talent level. I played running back my first two years under Coach Speegle. He was fired after my sophomore year in 1962. The new Coach was Phil Cutchin, a Bear Bryant protégé. I think he was Bryant's assistant head coach at Alabama. Do you remember the Junction Boys? That's when Bear Bryant took his Texas A&M players to Junction, Texas, in the 1950s for fall camp, and he ran a bunch of them off. I think they started with over one hundred players and ended up with around thirty-five.

"Well, Coach Cutchin tried the same thing at Oklahoma State. He ran off numerous players with his fall camp. We started with about two hundred players and ended up with about thirty-seven. People were leaving right and left. I survived the fall camp, and I was switched to defensive back my last two years. There were some racial things that went on at Oklahoma State under Cutchin.

"A white player back then, Chic Dambach, described an incident in graphic detail about what happened to my black teammate Earl 'Bud' Jones in a book he wrote. Out of the fifty or so freshmen I started with, only about five or six ended up playing all four years, and I was the only black player. After Oklahoma State, I served in the army for twenty-three years, and then after that I became an educator in Washington, DC."

In his book, *Exhaust the Limits: The Life and Times of a Global*

Peacebuilder, former Oklahoma State football player Charles "Chic" Dambach, described the treatment of Jones by Coach Cutchin and his staff: "My teammate and friend Earl "Bud" Jones injured his knee, and it would probably end his playing career. Under NCAA rules, injured athletes kept their scholarships until their graduation date, but you lost your scholarship if you quit. White athletes had no problem, but the coaches did everything imaginable to force the black players to quit and forfeit their scholarships.

"His injury came the week before we were to play Tulsa. . . . [S]ince Bud couldn't practice on his bad knee, the coaches told him to play the role of Tulsa quarterback Jerry Rhome and stand in the 'pocket' where the quarterback would—behind the offensive line, ready to make a pass. Jones would provide a target for the defensive line to practice their pass rush. . . . Everything seemed normal until defensive line coach Jim Stanley gave more specific instructions to the defensive linemen. 'Your job is to attack Jones, and the play will not stop until everyone hits him as hard as possible—*with your helmet on his knee.*'

"His demand was deplorable, so no one took him seriously . . . they didn't hit Jones hard or on his knee, and Coach Stanley was furious. In a rage, he stormed up to each defensive lineman, grabbed their face mask, and screamed, 'I said hit him hard and hit him in the knee!'

"It took a few rounds for the defensive linemen to comply, but they finally did, out of self-preservation. Action never stopped until all five defensive linemen had hit Bud hard on his knee . . . after each round, Coach Stanley roared at Jones, 'Are you quitting, nigger? When you gonna quit, nigger?' Bud was knocked to the ground each time, but he picked himself up and defiantly stood his ground.

"Finally, Jones could no longer even rise to his knees. He lay on the ground but the attacks and the unrelenting taunts continued. Finally, after at least thirty minutes of this torture and torment had passed, head coach Cutchin descended from the lofty tower he used to monitor the whole practice field. He came straight to our area walking fast and his face taut with fury. He looked down at the proud and fallen Earl 'Bud' Jones and simply said, 'Get out of here, nigger.'

"The rest of us moved on to continue the practice session in another part of the field, while Jones slowly crawled off into the locker room. I let my friend down that day, and I never recovered from the guilt. If any of the white players had 1 percent of the courage, integrity, and character of Earl 'Bud' Jones, we would have walked off the field in solidarity with him. Instead, in collective shame, we went on with our practice, and Earl disappeared."

Many years after the aforementioned incident, Earl "Bud" Jones recalled growing up in a segregated Arkansas and, as expected, recalled his shameful treatment. "I come from North Little Rock, Arkansas," he said. "Coincidently, I was in eighth grade when the 'Little Rock Nine' tried to integrate Little Rock Central High School in 1957. My eighth grade English teacher was Mrs. Patillo, the mother of Melba Patillo, one of the nine black students. We would get a blow-by-blow account of what was happening at Little Rock Central from Mrs. Patillo. Integration happened for those nine kids at Little Rock Central, but the rest of the state was 100 percent segregated. I didn't see my first white athlete until I went off to college at Oklahoma State.

"There were pros and cons to segregation. One pro was all the teachers were black and they cared about and knew how to treat black kids. We had about 96 or 97 percent of our seniors graduate from our black high school. Out of 143 seniors in my class, 140 graduated. The con was our facilities in school and in athletics—they were second or third rate.

"Back then, it really was true about the village raising the kids. Corporal punishment was also in vogue. The parents cooperated with the teachers. In the black community, if someone saw you doing something wrong, they would either correct you or they would tell your parents. The community saved a lot of kids. I have no love or respect for integrated schools. I bet 50 percent of the black kids drop out nowadays. I call it desegregation, not integration. There has never really been integration. Now segregation occurs inside of the schools. Kids get tagged as inferior, and they ended up being babysat and not really learning anything. They either drop out or, if they get a diploma, they get an inferior education as to what we used to get with segregated schools.

"After high school, I had a couple of offers from black colleges. I happened to get into Oklahoma State because they were recruiting one of our track athletes, and we kind of went there as a package deal. Oklahoma State had always been kind of a laughingstock of the Big Eight. We lost to Oklahoma like nineteen straight years. Oklahoma State had never brought in more than two black players at a time. The year before I got there, which was when Wardell Hollis came, the coaching staff brought in eleven or twelve blacks to play. The staff that recruited all of those black players and me, led by Head Coach Cliff Speegle, were fired after the spring of my freshman year. The new coaching staff, led by Phil Cutchin, pruned the number of players down, both white and black. As far as I know, Wardell Hollis was the only black out of those eleven or twelve who came in with him as a freshman and lasted all four years.

"After camp that fall, only about thirty players were still left to play. A lot of them weren't good football players; they could just tolerate abuse. Cutchin came from Alabama, where he was offensive coordinator under Bear Bryant. He also brought some of Bryant's former Texas A&M players with him on his coaching staff. That first year Cutchin was there, they put us through twenty days of hell. It was a duplicate practice what Bear Bryant did in Junction a few years before. Ours was there on our practice field right next to the field house. They put black bunting around the fence so people couldn't see in. There were about twelve guys who ended up with knee injuries.

"They did some crazy things to weed out players. There was one assistant coach—his name was 'Jumbo' Jim Stanley. He was a crazy man. He was the hit man for the coaching staff. If they wanted to get rid of somebody, they used him. He had these long arms like a gorilla. He had no problem with physical torture. He saw players as disposable. I saw him as a crazy man who beat up kids.

"We had a black kid from Houston on the team, Jerome Bell. He was a receiver and punter. One time on the practice field he was so exhausted he literally couldn't get up. Coach Stanley went over to Jerome and started jumping up and down on his chest to make sure he wasn't faking injury.

"I was on scholarship for three years, but I never played. By the fall of 1965 it looked like I was finally going to get to play. At practice one day we were practicing punts on the game field. My roommate accidentally clipped me and tore up my knee. I spent my twenty-first birthday at the university hospital. My knee needed surgery, but the team decided against it. Then, the coaches made me show up for practice. Then, they started making me practice just four weeks after I hurt my knee.

"Then came the incident Chic Dambach described in his book. We were getting ready to play Tulsa and their great quarterback Jerry Rhome, and they had me pose as him so our defensive linemen could get some practice rushing him. The coaches had the linemen try and take me out by hitting my bad knee, so they could get me to quit, so they could have my scholarship. The coaches didn't care. After a while, I just couldn't go on any further. That's when Coach Cutchin came down from his tower and said what he said to me. What they did was call a 'Quit Party.' If the coaches wanted to get rid of you, they would find a way to make you quit. They eventually forced me to withdraw.

"Now, not all of the white guys on the team were racist. Some were. I went to a team reunion a while back, and I met with one of the guys for breakfast. He was one of the guys Coach Stanley used to help run me off. He cried and apologized for taking part in what he did. Some of the white guys loved Coach Cutchin, though. They saw their survival as a badge of courage they've carried with them all of these years. The blacks didn't see it that way, though. Those white players aren't interested in hearing about the racism and torture we went through. To them, since they didn't experience the same thing we did, they didn't think it was so bad. You have to remember too that a lot of these whites grew up with this attitude towards blacks, a kind of indifference.

"In the end, I did get my degree in 1967, and then I spent the next thirty years working for AT&T in their research department."

Jerome Bell, the player from Houston that Jones spoke about being the object of Coach Jim Stanley's wrath, gave his take on the Oklahoma State coaching philosophy. Bell graduated from Wheatley High School in the spring of 1962 and then went to play for the Cowboys. "I was a punter and wide receiver at Houston Wheatley," Bell recalled. "I got to play in the Turkey Day Classic against Yates. There was one game I swear I averaged about eighty yards a punt. I came from a totally segregated society. You know, I believe we got a better education in segregation than we would have if things had been integrated. Our black teachers pre-pared us well, and I did well in college.

"When it came time for me to choose what college I wanted to play football at, I knew I wanted to get out of Texas. I visited Oklahoma State twice, and I signed a letter of intent there. I figured I wouldn't face rac-ism there. Boy, was I wrong! It was just as bad or worse at Oklahoma State. My roommate, Bob Kelly, was a black guy from West Virginia. He left because he was not used to that demonstrative racism.

"Bob left after our new coaching staff, led by Phil Cutchin, came in around 1963. We had been recruited by the previous coaches. They started running players off right and left. Cutchin and Sammy Baugh, one of the assistants, were a couple of bad actors. They proved that they were the outstanding rednecks that they were. Baugh had never coached at the college level before. They brought him in to supposedly teach me something about punting, since he set punting records in the NFL. I think they brought him in to help run me off. Let me give you an example. I was a wide receiver besides punting, and Baugh had a special play just for me that he nicknamed, 'Bastard Pass Left.' He was referring to the fact that I had a son born out of wedlock the year before in 1962. He didn't call me 'nigger' because that was too risky. He would just make the comments about my 'bastard child.' To me, it was pure hate.

"I was the punter at the start of the 1963 season, and I played some wide receiver. I played in the first couple of games against Texas and Arkansas, even though I had a punt blocked against the Longhorns. By the time we got into conference play, about game three or four, that's when they turned against me. The incident with me that Bud Jones talked about, what happened was the coaches started running us to death. They made it damn difficult for us to get an education because we were exhausted all of the time. I was one of the last ones they attacked. They waited until we were exhausted from all the running, and then they attacked us. They got me so tired that day that Earl talked about I just couldn't move. The coach threw me to the ground. He didn't exactly stand on my chest, but it was close to it. I couldn't fight back I was so tired from running all of those wind sprints. I had never quit anything before in my life, but they mishandled me and made me quit. It was a bad situation. Maybe I should have stayed in Texas."

A growing amount of civil unrest manifested itself by the mid-1960s with the civil rights movement; the assassinations of John F. Kennedy, Martin Luther King, and Robert Kennedy; and the Vietnam War and its resulting public protests and civil disobedience. Student unrest seemed to prevail on a growing number of college campuses and into college athletics. The latter happened in different forms of protests, such as walkouts and sit-ins. Many of these happened between 1968 and 1970, not long after events like the assassination of Dr. Martin Luther King Jr. in April 1968 and—at the Summer Olympics in Mexico City—the fist-raising "Black Power" protest on the medal stand by African American sprinters Tommie Smith and John Carlos.

In this noteworthy transition era, many old-school football coaches either refused or were unable to adapt. Grant Teaff, the head coach at three schools, including Baylor University, cited one early issue—the facial hair of African American players. "My experiences at McMurry College were great preparation for me dealing with minorities later on," Coach Teaff recalled. "My next head coaching job was at Angelo State in 1969. I had a pretty fair amount of black players on the team. Back then, I was very strict. My players could have no facial hair.

"Well, I had a black player from Lubbock, and he had some hair stubble on his face. Of course, I wanted him to be clean-shaven. My player said to me very calmly, 'Can I explain this to you?' The player told me that black men would get this stubble and it was hard for them to shave; it would really irritate their skin. He didn't protest or make a fuss about it. When he explained it, he made sense. I trusted this player. I changed my rule and changed my thinking. I was ignorant of the black culture. In 1969 it was an interesting time in America. It was a time of transition. Some coaches did well and adapted, and some didn't."

Not all coaches handled early issues like this one the same way Teaff did. The facial hair controversy came up again at other colleges in 1969. One incident unfolded at Oregon State University. African American linebacker Freddie Milton grew a goatee and a mustache after the end of the 1968 season. Early in 1969, Milton's coach, Dee Andros, spotted him on campus one day, observing the new look. Andros was old-school, with a strict facial hair policy, and ordered Milton to shave if he wanted to keep playing football. Milton refused and was suspended. Tensions mounted in the form of student protests, a march across campus, a call to boycott classes, and a Black Student Union walkout. Milton eventually left Oregon State and finished his college football career at Utah State.

The incident left a mark on the Oregon State football program, prompting reluctance among black recruits to accept scholarships there. Andros's reputation was damaged, as was Milton's. Pro teams were leery of signing Milton, although he eventually went to Canada, while Andros was accused of being a racist due to his obviously outdated and uncompromising old-school stance.

In 1970, the Beavers did not sign a single black athlete to scholarship status. Andros compiled a 26–13 in the four previous years, yet fell to just 8–36 from 1972 through 1975—a demise attributed to his inability to attract black players to campus. Unfortunately, this was not the sole example of facial hair causing backsteps. Similar incidents took place at UCLA, Stanford, and Purdue.

In 1968 and 1969, the Big Ten Conference, using the Michigan State model, was thought to be at the forefront of assimilating black players into their programs. However, Indiana, Iowa, and Wisconsin all experienced incidents with African American players that led to misunderstandings and suspensions.

At Indiana in 1969, Coach John Pont suspended ten black players who failed to show up for a practice, thereby eliminating themselves from the team. The players were boycotting practice over what they believed to be unfair treatment. The incident affected both the young men's football careers and the school's football program. The Hoosiers were expected to be contenders for the conference title but instead finished with just a 4–6 record. A year later, Indiana fell to 1–9. Pont was fired two seasons later.

At Iowa, also in 1968, Hawkeyes Coach Ray Nagel kicked sixteen black players off the team when they didn't show up for a spring training practice. Just days earlier, Nagel had two black players, sophomore Charles Bolden and junior Greg Allison, held out of spring drills for "personal reasons." This incident, along with the black players being dissatisfied with several elements of their education, plus some of the players' dislike of Nagel, led to the walkout. One of the black players involved in the protest was running back and future NFL head coach Dennis Green. Eventually, seven of the sixteen players were reinstated by a vote of the Iowa players. Four players did not request reinstatement, and five were turned down.

One of the suspended players not readmitted to the team was Houston native Kenny Price, who went on to play in the NFL. Price sat out the 1969 season, but returned to Iowa in 1970 to finish out his eligibility. Former NFL player Bert Askson, who knew Price back at Kashmere High School in Houston, said, "I think that Kenny was one of the guys who organized the walkout in the beginning, and that's why he wasn't voted back on the squad."

Frank Gilliam was an All-America receiver at Iowa in 1956 and in 1966 was the first African American assistant coach ever hired by a Big Ten school. He said, "The suspensions were for the team's benefit. Our Board of Regents supported us and the rules we had for our football program." Gilliam downplayed race as being a significant factor in the player protest, pointing out, "I had no problems myself at Iowa when I played and coaches there. It helped, though, that people there already knew me, and I had been coaching already. Iowa was looking to integrate their staff. The race issue really wasn't discussed. I was qualified to coach there. The president of Iowa knew me well, as did the athletic director, Forrest Evashevski, since I played for him."

African American players recruited from Texas were at the center of a controversy at Wisconsin at the end of the 1968 season. This carried over into 1969. The head coach at Wisconsin during this period was John Coatta, who played quarterback for the team he proceeded to coach back in 1949–51. As the starter, quarterback Coatta led the Badgers to an 18–7–2 record. He got into coaching and served as an assistant coach at his alma mater before he became head coach in 1967. Coatta's success as a player did not carry over into his coaching tenure. The Badgers went 0–9–1 in 1967, 0–10 in 1968, and 3–7 in 1969, his final season. This means Coatta started his coaching career with twenty-three games without a win, an NCAA record. His career 3–26–1 record ranks as the worst in Wisconsin coaching history.

One of the first things Coatta tried in 1967 that got his tenure off to a poor start was an ill-fated attempt to show his authority—he cut his best linebacker, Lucius Blair, an African American from Houston Yates, because he was late for reporting to practice.

Lewis Ritcherson Jr., who later became the center of the controversy at Wisconsin, said, "Why would he get rid of Lucius, who was probably our best defensive player? Couldn't you choose someone else to make a statement with? It was not a good start for us, and things only got worse."

Blair reflected on the incident: "I had a good freshman year, I was scheduled to start at linebacker. I got up to Wisconsin late, and I missed a meeting. I was told I was no longer on the team. There wasn't much I could do. I transferred to Tulsa and finished out my career there."

After Wisconsin was winless in 1967 and lost its first nine games the following season, controversy erupted. The cause: black players' contentions that their coaches discriminated in their choice of starting players. These players threatened to sit out their last game in a winless season against Minnesota on November 23. Ultimately, they went ahead and played for a lost cause, 23–15. Senior Tom McCauley, a white defensive back, described the scene in the dressing room before the game, when Coach Coatta left his players alone: "We all sat there quietly, and then I said, 'This is a bunch of baloney.' I said that they were all treated fairly at Wisconsin . . . if you don't want to play ball, don't. If you do, go out there and play right along with the rest of us. They did."

McCauley then denied racial tensions were a cause of the season with no games in the win column. "Maybe it was there," he said. "But I know it didn't affect me." He ventured to say that some of the black players were blaming the coaches for their own failures: "They wanted the glory; they weren't getting it. If they only went out there and played football, it would have been all right. It was a question of fourteen or fifteen little guys following three or four guys." The leaders of the player unrest included quarterback Lewis Ritcherson and leading receiver Mel Reddick.

McCauley said a focal point of the unrest was who should start at quarterback—Ritcherson, the black player, or John Ryan, the white player. "Lewis started the first game and did a terrible job," McCauley said, "and then they said Lewis was being discriminated against because he was a Negro. I think they gave him more of a chance because he was a Negro."

All Big Ten linebacker Ken Criter, who was white, said the team's racial problems were "definitely part of" the team's problems.

The problem carried over to the Tuesday after the Minnesota game. Eighteen black Wisconsin players did not attend the team's end-of-season banquet. Several people tried to minimize the racial problem, including athletic director Ivan B. Williamson, who said, "I don't believe we have a problem in this area, any more than exists in general at any other institution." Quarterback John Ryan said, "I don't think any rift existed until the boycott last night. I don't really know the situation between the black players and the coaches."

Coach Coatta apologized to the people at the banquet for the absence of the black players, saying, "I'm sorry we couldn't have been together at the end as we were in the beginning. Some of this protest cropped up last week, and I guess tonight is part of it. I'm sorry it happened."

The black players submitted their grievances to Wisconsin's athletic board. Among their demands were that four coaches be replaced; that Coatta review his relationships with his black players; that black players not be "stacked" at certain positions, which opened up more positions for white players; and that there be an improvement in academic counseling services for the football players, both white and black.

On December 5, more problems arose when one of the unpopular coaches, assistant Coach Gene Felker, resigned, blasting what he termed "weak, frightened administrators, black athletes, and their grievances." Felker also said, "The cards were stacked against Coach John Coatta two years ago. He had to inherit a black coach who had a five-year personal contract with university President Fred Harrington, while Coach Coatta was given just a three-year contract and each white assistant was given a one-year contract."

The coach to whom Felker referred was none other than Lewis "Les" Ritcherson Sr., a legend in the PVIL coaching ranks before he came to Wisconsin in 1966 after compiling a 132–38–3 record in sixteen seasons at Waco Moore High School for fifteen years. A Waco Moore graduate himself, Ritcherson played his college football at Wiley College in Marshall, Texas, and was a part of their Black College National Championship team in 1945. Ritcherson returned to Moore High and became its head coach in 1950. He won outright state titles in 1952 and 1964. Ritcherson's 1951 and 1960 teams tied for the state crown, and his 1954 squad lost in the finals. He was the second African American assistant coach in the Big Ten after Frank Gilliam at Iowa.

"Most coaches," Coach Ritcherson opined, "never had the opportunity to coach Negroes and are at a big disadvantage. The coach wants to be helpful, but he doesn't know how to cope with the situation. There is a black/white problem that the head coach doesn't realize. I went to Wisconsin to help the cause. For that I was happy. I was only the second black assistant coach in the Big Ten. Frank Gilliam had been hired at Iowa the year before me. I had it rough, though. White folks are still white folks. It would be years before there was a black head coach in college. But I helped make progress for blacks in the Big Ten Conference and at Wisconsin."

Leonard Fields was another black Wisconsin player who had Texas roots, coming to Wisconsin via Galveston Central High School. "My college choice boiled down to two schools: UCLA and Wisconsin," Fields said. "Coach Ritcherson came down from Wisconsin to try and get me to come there. I had played against his Waco Moore team and his son in the playoffs. He told me he would be like a father to me. I decided on Wisconsin. One thing that bothered me about going to Wisconsin was the losing. In high school I had lost only two games in three years. Losing at Wisconsin wasn't what I was used to.

"We did have problems with the coaches. The boycott was a mess. I was a captain, so Mel Reddick, another black player, and I tried to calm things down. There were some picket lines on campus after the boycott, and we decided to break them. That just caused more problems. It left a bad taste in everybody's mouth. In the end, though, I guess the boycott helped a little. The university gave in a little bit to the black players, and they tried to understand our culture more."

Bill Gregory from LaMarque was another African American player from Texas who was caught up in the boycott. He said, "I think the boycott came from the dissatisfaction of a losing season and the way the black players in general were being treated. To spotlight that, we voted for Lewis (Ritcherson) to be MVP for the season. The coaching staff chose who they wanted. Once it was determined what had happened, that's when we didn't go to the banquet. To me, Lewis was the focal point of the whole incident. We felt he should have been playing more. I'm not sure that the problems at Wisconsin were overt. We didn't have any name-calling or anything like that. Things were more covert. In the end, however, it's still all the same."

Lewis Ritcherson Jr. graduated from Waco Moore High School in 1966, having quarterbacked his team to the 1964 PVIL state title as a junior. As a senior, Ritcherson was one of the most sought-after recruits in the country. "I looked at a lot of colleges before deciding on Wisconsin," the coach's son recalled. "USC, UCLA, Washington, Oklahoma. I was offered scholarships by Grambling and Southern. I considered going to Southern. My dad had ties there, and some of my teammates from Waco Moore had gone there. The University of Houston offered me money, as well as Baylor and SMU. If I had chosen either Baylor or SMU, I possibly could've been the one to help integrate the Southwest Conference, because that was the same year SMU brought in Jerry LeVias.

Bill Gregory, University of Wisconsin, circa 1968. Courtesy of Wisconsin Badger Athletics.

"In the end, it came down to UCLA and Wisconsin. We were not a package deal, my father and I. He already had the job at Wisconsin before I decided to go there. His getting the job didn't depend on me going there. Having my dad at Wisconsin was obviously a factor in me going there, but my mother was the biggest influence. She wanted me close to her.

"Things started well at Wisconsin. I was MVP of the freshman team, but then the coaching staff got fired. Milt Bruhn was replaced by John Coatta. Bruhn was the one who hired my dad. The new coaching staff was a completely different regime from the old one. They were a different breed. My dad was smart. To protect himself, he got himself a five-year contract after Bruhn was fired. He wasn't sure if he was going to be kept around by the new staff, so he got the contract from the university president. Those other coaches who complained later about my dad having a five-year contract and them only having one-year contracts weren't as smart as my dad. He covered his bases.

"The new coaching staff moved me to receiver my sophomore year. I had a good spring training at quarterback in 1967, but the new coaching staff moved me anyways. I wasn't happy about it, and it ended up being a wasted year. Plus, I didn't get to play quarterback for a year. However, I had a good spring in 1968 before my junior year after I was switched back to quarterback, and I started the first game of the year against Arizona State. The first pass I threw against Arizona State was intercepted, and I only played three series before I was pulled. It was baffling to me and a lot of the other players on the team. I had words on the sidelines with the coaches. After that, I only played sporadically the rest of the season.

"Our next game, the new quarterback, John Ryan, threw seven interceptions. After the third one, I started warming up because I was sure I was going into the game. I never got in. The next game, they started another guy, and he threw three interceptions. I got to play against Utah State a little, and when our quarterback got knocked out for a series against Michigan, I went in there and moved the team fairly well. I felt there was a double standard. I threw one interception and I was out of the game. One of the other quarterbacks throws seven interceptions, and he stays in the game, and the other one throws three and he stays in the game. I just would have liked to stay in the game long enough to throw three interceptions! You couldn't hide the fact there was this double standard, though. All I wanted was a chance. A lot of my teammates, black and white, didn't feel I got a fair shot.

"The boycott more or less came out of this issue. There was some talk about the black players not playing in our last game of the year against Minnesota, but we ended up playing. The boycott came at the football banquet a few days later. A lot of it stemmed from the fact the black players chose me as MVP for the year, but the coaches chose who they wanted. That's when eighteen of us black players boycotted the banquet.

"Mel Reddick, one of our best players, organized the boycott. Everything came to a head then. The coaching staff finally realized they had a big problem on their hands. My dad was caught in the middle of this. We tried to keep him distanced from the boycott. He was in a tough situation. He had been hired by the previous coaching staff, and I don't think the new staff really wanted him around. Sometimes they wouldn't include him in meetings. He told me one time he walked into a meeting room, and there were the names of players they were going to get rid of. My name wasn't on that list because I was always academically in good standing. That was another thing that ticked the coaches off about me. Back then at Wisconsin and a lot of other schools, the coaches would pick your academic schedule for you so you would get easy classes so you could stay eligible. After my freshman year, I started going to a real

Lewis Fields, #74, from Galveston Central High School, with Lewis Ritcherson Jr., #10, and Head Coach John Coatta. Courtesy of Wisconsin Badger Athletics.

counselor because I wanted to graduate with a degree. I did graduate in four years. I was one of the few who did.

"My senior year was a waste. I had a back injury that set me back a little bit, but I didn't play at all that year. I met with Coach Coatta before the season, and we had a long conversation. There were some harsh words, and the whole meeting didn't end well. I knew after that meeting I wasn't going to play. What was strange was years later I ran into Coach Coatta at a coaches' convention, and he apologized to me for the way he dealt with me. I didn't know what to say when he said that. I was speechless.

"Going to Wisconsin was great as far as getting a degree. The Wisconsin diploma opened doors for me. It is recognized as a great college. Football-wise, things could've been better. I didn't like the losing. We were never a team. There was no camaraderie, and it was obvious the way things were going under Coatta's regime, it wasn't going to get any better. I might as well have gone to Baylor or SMU. I think about what could have been sometimes, but it is what it is."

Thus, as the incidents at Oklahoma State, Iowa, Wisconsin, and other institutions show, sometimes players left Texas for better opportunities only to meet with further disappointment and discrimination. Fortunately, as Texas colleges were slowly integrated by the end of the 1960s, African American players could now stay in their home state to play. By the end of the 1960s, all that remained integration-wise was the integration of the high school ranks in the Eastern part of the state. The next two key colleges were the University of Houston and Southern Methodist University (SMU).

14

The Coogs and the SWC

If you keep giving the ball to that little nigger, I'm going to pull all of my money out of this university!
—SMU BOOSTER TO MUSTANG COACH HAYDEN FRY

When Warren McVea integrated the University of Houston football program in 1964, it was significant because UH was the first major four-year college in Texas and the South to do so. The UH schedule continued to include still-segregated teams. North Texas State, Texas A&I, West Texas State, Lamar, and McMurry all integrated before UH, but they didn't play southern schools. North Texas potentially could have played Mississippi and Mississippi State back in 1957, but those two schools cancelled their games with the Eagles when they found out they had Abner Haynes and Leon King on their team.

Bill Yeoman, the coach who integrated UH, played college football at West Point under Colonel Red Blaik. Growing up in Glendale, Arizona, Yeoman would later remark, "I never paid attention to what people were. In Glendale, we had Poles, Russians, and we had a fair amount of Japanese around who helped with the nearby farms. I never cared what people were. My parents instilled that in me from an early age."

When Yeoman took over the head coaching chores at UH in 1961, he had an eight-year stint under Duffy Daugherty under his belt and faced the same dilemma as Joe Kerbel at West Texas State one year earlier. Yeoman knew he needed better talent on his all-white football team if he was ever going to compete on a national basis. He, like Kerbel, knew he had to recruit the best athletes possible. The color of their skin didn't matter. The famed coach vividly recalled his initial steps: "I got up in front of all of these black leaders at the Shamrock Hilton Hotel one evening and I said, 'I'm prejudiced!' They all looked at me, stunned. Their eyes lit up with concern until I then said, 'I'm prejudiced against bad football players!' That broke the ice, and the black community in Houston was in my corner after that." After the UH student body was integrated by President Philip Hoffman in the summer of 1962, the athletic department followed suit. What Yeoman had to decide, however, was who they were going to choose to integrate the Cougar football program in the spring of 1964.

There was no better known high school running back than "Wondrous Warren" McVea, as he was known. He was unquestionably the most sought-after recruit in the nation. A native of San Antonio, McVea attended Brackenridge High School. Playing halfback as a junior, McVea led the Eagles to an 11–3 record and a Class 4A state championship in 1962, with a 30–26 victory over Borger. In McVea's senior season, Brackenridge compiled an 8–3 record and lost a bi-district playoff game to San Antonio Lee and their star halfback Linus Baer. In what many consider the greatest high school football game ever played in Texas, Lee squeaked out a 55–48 victory. This being McVea's final high school game, in which he was inserted into the quarterback position for the first time, he ran for 215 yards on 21 carries, scored six touchdowns, and scored thirty-eight of his team's forty-eight points. That season McVea totaled 1,332 yards rushing on only 127 carries, an astounding 10.4 yards per carry. He scored forty-six touchdowns and thirty-nine extra points. His 315 single-season point total and 591 for his career were at the time Class 4A records.

At the end of the 1960s, Dave Campbell's prestigious *Texas Football* magazine chose McVea as the best runner of the 1960s from a panel of six-hundred coaches, writers, and observers. In 2004 interviews both Campbell and Dan Cook, a fifty-plus-year sports editor and television journalist

Warren McVea, University of Houston, circa 1963. Courtesy of Vic Castillo.

from San Antonio, both thought McVea was the best high school football player they ever saw.

Every major college coach in the country wanted McVea. During the 1963 season, Oklahoma coach Bud Wilkinson came in person to watch McVea play. Apparently McVea ran wild in the game, and Wilkinson said afterward, "I'd lock him in the trunk of my car and head for Oklahoma, but, from what I saw tonight, I'm sure he'd get out."

McVea was also a sideline guest of the Texas Longhorns on January 1, 1964, when the Horns won their first National Championship with a 28–6 rout of Navy in the Cotton Bowl.

The University of Missouri, a school high on McVea's list, got former President Harry S. Truman to write McVea a letter trying to convince him to become a Tiger. In fact, Dan Devine, the Missouri coach, said, "I've never seen anything like it. Every place I go I hear of this kid. It seems like everyone has heard of him."

When Yeoman decided to recruit McVea, he realized he would need help from Houston's black community leaders. He turned to Lloyd C. A. Wells, also known as "the Judge." A native Houstonian from the Fifth Ward neighborhood, Wells worked as a photographer and spent many years writing an influential sports column for a couple of Houston's black newspapers, *The Forward Times* and *The Informer*. Wells used his column to bring about the elimination of segregated seating at the Texas League's Houston Buffs games and in Jeppesen Stadium at Houston Oilers games.

What Wells was best known for in the Houston area was serving as an advisor and surrogate father to young black athletes as early as high school and later to college and pro players. Jim Kearney of Wharton, a small town south of Houston, went to Prairie View A&M, where he played quarterback. Eventually he played defensive back for the Kansas City Chiefs because of Wells. "Oh, he was the man," Kearney said. "In Houston, nobody was bigger than Lloyd. *Nobody*. He was quite the man. He became a person we could go to and talk about problems. He had seen the world; he knew the score."

Apparently it was UH Sports Information Director Ted Nance who brought Wells to Bill Yeoman's attention. "Ted Nance was very important in getting me recruited," McVea recounted. "He's the best that's ever done his job. Apparently Ted went to Coach Yeoman and said, 'You don't have a chance to get Warren. He's never even heard of the University of Houston.' I was planning on going to USC—all the tailbacks and the Heismans.

"Coach Yeoman didn't know what was going on in the black community in Houston, but he knew Ted did, so he got leaders in the black community to recruit me. He got Lloyd Wells, of course, and other business leaders. I already knew a little about Lloyd Wells. A lot of people thought the only way I would go to UH would be through Lloyd. I guess that's somewhat true."

Nance underscored that belief: "I told Coach Yeoman about Lloyd Wells. I had gotten to know Lloyd because he was a columnist for one of the black newspapers in town, and we were the first college in the South to admit black media to our games. Once Coach Yeoman met with Wells, he in turn introduced him to the black leaders of Houston."

It was not just Wells who convinced McVea to come to Houston. While Wells was a catalyst, it was a collaborative effort of many people. On Yeoman's staff, Chuck Fairbanks was one of the coaches involved. "Warren was a great young man to be recruited to U of H," Coach Fairbanks said. "He was a phenomenal player. To this day, he is probably the greatest instinctive runner I have ever seen or coached."

Fairbanks continued, "Tom Boisture was another Yeoman staff member instrumental in recruiting Warren. We both helped recruit Warren. Before Warren came, we were struggling for recognition as a college and as a football program. When Warren decided to come to the University of Houston, he made it acceptable and popular for blacks and whites to come to UH. I have a great appreciation for what Warren went through being our first black football player. He was the right person to do it, though. He was very outgoing and wouldn't let little things bother him."

The last piece of the McVea recruiting puzzle was, of course, Bill Yeoman. "After I visited with Warren and saw how he acted around his mom," the coach remembered, "I knew we had a chance to get him. We were the closest major college to San Antonio that actually had integrated. I knew he wasn't going to go too far from home. To tell you the truth, my main worry was St. Mary's University in San Antonio. Some were saying that they were going to recruit Warren and resurrect their football program."

McVea echoed Yeoman: "I was a mama's boy; we had nine in our family. A lot of times I would come home after a recruiting trip after only a day or so because I was homesick. Coach Yeoman was the only coach who picked up on this and the loneliness I felt.

"I had never seen a coach like Coach Yeoman. He hardly ever said anything. He was also one of two coaches who picked up on the importance of religion to our family (Coach Dan Devine of Missouri was the other), and Coach Yeoman really focused on winning over my mother."

McVea signed his UH letter of intent in the summer of 1964. When he arrived on campus in the fall, he was for the most part readily accepted by his Cougar teammates, the student body, and UH fans. While not incident-free, the UH community appeared to welcome its newest star.

Native Houstonian Bill Worrell experienced McVea's arrival from a unique perspective. Worrell was a UH cheerleader, a member of the Cougar baseball team, and a resident of Baldwin House, the athletic dormitory. "Warren was well liked," Worrell remembered. "I had several classes with him. Put yourself in Warren's shoes. What would it be like for me at Grambling?"

Gus Hollomon came to Houston that same year. A defensive back, Hollomon eventually set the UH career interception record. He said, "This was all new territory for us. We wanted to make it work, and the coaches worked hard to make Warren feel welcome. It really worked out well. Now if Warren would have been a jerk, it may have been different. Warren was just a fellow player and athlete to us."

Jody Powers, a white freshman teammate, said, "We were happy to have Warren join us. He had gotten a lot of press. At first Warren was somewhat quiet and shy. We always wondered how it felt to be in his shoes. When he first got there, we did have a couple of rednecks on the team, but we kept them in check. At first there were some dumbass remarks. A lot of the credit for the way Warren was treated had to do with Coach Yeoman. He created an environment of acceptance. Leadership determines the environment. It was understood that Warren was to be treated as an equal."

"When I got to campus," McVea said in retrospect, "Coach Yeoman let it be known in his own way that I was to be left alone. Coach Yeoman put everything to rest. I asked him awhile back if he was nervous about our situation, and he said no, he hadn't given it much thought; he just did it.

"Once I got started at UH, there were a couple of incidents. One time when I was in line at the bookstore, I could hear some people saying some racial things. Sometimes, if I was in a crowd somewhere, I would hear the word 'nigger!' shouted from someone in the crowd. Early on, sometimes my teammates would accidentally say the "N" word around me. It was never directed at me, and they would always apologize. That was about it. I must say pretty much all my classroom instructors were helpful to me."

Once McVea started playing varsity football in 1965, he became the first African American to play major college football in the South. The Cougars typically played a major college schedule as an independent. They typically played half of their games against still-segregated Southeastern Conference foes, such as Ole Miss, Mississippi State, Kentucky, Tennessee, and Georgia. Other southern opponents were Miami, Florida State, Memphis, Tampa, Wake Forest, and North Carolina State. McVea was the first African American to ever take the field against Ole Miss, Mississippi State, Kentucky, Tennessee, Miami, and Florida State. In addition, the Cougars also played other national powers like Texas A&M, Penn State, Auburn, Michigan State, and the University of Texas.

What McVea did the year before Jerry LeVias showed up on the SMU campus in 1965 was show that a major college in Texas and the South could be integrated mostly incident-free. While McVea faced some challenges on the road, especially at the University of Mississippi in 1967—where he received death threats—the star running back experienced little to no discrimination, racism, or retaliation on the football field. McVea even said, "I never experienced any problems on the field, such as name-calling, rough play, or spitting on me."

Unfortunately, when Jerry LeVias of Beaumont integrated the Southwest Conference in 1966, he experienced all of the hardships on the field that Warren McVea did not have to endure, and then some. LeVias was the first scholarship African American football player in the Southwest Conference when he made his varsity debut for the Mustangs on September 17, 1966. Technically LeVias was not the *first* black athlete to take the field in a Southwest Conference game. One week before, a nonscholarship player—or "walk-on"—got into a nationally televised game. Running back John Westbrook of the Baylor Bears was sent into the game against Syracuse on a day when the Bears upset the Orangemen, 35–12. The game, originally scheduled for September 17, was moved up a week to accommodate the ABC television audience.

Westbrook was a product of Booker T. Washington High School in Elgin, just outside of Austin. Offered scholarships by North Texas State and Bishop College, Westbrook decided to walk on at Baylor, in part because they offered the religion and psychology courses he desired. Despite playing a total of only three minutes during his freshman year, Westbrook had worked himself up to a backup role in his first varsity season.

In the fourth quarter of the game against seventh-ranked Syracuse, with Baylor up 28–6 and a fair number of the Baylor contingent chanting "We want Westbrook!," Coach John Bridgers put in his backup running back. When Westbrook entered the game, Baylor speech professor and stadium public address announcer Dr. George Stokes proclaimed to the home crowd, "Ladies and gentleman, another Baylor first: Colored football for color television!" (referring to the newness of color television in 1966 and obviously the newness of Baylor having an African American football player).

Tom Kennedy, sports editor of *The Baylor Lariat* and future columnist for *The Houston Post*, was selected to be the spotter for ABC telecasters Chris Schenkel and Bud Wilkinson for the game. "Our stadium announcer was a long-time speech professor, Dr. George Stokes," Kennedy remembered. "He was always making what he thought were these clever little comments on the PA. When John Westbrook came into the game in the fourth quarter, I will never forget Stokes making what he thought was a clever announcement. I was stunned. So were these two famous announcers—they were speechless—only for a few seconds. They didn't want empty air time. Bud Wilkinson looked at Chris Schenkel, and they both shrugged their shoulders. Instead of gushing about what should have been a positive historic moment for Baylor and the Southwest Conference, their somewhat taken-aback responses made everything anticlimactic. Off-camera they continued to nod their heads as if to say 'What did you expect?' Instead of telling the viewing audience that Baylor had embraced integration, they didn't know what to say, so they said very little.

"I took Dr. Stokes to task in my next column in *The Lariat*, but that was nothing compared to the reaction of another individual I highly admire and respect. Walter Abercrombie was playing football in the Waco public schools at the time and was especially excited when his hero, John Westbrook, also a preacher man and fellow African American, took the field for the Baylor Bears. Walter remembered the 'color football' comment and how it embarrassed and even angered him. Walter played running back at Baylor in the late seventies, early eighties, and then with the Pittsburgh Steelers. Walter is now the executive director of the Baylor 'B' Association, which is the organization of the school's former letter winners. Well, it turns out Walter was in the stadium that day also. He told me he remembered that comment by Dr. Stokes. Walter said he never felt so angry or embarrassed for Baylor. It turns out John Westbrook was Walter's hero growing up. John had come to speak at Walter's church in Waco when he was a kid. Walter said John Westbrook was one of the primary reasons that he wanted to be a Baylor Bear. When he saw this strong black man take the field that day, he knew this goal was within his grasp."

Sure enough, Abercrombie was All-Southwest Conference and a member of Baylor's 1981 Cotton Bowl team. He held school rushing records for a number of years and was an NFL star after being drafted by the Pittsburgh Steelers. As for Walter's hero, John Westbrook, he played only sparingly during that 1966 season and beyond, due in part to a knee injury. Thus the majority of Southwest Conference integration centered around Jerry LeVias.

The fleet-footed LeVias was another product of the Beaumont Hebert powerhouse program of Coach Clifford Ozen in the late 1950s and early 1960s. LeVias played quarterback, defensive back, and returned kicks and punts for the Panthers. He was also a cousin of Hebert products and future Pro Bowlers Miller and Mel Farr. He also was a track star, and his high school sprint relay team (along with his cousin Mel Farr) set a national high school record. Every major college in the northern and western United States recruited LeVias—and even some Texas schools made their pitches.

The highly recruited standout wound up at Southern Methodist University, enabling Coach Hayden Fry to make history. LeVias was a three-time All-Southwest Conference choice, and during his 1968 senior season he was an academic and consensus football All-American. Levias set SWC marks in career receptions (155), receiving yards (2,275), and career touchdown receptions (22). After his SMU career concluded, he was a second-round draft pick of the Houston Oilers and made the Pro Bowl as a receiver and kick returner his rookie year in 1969. LeVias was elected to the College Football Hall of Fame in 2003.

Jerry Levias discussed growing up in Beaumont and being recruited to play at SMU. "We were aware of segregation growing up," he recalled. "It didn't really bother us, though. We were wrapped up in playing sports and in our community. Things like black people demonstrating were just getting started when I was growing up. I was mostly involved with what was going on at my black high school, Hebert. I loved Hebert. We had some great teachers. Another great teacher and coach I had back in junior high was Enous Minix. He set standards for us, and he made us live up to them. We didn't miss that much growing up in Beaumont. We had great coaches and academics. Everyone wanted to be a Hebert Panther. Our academic environment was one of learning.

"Then there was Coach Ozen. He was a huge man. We used to say he was like Elwood the football player in the Old Pro Falstaff beer commercials in the 1960s. You would never see all of Elwood in the commercial because he was so big. That's about how big Coach Ozen was. I remember when it was cold out during practice, he would wear shorts and short sleeves. He also had that board he would hit players in the rear with if they were messing up. That board looked like a toothpick in his hands. One thing about Coach Ozen was you didn't want to disappoint him. You would never mess around at practice, either, out of the respect you had for him. You also didn't quit, at least not during the season. You could quit after the season was over, but not during.

"We did mix with whites a little on weekends. We would play a little sandlot football, two-handed touch. Gus Hollomon and Johnny Fuller, two of the better white players in Beaumont back then, used to come play.

"Everything was football. My cousins were Miller and Mel Farr. It helped in the sandlot games being related to them, because that meant I would be chosen. Football was king. If Coach Ozen was driving around Beaumont and he saw a bunch of young black kids, he would throw a football out of his car into a ditch so they would take the football and start playing with it.

"I actually started out as a water boy for Coach Ozen and Hebert. I lived right across the street from the Hebert practice field, and I would bring water for the coaches. Players back then were not allowed water at practice. I used to put ice from our freezer in the coaches' water.

"Back then, the ultimate football game every year was the 'Soul Bowl.' It was Charlton-Pollard versus Hebert. There were 20,000 to 25,000 at that game every year. No one got sick that day, no one died. If a household had a husband that went to one of those schools and a wife that went to the other, there could be all kinds of fights. There were some big wagers on the game. The whole town was up in arms every year about the 'Soul Bowl.' We did beat Charlton-Pollard my senior year!

"As far as my recruitment, I was gone pretty much every weekend the spring of my senior year. In fact, I didn't get to run track because I was gone so much. There was really no limit on the number of visits you could take. I had ninety scholarship offers. Toward the end of spring I was tired of traveling and all the visits.

"One day, Coach Ozen called me down to his office. He said someone was here to see me. Out of respect for him, I came down there. I was just doing him a favor. Our athletic director, Sparky Adams, was also there. The coach that came to see me was Hayden Fry of SMU. He wanted to talk to me about going there. I had never heard of SMU. The main thing Coach Fry talked to me about was getting an education. He was the only coach out of all the ones that had talked to me who focused on my getting a degree. Since I was a good and serious student, this got my attention. He didn't even mention anything to me about integration.

"Coach Fry eventually came to my house to meet my family. He first met my grandmother, and she really liked him. Then, Coach Fry went straight to the kitchen. All the other coaches who came to visit me focused on my dad, but Coach Fry focused on my mom. He went into the kitchen and started talking to her about how to prepare pinto beans so they wouldn't give you gas. So, of course, she really liked him. I did too. Once again, Coach Fry talked to my parents about my getting an education, not integration. If he would have mentioned integration, I probably wouldn't have gone to SMU.

"I didn't even realize until later that I would be the first black in the Southwest Conference. A story came out in the newspaper later about it, and that's how I found out about it. The headline in the Beaumont newspaper said, 'LeVias to Become First Negro Athlete in SWC History.' They had told me I was going to be a pioneer, but I had no idea I was going to be the first. I had seen stories on TV about how black people were being shot and hosed down and attacked by dogs. I didn't want any part of that. I didn't want to be put in that position.

"Back then, the Southwest Conference had a big reputation as a football conference, kind of like the Southeastern Conference today. In those days, you had all this money in Texas, mostly from oil. A lot of these oilmen went to SMU, TCU, Baylor, Texas Tech, all the SWC schools. It was kind of prima donna football, run by a bunch of oil millionaires. It's what people talked about at the water fountain on Monday mornings, Southwest Conference football. It was like their own private club. They really didn't want me in their private club. I think that's where a lot of the problems were with my integrating the conference.

"I know Warren McVea had integrated the University of Houston the year before I did, but not too many people cared. UH wasn't in the Southwest Conference; they were an independent and no one paid any attention to them. Mac and I stay in touch, and I know he had it a little easier than me as far as integration, for the reasons I just mentioned. Mac has even said to me, 'I couldn't have gone through what you went through. What was wrong with you for putting up with all of that?' Warren didn't have the temperament to do what I did."

Hayden Fry recounted an incident at the start of the 1967 football season that clearly illustrated what LeVias was talking about. After SMU's Hispanic quarterback Ines Perez and Levias had led SMU to a last second win over Texas A&M, a prominent Aggie booster went up to Coach Fry and said, "You should feel great, Coach Fry. You beat us, but it took a Mexican and a nigger to do it!"

Jerry Levias, SMU, circa 1967. Courtesy of SMU Athletics.

LeVias mentioned a similar conversation he overheard one day. He said, "I was sitting outside Coach Fry's office one night and he had a big SMU booster in there who told him, 'If you keep giving the ball to that little nigger, I'm going to take all of my money out of this university!'

"My first year at SMU was tough. All I could do was practice and not play ball, since freshmen couldn't play varsity. I had to go against guys like John LaGrone, who was an unbelievable player, an All-American.

"My sophomore year, when I was on varsity for the first time, the world discovered me. Things got even tougher. Sometimes I wanted to quit. I didn't want to disappoint Coach Fry, though. He had stuck his neck out for me. Just think of the courage it took for him a few years earlier when he applied for the SMU job, and he told them he wouldn't take the job if he couldn't recruit black players. You're an up-and-coming coach, you have a chance for a prestigious job at a Southwest Conference school, yet you're willing to not get the job because you refuse to back down from your beliefs? How could I quit? My dad also told me, 'You're a man of your word—you can't quit.'"

Many times, because of the abuse heaped on him, LeVias often thought about quitting during his three varsity seasons. He was tormented almost everywhere he played. At Texas A&M, they pulled out hangman's nooses, and a student let loose several black cats onto the field. At TCU, LeVias got a death threat, and the FBI set up a human barricade around him and positioned snipers on top of buildings around the stadium.

The death threats continued throughout his SMU career, yet LeVias didn't worry about being killed. "The only thing I feared in life was disappointing Hayden Fry," he remarked, "When they threatened to shoot me, I didn't care. I just wanted to play good football and make Hayden Fry happy."

LeVias experienced problems on the field from opponents too. In 1966, his sophomore year, the Mustangs needed to defeat Baylor to reach their first Cotton Bowl in eighteen years. SMU won the game in the final seconds, 24–22, on a field goal set up by a long gain by LeVias down to the Baylor fifteen-yard line. Instead of being joyful after the victory he contributed to, LeVias was found alone, crying in the equipment room. The Baylor players had punched him in the bottom of pileups and called him a nigger and a spook during the entire game. It is ironic this came from the same Baylor players who had an African American of their own, John Westbrook, on their team.

Another incident in LeVias's senior season in 1968 against TCU in Fort Worth almost sent him over the edge. After he caught a pass over the middle, a TCU defensive back came up and spit right in his face. The player then called him a nigger. LeVias came off the field, threw down his helmet, and said, "I quit."

Coach Fry came over to his star player and said, "Jerry, don't let that one dumbass whip you. If we win this game, we've got a chance to win a championship. If you quit now, they're going to think they beat you down."

LeVias said, "When it became time to go back into the game, I made a bold statement. I told Coach Fry, 'I'm going to run this punt all the way back.'"

So, in a bit of redemption, LeVias got the last laugh when in the fourth quarter with the game tied at fourteen, he fielded the TCU punt at his own eleven-yard line and zigzagged eighty-nine yards for a touchdown. The

Mustangs beat TCU on their way to a 7–3 regular season that earned them a berth in the Bluebonnet Bowl, where SMU beat Oklahoma 28–27 in one of the most thrilling games in the history of the Houston bowl game.

Jerry Levias reflected further, "One person who doesn't get enough credit for my surviving at SMU was Rufus Cormier. Rufus came the year after I did from Hebert too. He was my fullback at Hebert and a linebacker on defense. He was a great player. He ended up being a lineman at SMU, and he was the MVP of the Bluebonnet Bowl in 1968 when we beat Oklahoma 28–27. He tackled Oklahoma's great running back, Steve Owens, four times behind the line of scrimmage that game. Supposedly, those were the only times in his career he ever lost yardage on a run.

"Rufus was an academic guy too. He went that route after SMU and went to Yale Law School. He was a classmate of the Clintons and Clarence Thomas. He later became the first black partner of the Baker and Botts law firm in Houston, and he was also the first black member of River Oaks Country Club. Rufus was a real stabilizing force for me at SMU. He's just an unbelievable person.

"So Rufus and Coach Fry were my two main people at SMU. Coach Fry and I still speak at least once a month. He always kids me and says, 'Levi, if I'm gonna be your daddy, I have to make sure my tan stays just right.'"

Rufus Cormier said, "I had some great teachers growing up. They made a huge difference in my life. I loved school. My father also emphasized education, even though he only had an eighth-grade education himself.

"I was in band at Hebert for a while, but when I found out you had to buy the instrument you played, that's when I went out for football. I started out as a linebacker. Jerry had already made a name for himself, so when I went out for the team as a sophomore, Jerry was a junior and already well-known for his football exploits.

"Well, I wanted to make an impact out there in football. On the first play I was out there, Jerry came to my side of the field and ran right by me for a touchdown. When Jerry went into the end zone, I was behind him, and when I caught up with him, I just laid him out. Needless to say, Coach Ozen was not happy. He grabbed me and said, 'Boy, what's wrong with you? Are you crazy? Do you know who that boy is?' I said, 'Yes sir.' Coach Ozen replied, 'If you do anything like that again, I'm going to kill you!'

"After I hit Jerry like that, I was ready to go back to band," Cormier chuckled. "My football career was almost over after one play. Coach Ozen used his board on me after that incident.

"Things were very segregated in Beaumont. We basically led separate lives, whites and blacks. There was very little interaction. My father also forbade me from places where there could be potential problems. He discouraged us from riding on city busses, and he wouldn't let us go to the white movie theater. For the most part we just stayed in our neighborhood.

"I played in the Soul Bowl, Hebert versus Charlton-Pollard. The place was packed every year. The stands were full and people surrounded the field by standing on the track. We beat Charlton-Pollard my junior year, when Jerry was a senior, and we lost to them when I was a senior.

"Hayden Fry came and talked to me about going to SMU. Jerry was an influence for me going there too. The truth is, however, I went to SMU because it was warm. I went on recruiting trips to the Big Ten and Big Eight schools, and I was freezing to death on those visits. I talked to the University of Houston a little about going there, and to Lamar College in Beaumont, but I ultimately chose SMU because of the warm weather.

"Jerry said I was a stabilizing force for him when I got there. Well, it was mutual. Jerry had a splendid year as a freshman. He learned about the team and the school. So when Jerry was a sophomore and I was a freshman, we spent a lot of time together. One thing that helped was that Jerry was a fabulous player, and because of that we had access to places we otherwise couldn't have gotten into. So Jerry was good to have around! Our situation, there not being very many blacks on campus and us being the only two on the varsity football team, just kind of led us together, plus the fact we were already friends."

Once the University of Houston in 1965 and Baylor and SMU in 1966 integrated their programs, the integration of college football in Texas was on its way to completion.

The University of Houston made it acceptable for blacks to attend and play football at major four-year institutions in Texas, while the integration of the Southwest Conference by Baylor and SMU made it acceptable for the rest of the SWC schools to integrate, like Texas, Texas A&M, and Arkansas.

When the Longhorns and Razorbacks each fielded their first African American varsity player in the same season, 1970, the integration of Texas and Southwest Conference college football was finally complete. All that remained now in the late 1960s was for the high school gridirons of the Lone Star State to be fully integrated.

15

Everyone Joins the Fold

When integration came in 1967, my sophomore year, it was a big deal for the school, the players, and the coaches. We could prove to everyone we had a good team. We wanted to compete against everybody.
—DELVIN WILLIAMS, HOUSTON KASHMERE PLAYER
AND FUTURE ALL-PRO RUNNING BACK

The inroads with the desegregation of school districts and colleges in other parts of Texas in the late 1960s gradually led to changes in the conservative, slow-to-change eastern portion of the Lone Star State. When the University of Houston and SMU integrated in 1964 and 1965, respectively, that also facilitated the integration of programs in East Texas, Dallas, and Houston school districts and football programs by the 1967–68 Texas Interscholastic League school year.

No matter which part of the state was still an integration holdout by the late 1960s, the assimilation did occur, and players now have their unique stories to tell about their experiences and how they adapted and persevered in spite of the odds.

Even in the more progressive west side of the state, some stubborn holdovers held forth. In the Panhandle, for instance, the two major school districts in Lubbock and Amarillo followed numerous smaller districts and finally integrated in 1965 when Don Burrell suited up for the Lubbock High Westerners, leaving only Amarillo to be desegregated.

The turning point for Amarillo High School came in the 1966–67 school year. However, Carver High, the African American high school in this northern Panhandle city, remained open. School choice went into effect—black students could go to Amarillo High or Carver. Morris Overstreet was the young African American who integrated Amarillo High School. A junior wide receiver, Overstreet went on to play at Angelo State University before obtaining a law degree from Texas Southern in Houston in 1975. By 1990 Overstreet became the first African American elected to a statewide office in Texas—the Texas Court of Criminal Appeals. In 2016, Justice Overstreet lost the race to become the Democratic nominee for Harris County district attorney.

"It's hard to make a comparison at the time with something you didn't know," Overstreet said, reflecting on those early days of integration. "Later on you can look at the conditions and see the effects of segregation. To me, segregation is different from discrimination. Discrimination is where someone has treated you different. Now, segregation is rooted in discrimination, and part of it is discrimination. Later on you can look back and see the effects of it.

"We never got new books. Where you sign and date it in the front of the book, it was always full of names. I would ask, 'Why do we have to get the used stuff?' We got inferior equipment in football. Now, the varsity got new uniforms and some other new things, and that was because of our football coach, Johnny Allen. He was very successful, and he brought a lot of favor and publicity to the school district. But at the time, how did you know? There was nothing to compare it to. We knew the stuff wasn't new. When you were older you could make comparisons. The whites had newer, different, and more equipment.

"I had a lot of good influences growing up. Before the phrase, 'It takes a village to raise a child' became popular, that's what was really happening in Amarillo. Parents, teachers, friends—they all helped influence and raise the black kids in the area. Take one of my coaches, Ike Avery. I saw him every day of the week but Saturday, and sometimes then too. I saw him at school, practice, games, Boy Scouts, church, you name it. I also saw our principal, Mr. Champion, all of the time too.

"When integration came along, we had the choice of staying at Amarillo Carver High School or going to Amarillo High School, the white school. That was in 1966. The next year, 1967, Carver was to be closed down, and then all of the blacks would go to the white school. In 1966, however, we could choose which school to go to. The seniors stayed at Carver. Ron Shanklin, who later played receiver with the Steelers in the 1970s, was the star of the Carver team, and he influenced the other seniors to stay there.

"I was a junior in 1966, so I had a decision to make. I thought to myself, 'What are the advantages of going to Amarillo High?' The big advantage I could think of was I would be seen by more colleges in hopes of getting a football scholarship so my college would be paid for.

"The principal at Amarillo High, Ross H. Larsen, wanted things to go smoothly with integration. It was mandated and it had to happen. He was committed to making it work. Everyone was nervous about integration, including me. I changed my mind a couple of times over the summer about which school I wanted to attend. I figured I could try out at Amarillo High, and if things didn't work out, I could go back to Carver. Warren Harper was the football coach at Amarillo High. He helped make it work too.

"We were pretty good the two seasons I played there. My junior year we went 6–4, and my senior year we went 10–0, but lost in the first round of the playoffs to Amarillo Tascosa. After that season, Coach Harper went to coach at the University of Oklahoma for a few years.

"They even hired one of the coaches from Carver, James Nash, to help with the transition. We roomed by position on road trips. I was a receiver, so I had some white roommates on trips. There were no problems. There weren't any problems eating at restaurants either. I later found out that Coach Harper had always cleared things in advance so there wouldn't be a problem. He would always call ahead. I didn't have any issues on the field with anyone either.

"There was one other good thing about Amarillo, even though it was home to a chapter of the John Birch Society. If people didn't like you in Amarillo, they let you know it. There was no hiding it. There was nothing behind your back or covert about anything."

Before mass integration came to the UIL in 1967, some school districts in the eastern part of Texas integrated early, or at least gave African American students the option of attending the white school or the black school in their respective hometowns.

Down in the Houston/Galveston segment of the Gulf Coast, Bill Gregory—like Morris Overstreet—had to choose which school to attend in LaMarque in the fall of 1966. It would be his senior year. Gregory remembered the "integration" plan and what happened: "I didn't realize I was in a segregated environment. We lived in separate neighborhoods, but I didn't think about it in terms of black and white. I didn't think about having to live, 'across the tracks.'

"My parents played it down and didn't make a big deal about it. My world, I realized later, was pretty much totally segregated. I did have some contact with whites at Bostic's Restaurant in LaMarque. My dad was a cook there, and I was a busboy there in high school. I worked with whites at the restaurant. The only other real contact I had with whites in LaMarque before I went off to college was in my junior year at Lincoln High School. We got a principal who was Anglo. He was there for only a short time. Then my senior year we had an Anglo English teacher. She didn't last the year. My contact with whites was pretty much limited to that.

"The summer between my junior and senior year, 1966, that all had the potential to change. The school district of LaMarque kind of integrated. They drew a line through town. On the right side of the line, the white side of town, students would go to LaMarque High School. On the left side of town, where the blacks lived, those students would go to Lincoln. There was an area in between the two lines where anyone living there could go to either school. I lived in that middle section. The whole thing was athletics-motivated. LaMarque High School wanted to get a few black athletes, myself included, who lived in that middle section to go play at the white school.

"The coaches at neither school knew which school I was going to because I missed the first two weeks of fall practice, since I was still working and I also wanted to stay out of the heat. The coaches at Lincoln kept asking me where I was going to go. To me it was a no-brainer. I was going to stay at Lincoln for my senior year. I had no inkling or thoughts about playing at LaMarque High School. The whole incident was a little like college recruiting. They were trying to get the cream-of-the-crop players from Lincoln. I can't blame them—that's just the way it was."

Perry Pruett hailed from Grand Prairie, which is bordered by Dallas to the east, Arlington to the west, and Irving to the north. Grand Prairie had a population of about forty thousand in the mid-1960s. Besides Pruett, Grand Prairie was also home to future NFL Hall of Fame receiver Charley Taylor and his half-brother, Joe "Turkey" Jones. A defensive back, Pruett played his college football at North Texas State and appeared in eleven games with the New England Patriots during the 1971 season.

In 1966, Pruett helped integrate Grand Prairie High School and its football program. "Growing up in Grand Prairie, segregation was like living in a different world," Pruett said. "I realized I grew up in a different world. We had our own stadium at Dalworth High School. I grew up thinking our little pasture that we used to play in was our Cowboy Stadium. Our goal was to make it to Prairie View University and the state championships. My older brother and Charley Taylor were our predecessors. They were ballers, and they started 'it' at Dalworth. Charley always had that 'it' factor. We all admired him. I didn't have the sense to know exactly how good he was. We knew he was good, but we had no idea he'd go to the Hall of Fame.

"My life also revolved around John Tyre Park. It's still open. It had a pool for the black kids. Kids would come from Dallas just so they could swim there. That pool was my world. My concept of sports was in that small radius. I was blissfully ignorant.

"Then, integration hit. Grand Prairie was a little bit ahead of its time. When they decided to integrate my senior year of 1966–67, they did it cold turkey—all twelve grades at once. When integration hit, reality hit. I was not in my little world anymore. The change was stark. I was now bussed to Grand Prairie High School. I was brutally introduced to new rules and regulations as far as things went.

"When the other black players from Dalworth and I tried out for football in the fall of 1966, they told us we couldn't be on varsity if we hadn't been to spring training. The schools hadn't integrated yet, so how could we have done that? The coaches said we could come off the bench, but we couldn't start. We had to reestablish ourselves as athletes. We had been state champs in track at Dalworth for two years. In football in 1965 we had gone to the quarterfinals. As seniors, if we had played at Dalworth, we would have been favored to win state in football.

"Now, all of a sudden, I couldn't play. I was nine months from deciding on where I should be playing in college. I had always thought I would go to a black school like Bishop or Wiley or TSU. I had never even thought about going to an integrated school. You know, though, once we got past the adults interfering and it got down to just us kids, it all worked out. Everyone just wanted to win. I don't think the coaches felt that way. They let politics get involved.

"Our coach was Travis Rhodes; he was from some little Podunk school in Oklahoma. He didn't have any use for the black players. When we got on the field, though, there was no denying our talent. They eventually accepted that some of us were exceptional athletes. The good and pretty good black players, they didn't get to play at first. They got the shaft. The positions went to the white players.

"We eventually had a strike. We decided we wouldn't play. We were serious about the strike. The players understood about the best players playing. The coaches were crazy. We did work through the rough spots, and we ended up having a good season. I regret that I was still limited as to what I could do on the field, however. They only let me play defense. Our offense was 'three yards and a cloud of dust.' They wouldn't let me play offense. I got so vicious on defense in practice the coaches made me stop practicing because I was hurting people. I was frustrated. At Dalworth I never came off the field. I was the first freshman to start at Dalworth since Charley Taylor. In my young mind, the whole thing was horrible.

"Integration was a curse and a blessing. It was more of a blessing for me. It hurt that I didn't make all-state because of integration, but it opened a lot of doors for me. Going to class in a white school was different. I had a real schedule and a counselor. I didn't know until I got to Grand Prairie High School that you needed to take the SAT or ACT test if you wanted to go to a white college. If you wanted to go to a black college, you didn't have to take those tests. I ended up with football scholarship offers from all over the country because of integration. There was this knock on black players from small towns, whether they could they compete against athletes from larger schools. I found out I belonged. Confidence is the key. It helps you separate from others. If you let your confidence wane you plateau. Integration gave me confidence."

After UIL integration in 1967, some African American schools stayed in the PVIL until the organization dissolved in 1970. In addition, some cities decided not to close their African American high schools and had them play in the UIL, thus not truly integrating with the white high school(s) in their respective towns. Most of the black schools not totally absorbed by the white schools had immediate success. Aldine Carver went 6–4 in 1967. Beaumont Charlton-Pollard went 8–1 in 1967, missing the playoffs, and 10–1–1 in 1968. Beaumont Hebert made it to the second round of the playoffs with a 9–3 record in 1967, and went to the semifinals with a 12–2 record in 1969. In 1976, Hebert became the first former PVIL school to capture a state championship when the team defeated the Gainesville Leopards 35–7 in the Class 3A finals.

In 1967—Galveston Central's only season in the UIL—the team went 10–0, but lost in the first round of the playoffs. The three Fort Worth African American high schools distinguished themselves well in their first season of UIL competition in 1967. Dunbar went 7–2–1, Kirkpatrick was 9–1, and Terrell was 7–2–1. Houston Elmore, led by Greg Pruitt, went 7–2–1 in 1968, the team's first UIL season, and 10–1 in 1969. Houston Kashmere, sparked by future All-Pro running back Delvin Williams, was 8–1–2 in 1967, 6–4 in 1968, and 12–1 in 1969, Williams's senior season. Booker T. Washington went 7–3 in 1967, but 13–1 in 1968, making it to the Class 4A semifinals.

In fact, at the end of the 1969 regular season, Houston Kashmere was ranked number two in the state in Class 4A, Texas' largest classification for its schools at that time. Houston Elmore was ranked number one in Class 3A, and Lufkin Dunbar was ranked number one in Class 2A.

Wichita Falls, about 120 miles northwest of Fort Worth, was one such example of a city not closing their black high school and having it enter the UIL. Wichita Falls Washington High School entered the UIL and played for two seasons, with some success before shutting down. The Leopards went 7–2–1 in 1967 and 8–2 in 1968. Before the 1969 season, Wichita Falls ISD closed Washington because of upcoming mandated integration, and the seven hundred Washington students went to one of two schools, either Hirschi or Rider High School. The resulting influx of talent enabled the Wichita Falls Coyotes to capture the Class 4A state title with a 28–20 win over San Antonio Lee. The Coyotes got key contributions from several black players, including legendary running back Ronnie Littleton, quarterback Lawrence Williams, and middle linebacker James Reed. Ironically, just nine years before, all-white Wichita Falls High School had lost the state title to the first integrated team to win state, the 1960 Corpus Christi Miller Buccaneers.

Ervin Garnett, the Washington coach, was turned into a junior high principal when Booker T. Washington closed. Garnett repeated the oft-voiced sentiment of the integration era when he said many students lost the black teachers and coaches that had served as their role models. As Garnett put it decades later: "At Booker T., the black kids knew a whole community was watching after them. Even the marginal students were put in positions of responsibility to showcase their talents and give them confidence. One of my great fears was that those kids would be lost at a white school. They would be looking at mostly white teachers who were happy to pass them a C and get them out of their classrooms."

Roosevelt "Rosie" Manning played at Washington from 1965 to 1967, which meant he was there when the school entered the UIL in 1967. Manning, a defensive tackle, went to Northeast Oklahoma State after high school and was selected in the second round by the Atlanta Falcons in the 1972 NFL draft. Manning went on to play four seasons with the Falcons and the Philadelphia Eagles. Recalling the early stair steps in his successful career, he said, "I was at Washington from 1965 to 1968. The next year, 1969, was when they closed Washington. My first couple of years, we played all-black schools. In 1967, we went into the UIL. We used to say before the season before integration to our coaches, 'Can we play the white schools? Or at least practice against them, like Wichita Falls High School?' The coaches said we couldn't; we might get injured. I think the real reason was because things were still segregated. We really didn't have any problems that first season in the UIL. We had a pretty decent season.

"In Wichita Falls growing up, the blacks lived in an area called the Flats. It was across the railroad tracks, on the east side of town. Growing up, we pretty much stayed on each other's side of town. I never went over there. Now some guys from the neighborhood would go driving over to the white part of town and get in trouble, but I never did. We had everything we needed in the Flats. There were a bunch of black-owned businesses: grocery stores, filling stations, restaurants, and such. My mom told me to pretty much stay in our part of town, so I did. I had no run-ins with whites. We didn't go into town to play sandlot ball or anything like that. We would go out to Shepard Air Force Base and play against the white guys stationed there at the base. We had no trouble with them. I guess integration worked out OK, football-wise. The year after I left Wichita Falls, they won the state title with Ronnie Littleton."

Like Wichita Falls, another school district that had their black school enter the UIL as a whole was Wilmer-Hutchins ISD, just south of Dallas. Dexter Bussey went to the short-lived Dallas Kennedy High School. Kennedy opened in 1964 and remained open until 1969. Bussey, a running back, played at Kennedy from 1966 to 1969, so he saw integration. From Kennedy, Bussey went to the University of Oklahoma for a season but ended up at Texas-Arlington. Bussey was a 1974 third-round draft choice of the Detroit Lions, and over eleven seasons with the Lions rushed for 5,105 yards, good for third place on the Lions all-time list behind Barry Sanders and Billy Sims.

Bussey recalled his experiences: "In my neighborhood in the early to mid-1960s, there were some whites and Mexicans, but the whites moved out by the end of the decade. The churches and schools in Wilmer-Hutchins were not very diverse. I originally grew up in west Dallas and then went to Oak Cliff. In third grade, I went to the Wilmer-Hutchins area. It's not really in Dallas; it's a little south of there. In my neighborhood there, the segregation wasn't too bad. Now, I used to go visit my grandparents in Shelby County in East Texas. Traveling back and forth to there was where I witnessed segregation with separate fountains and restrooms when we would stop in towns along the way there. You had to be careful because you were in the South. You had to be cognizant of things.

"I was in the last class of Kennedy High School before it closed. It shut down in 1969, so it wasn't open very long. My sophomore year was when we integrated. We played in Class 2A that first year. We entered the UIL as an all-black school. We played other integrated schools. I remember a couple of times there was some name-calling on the field, but after the game there were no problems. We were not real good in football. We were competitive, but no championships. [Kennedy lost to state power-house Ennis High School in consecutive years, 93–0 in 1968 and 88–0 in 1969.] We were better in basketball and track. I just remember integration not being that big of a deal."

Lufkin Dunbar was another African American high school that joined the UIL—but not until 1968. The Dragons had the most immediate impact of any former PVIL team, making it all the way to the 3A state finals before losing to Daingerfield 7–6.

The legendary Elmer Redd was the football and track coach at Dunbar, and won two state titles in track and was runner-up four times. In football, Redd compiled a 146–36–3 record in seventeen seasons at Dunbar, including three state titles, one runner-up finish, and three other semifinals appearances. Before that, he was the head football coach at Arp Industrial High School, where he had a 32–2-record and one state title. After losing the heartbreaker to Daingerfield in the 1968 state finals, the following year, Redd's last as the coach at Dunbar, the Tigers made it to the semifinals before losing to Klein on penetrations.

In 1970, University of Houston Head Football Coach Bill Yeoman hired Redd to be his running back coach. "Elmer was a great football person," Yeoman said. "Elmer was loyal; he had a great reputation among blacks in East Texas homes. If he wanted a player for us, he usually got him. He had to have that respect in order to get into homes to recruit players there. I gave him a job at Houston, and he basically said, 'Leave me alone and let me do it.' And he did.

"Elmer was worth his weight in gold. He was a heckuva human being, and he knew how to treat people right. He would not tolerate any nonsense whatsoever from his players. The black kids at UH knew it was football and their studies."

Pro Football Hall of Fame safety Kenny Houston, who played for Redd at Dunbar in the early 1960s, shared his opinion: "Coach Redd was like a father and a coach. All of the parents believed in him. The black community lived and breathed Dunbar Tiger football back then. Coach Redd had this big green Cadillac. We had a curfew, even in the summertime. We would see his car coming down the street, and we would scatter. You may not run from your parents, but you would run from Coach Redd. He also didn't tolerate bad apples."

D. C. Nobles, as the quarterback, led Dunbar to the PVIL state championship as a sophomore in 1967, and then led the Dragons into their first two seasons in the UIL in 1968 and 1969 before Dunbar was consolidated with Lufkin High School in 1970. In 1969, Nobles led the Dragons to a 12–0–2 record, losing their state semifinal game to Klein on first downs. This was before overtime play began in the mid-1990s. Accordingly, if a Texas high school playoff game was tied at the end of regulation play, the winner was decided by which team had the most penetrations

Elmer Redd, legendary Lufkin Dunbar head coach. Courtesy of University of Houston Department of Athletics.

inside their opponent's twenty-yard line. If that was tied, the team with the most first downs won.

Nobles went to the University of Houston, following his Dunbar coach, Elmer Redd, who took a job as a UH assistant coach in late 1969. Nobles became the first black quarterback in Cougar history, and as a senior in 1973 he led the Cougars to an 11–1 record and a number nine national ranking. He then played in Canada for the Winnipeg Blue Bombers, and the Houston Texans and Shreveport Steamer of the World Football League.

Nobles spoke of growing up in Lufkin and playing football for the Dunbar Dragons. He remarked, "I really can't compare segregation in Lufkin to anywhere else. My parents died when I was young. I was raised mostly by my aunt, my dad's sister. She was a housekeeper. I would go to work with her when I was a kid. I used to play with the white family's kids. My aunt would tell me things like, 'Don't breathe on them!' She was afraid of what the white parents might do if they caught me doing that.

"When I got a little older, I remember walking down the street in Lufkin and the white kids would throw eggs at me, call me 'nigger,' things like that. One time, in high school, some white kids tied me up with a water hose and drug me down the road. Eventually, though, I ended up with a whole lot of white friends through the years. It's amazing how things have worked out. Just look at how things have changed in my lifetime. I started out having to go in the back door of places, and now I get to go in the front door.

"Coach Redd lived down the street from my aunt. He was so inspirational. He was a disciplinarian. I remember when he used to drive around to see if we were out after curfew. We were afraid to get caught because we would have to answer to him. When I was in eighth grade, one day, Coach Redd told me to hop on the back of his pickup truck. He ended up taking me over to the field house, and he gave me equipment to get ready for high school. On Sundays I would go back over to the field house, and I would dig out plays that the coaches had thrown into the trash can outside. I would go back home and run the plays by myself in my yard. I wasn't allowed to have friends over during the day.

"Coach Redd told me from an early age, 'You're going to be the first black quarterback down South.' He must have seen something in me. I was only 140 pounds going into high school. The other players would laugh at me and say, 'That skinny ole kid is going to be our quarterback?'

D. C. Nobles, Lufkin Dunbar quarterback, circa 1969. Courtesy of University of Houston Department of Athletics.

Coach Redd would say, 'You better believe it! He already knows all the plays.' Eventually Coach Redd had me move into his house with him. He was the father figure I so desperately needed. He was like my daddy. He left Dunbar the day after my last high school game in December of 1969. He went to coach at the University of Houston under Bill Yeoman. I signed with the Cougars in the spring of 1970. Coach Redd kidded me, at least I think he was kidding me, when he said, 'I'll mess you up if you go anywhere else to college!'

"In high school I had a great career. In 1966, when I was a freshman, we beat Wichita Falls Washington for the state PVIL championship. In 1967, when I was a sophomore, we won the PVIL state title when we beat Texarkana Dunbar 44–24. We won the first fourteen games of our first year in the UIL, in 1968. We then lost to Daingerfield, 7–6. It was the first time I had ever lost a high school game. I cried like a baby. In 1969, my senior year, we tied Klein in the semifinals, but we lost on first downs. So in four years of high school, we lost one game."

Houston Elmore High School, the African American high school in the North Forest ISD in the northeast part of Houston, was another school that didn't join the UIL until 1968. When the Tigers made their debut, they made their presence felt. They went 7–3–1 their first year, and lost to Silsbee 26–6 in the first round of the playoffs. The Tigers were 10–1 in their second UIL season of 1969, ranking as the number-one team in the state for Class 3A for almost the whole season. Elmore was upset in the first round of the playoffs by Brenham, 33–14, in a game played at Elmore. Two of the stars for that Brenham team were junior running back Roosevelt Leaks and freshman defensive tackle Wilson Whitley.

Leaks and Whitley later achieved All-America status in college—Leaks with the University of Texas, and Whitley with the University of Houston. These two African Americans came to Brenham High School when Pickard, the black high school, closed in 1967. Elmore was led by Coach Wendell Moseley, who eventually ended up on Barry Switzer's staff at the University of Oklahoma. Elmore was led by eventual Cleveland Browns and Los Angeles Raiders Pro Bowler Greg Pruitt, who was a senior, and junior quarterback Dyain Frazier.

From Elmore, Pruitt went on to become an All-America running back at Oklahoma, finishing third in the Heisman voting in 1971 and second in 1972. Pruitt was a second-round pick of the Cleveland Browns in the 1973 NFL Draft and went on to play nine seasons for the Browns, making the Pro Bowl four times before playing his last three seasons for the Raiders. He made the Pro Bowl for the last time in 1983, the year the Raiders won Super Bowl XVIII. Pruitt was elected to the College Football Hall of Fame in 1999.

"I grew up in Settegast Gardens," Pruitt explained. "Born and raised there. It's a black section in northeast Houston. Settegast Road is by there. We really didn't have much contact with whites living there. We had our black schools. Now, when Elmore was brought into the UIL, we did have some white teachers my last year there in 1968–69. We used to catch the bus to go downtown, and we would have some contact with whites down there. One thing I do remember growing up was I marched in a protest because they had a bond election in our school district and they didn't appropriate hardly any funding for the black schools. We marched and protested in our neighborhood. It worked because we got more money. Our neighborhood was very close-knit. Everybody looked out for everybody. People in the neighborhood would discipline us if we messed up. We were taught to respect our elders. We would accept their discipline, and then we would usually get whipped when we got home too.

"We really didn't have any problems when we integrated my senior year. I do remember, however, when we went to play at Cy-Fair High School. Their campus looked like a college. We won, as Dyain Frazier passed the ball all over the place. That was the first time I had played against whites.

"Speaking of Dyain, he was a heckuva quarterback and had a great arm. He was actually playing behind me because I was the quarterback, but our coach, Wendell Moseley, came to me before my senior season and thought it would be a good idea if I moved to receiver. He had talked to Bill Michaels, an assistant coach at Oklahoma. There were no black Division I college quarterbacks at that time, and Coach Michaels told Coach Moseley I would have a better shot at a scholarship if I moved to another position. We had a great quarterback in Dyain, so it all worked out.

"Coach Mosley was a great coach and an even greater person. He was devoted to the kids at Elmore. He had a chance to go to other schools, but he stayed with us until Elmore closed. I was lucky that all of my coaches at Elmore were great. It helped me fall in love with sports. I played all the sports growing up. I would go from one practice to another, and it was great."

Dyain Frazier passed for 2,345 his senior season of 1969, throwing for thirty-five touchdowns. For his career, Frazier had 4,486 passing yards, which at the time was a Class 3A state record, and seventy-three touchdowns, which was an all-time Texas record. For many years, Frazier held the Texas single-game passing record when he threw for 588 yards and five touchdowns in a 58–6 rout of Aldine Carver High School in Frazier's junior season of 1968. Frazier's shining moment came on October 17, 1969, when Elmore took on Cy-Fair High School at their place. The Tigers and Cy-Fair were tied atop the district 10–3A standings with perfect 6–0 marks, and the winner would most likely represent their district in the playoffs. Elmore used a furious fourth quarter comeback to nip the Bobcats, 54–51. Frazier ended up passing for 399 yards and six touchdowns, including the game winner with 1:37 left to play. Elmore scored the last twenty-two points, all in the fourth quarter. Frazier bypassed a college football career in favor of baseball, as he was a second round pick of the Chicago Cubs in the 1970 MLB Draft. A southpaw pitcher, Frazier lasted for six minor league seasons.

"I lived at 7122 Little Street," Frazier said, recalling his growing-up years in Houston. "Gregg Pruitt lived on Cinderella Street. We were the best of friends. When we integrated in 1968 and went into the UIL, one thing I remember is that we had one white kid that went to our school. Coach Moseley called me into his office one day and said, 'I need you to do me a favor. I need this young man to hang with you.' He wanted him to hang out with Gregg too. Since we were well-known at school, Coach Moseley thought we could help protect him. I can't remember the kid's name. He ended up being a good friend. We would go to class together. He didn't play football, but he would always come to practice to watch me. He would come in our locker room too. He became one of my biggest fans. It was like he was one of the team. Eventually everyone loved him. He was just a good guy. He was accepted by all of the black kids. He never had to put up with any kind of name-calling or anything like that.

"I do remember the first time we played against a white school, Cy-Fair, in 1968 when I was a junior. We played at their place. We weren't sure what to expect, a black school going to play at a white school. We beat them 34–8, and we didn't run into any problems. We went to play at Cy-Fair again when we faced Brenham there in the playoffs. We rode a coach bus to the game with a police escort. Luckily, we did not experience any name-calling, like people calling us 'nigger' or throwing rocks at our bus—nothing of the sort. There was none of that Mississippi or Georgia stuff. It wasn't like the deep southern states in Houston.

"When we got to Cy-Fair, we were greeted warmly. There were fans saying, 'Who's Frazier? Which one is he?' They had heard about some of my earlier games passing the ball that season. The place was packed, and some of the Cy-Fair people actually rooted for us. We beat Brenham 18–13.

"Unfortunately, our season ended in the second round of the playoffs in 1968 when we lost to Silsbee, 26–6. Gregg Pruitt got hurt on the first play of the game. A linebacker hit him in the chest, and Gregg started spitting up blood. It was also raining, and that slowed down our passing game, which was our bread and butter. We were throwing forty to sixty times a game, which was unheard of in the 1960s. Coach Moseley even put it in where I could audible at the line of scrimmage.

"My senior year we went 10–0 and were ranked number one in the state. We beat four Class 4A teams in a row in nondistrict play. However, we lost 33–14 in the first round of the playoffs, at home to Brenham, the same team we had beaten the year before. Brenham had a good team. They had Roosevelt Leaks on their team, and he ran all over us."

When integration finally arrived in 1967, Houston Independent School District was an example of a school district that was proactive when it came to the assimilation of players and schools into the UIL. The athletic director who led HISD into these uncharted waters was Joe Tusa. Tusa had coached football for three seasons at his Houston ISD alma mater, Reagan High School, before stepping into the athletic director's chair in 1965 after a stint at Waltrip High School as an assistant principal. Tusa guided the HISD athletic department until his retirement in 1989 after seeing HISD through integration, and then Title

IX and the establishment of girls programs through his tenure. Today, one of HISD's football facilities, Delmar Stadium, has been renamed Delmar-Tusa Stadium.

"I took over as athletic director at HISD in 1965," Tusa said. "When integration came along a couple of years later, there were some concerns. The Texas Southern University riots had taken place back in May. I met with Herman Short, the Houston chief of police, and he asked me to help put on a summer recreation program for the kids in Houston, where the races could mix some. Chief Short felt it would help us through some difficulties. The program absolutely helped. It would be an outlet for the kids. When I set it up, I put both black and white administrators in charge of it. We had a program in the Fifth Ward and also Southwest Houston, among other places.

"Another thing we did to help with integration was we started setting the stage in some other sports. In basketball, we started inviting some black schools on a voluntary basis to the Jaycee tournament we had every year in December. We did that in 1966, about a year and a half before we integrated football. We did the same thing with track meets. In 1966 we started inviting black schools on a voluntary basis. Then, we started integrating our coaching staffs at our thirty-six middle schools and twenty-five high schools.

"Because we prepared for integration with these steps, it all went pretty well, considering. We laid the groundwork. For example, we also went to black churches and the black YMCA on Wheeler Street over by TSU, and talked to leaders in the black community. They were apprehensive at first, but it worked. People started understanding what we were trying to do was what was best for the kids. We opened up the opportunities for kids to go to college. We changed college sports in Texas. Blacks didn't used to go to white colleges in Texas, but we helped change that.

"The one big event I remember from that first year of integrated football in the fall of 1967 was the first playoff game between an all-black school, Kashmere, and an all-white school, Bellaire. The winner would be the city champion. We played the game at Jeppesen Stadium, which held over thirty thousand people. We filled the place that night. Before the game, the stadium officials came to me and said, 'What do we do? We have all these people that want to get into the stadium.' I said, 'Let them in.' There were people everywhere. They lined the track around the stadium. There were more Kashmere fans than Bellaire. We allowed some of the Kashmere fans to come over to the Bellaire side and fill some empty seats over there. You know what? Bellaire won the game, and we didn't have a single problem.

"Overall, we had very few problems with integration. Houston became one of the only cities in America that still plays its games at night after dark. Most cities have to play their games during the day to avoid problems. In some cities, they don't allow spectators at the high school games to prevent problems. We didn't have any of that stuff go on in Houston."

Nate Hawkins went to Booker T. Washington High School in Houston and played the first year of full UIL integration in 1967. Hawkins attended the University of Nevada–Las Vegas after high school and became the first football player ever drafted from the Rebels in 1972 when the Pittsburgh Steelers picked him in the sixteenth round. Hawkins ended up playing one season in the NFL with the 1975 Houston Oilers.

"Growing up in the 1950s and 1960s in Houston was pretty much like everywhere else," Hawkins said. "You had black and white restrooms all over town, and some parts of town it was all white and some parts it was all black. I grew up in the Studewood area of Houston on Thirty-Fifth Street. Booker T. Washington was on Thirty-Ninth Street.

"I played the first year of integration in HISD in 1967. I remember the coaches, how proud they were of their players and their program. They said 'This is what we got; we want to show up and show out.' The coaches had a lot of pride; they wanted to show everyone what they had. I played both ways in high school. I played tight end and defensive end. There were three games that first year of integration where I scored the winning touchdown. We beat Waltrip High School 7–0 when I took the ball out of the defender's hands for a touchdown. We never had any problems at the games. There may have been some problems in the stands, but I really couldn't tell you whether that was the case.

"We did start playing on Friday nights instead of Wednesday or Thursday at the black schools. We also got to play at all of the HISD stadiums around town. The black teams used to play at Jeppesen and Dyer Stadiums before integration. Now we could play at Delmar, which was right next door to Dyer Stadium on the northwest side of Houston. Delmar was where the white teams played. We also got to play at the new stadium out on South Main Street, Butler."

Delvin Williams played for Kashmere High School the first three seasons they were in the UIL, from 1967 to 1969. "I had no interaction with

whites growing up," Williams said. "In fact, I didn't have any daily interaction with whites pretty much until I went to college. My senior year
at Kashmere we did actually get a few white teachers. I played against
whites on other teams in high school, but I had no real personal contact
with them.

"I never really experienced any direct discrimination. There's no incidents that I remember that stayed with me. I pretty much stayed in
Kashmere Gardens growing up, or the Fifth Ward. Sometimes we would
go downtown to shop, but not that often. Sometimes I would go with my
uncle to the Tanglewood and Memorial areas, real nice white areas of
town, to help him cut lawns. We weren't involved in any type of protests,
like the march on Washington or anything like that. My parents were
afraid of the potential violence of being involved in anything like that.
When you don't know what things should be and how things should be
because you've been sheltered in segregation, you just kind of accept it.
We just didn't know any different growing up.

"Kashmere High School was built in 1957. It wasn't bad. We had a
swimming pool there. The new Kashmere, which was nice, we moved
into my junior year, but it didn't have a pool. Our school supplies and
football equipment were not very good. They were both used. When the
Kansas coaches came to talk to me, they looked at my books and mentioned that they were three editions behind. They didn't think too much
of our football gear either. Once again, we just didn't know any better.

"When integration came in 1967, my sophomore year, it was a big deal
for the school, the players, and the coaches. We could prove to everyone
we had a good team. We were forewarned about integration and that
there could be some problems, but there was no fear about it. We wanted
to compete against everybody.

"There's a couple of games from 1967 that I remember. We had a game
at Delmar Stadium against Sam Houston High School, which was all-
white at the time. They were in our district, and their school wasn't too
far from Kashmere. Whoever won the game would have the upper hand
in getting to the playoffs. There were going to be tensions at the game.
The athletic director for Houston schools, Joe Tusa, had some concerns
about playing the game at night. The game was intense, and we had a
squabble in the first half with them. Tusa, who was at the game, called
the two head coaches out onto the field together and warned them to

clean it up. The teams and fans calmed down, and we went on to beat Sam Houston and headed to the playoffs.

"We played Bellaire in the playoffs for the city championship at Jeppesen Stadium on the University of Houston campus. Once again, it was all-white against all-black. The crowd was huge. There were fans lined around the field on the track. We lost to Bellaire. I don't remember the score. I don't understand why we didn't pass more that game. We kept trying to run up the middle in that game, but they were stuffing us. Still, even though there was potential for problems with the large crowd and importance of the game, there weren't any. We never really had much in the way of problems after integration.

"You know, the black teams that came into the UIL did pretty well right off the bat. We made the playoffs that first year; then in 1969 we were 12–0 and ranked number two in the state for much of the season, but we lost to Beaumont Hebert in the quarterfinals, 29–12. We had beat them 26–7 earlier in the year. We lost to them in a rainstorm, and we fumbled the ball thirteen times and had eight turnovers in all. Then, in 1968, Booker T. Washington went to the semifinals with a 13–1 record. The black schools proved they could compete against any and all competition."

D. W. Rutledge was playing for Sam Houston High School when the team took on Kashmere in the 1967 game Delvin Williams described. Rutledge eventually went on to become one of the greats in the Texas High School coaching ranks, ringing up a 197–32–5 record at Converse Judson High School, just outside of San Antonio. Rutledge's teams won state titles in 1988, 1992, 1993, and 1995. In 2001, Rutledge became the director of the Texas High School Coaches Association, a position he still held in 2017. "There was a lot of electricity as you went into the game, and it just got worse," Coach Rutledge remembered. "There was no doubt there was prejudice against some people. There was tension." After Joe Tusa met with the coaches and took control of the situation, things calmed down, and Kashmere took the contest 14–6. Rutledge concluded, "We had a great ball club, but they just blew us away. You had to respect them. They were good."

By the end of the 1960s and heading into a new decade, athletic programs for high schools in the state of Texas were now integrated. In 1970 the PVIL was dissolved, and all schools were under the governing body of the University Interscholastic League. Although the transition was not always smooth, the 1960s had brought much change and progress with the integration of high school athletics. Along with college football being concurrently integrated in Texas at the same time as high schools, Texas helped lead the South, and the country as a whole, into a new era in athletics and race relations.

In addition, it didn't matter what part of Texas these players were from—North, South, East, West, the Panhandle, or the Rio Grande Valley. The demographics of their town or region didn't matter either, or whether they integrated a high school or a college. These players sometimes grew up in a segregated situation or, after they helped integrate a school or football team, faced other challenges like going on a road game and staring down prejudice, sometimes even facing discrimination in their new surroundings from classmates, teammates, and coaches. But in the end, these integration and football pioneers did have one common thread: they overcame the odds to become very successful in their chosen sport of football, and more importantly, many of these players turned into productive citizens after their football careers were over. Their stories in their own words speak levels about their perseverance, and their success is a testament to their overcoming the odds in the face of prejudice, inequality, and bigotry.

Bibliography

Personal Interviews

Adams, Willie—May 14, 2015
Alcorn, Lee—March 9, 2016
Alderman, Donald—March 10, 2016
Aldridge, Allan—April 17, 2015
Allen, Ralph—August 7, 2015
Anders, Herbert—June 3, 2015
Askson, Bert—March 9, 2016
Bahnsen, Gene—June 9, 2015
Bahnsen, Ken—June 10, 2015
Baker, Melvin—September 1, 2015
Barnes, Benny—August 18, 2015
Baylor, Raymond—July 23, 2015
Bayuk, John—June 9, 2015
Beatty, Chuck—May 26, 2015
Bell, Eddie—July 10, 2015
Bell, Jerome—October 7, 2015
Benys, Victor—February 26, 2016
Berry, Jay—September 15, 2015, September 18, 2015
Blair, Lucius—February 26, 2016
Blanks, Clarice—April 21, 2016
Blanks, Sid—April 21, 2016
Bookman Sr., Leroy—August 29, 2015
Bookman Jr., Leroy—January 1, 2016
Bookout, George—September 28, 2016
Boyette, Garland—May 17, 2015
Branch, Cliff—June 8, 2015
Brooks, Charlie—February 24, 2016
Brown, Charles—July 31, 2015
Brown, Charles W.—February 1, 2016
Brown, Ray—June 5, 2015
Brown, Robert—January 27, 2016
Bryant, John David—August 12, 2016
Buetow, Billy—March 11, 2016
Bullock, Dale—March 15, 2016
Bunn, Melvin—June 18, 2015
Burchers, Jack—May 9, 2015
Bussey, Dexter—August 17, 2015

Campbell, Carl—August 23, 2016
Cantu, Roy—July 15, 2015
Carr, Leon—July 24, 2015
Castillo, Vic—April 28, 2015
Clarke, Frank—May 26, 2015
Clay, Moses—March 1, 2016
Coffer, Joe—June 17, 2015
Coffey, Junior—December 21, 2009, July 24, 2016
Cormier, Rufus—October 5, 2016
Culak, Mertes—March 5, 2016
Culwell, Gwen—April 26, 2016
Daniels, Clem—July 6, 2015
Davalos, Rudy—April 26, 2016
Davis, Lonnie—August 2, 2015
Deckard, Kenneth—August 3, 2015
Delgado, Art—August 16, 2016
Doan, Bobby—July 25, 2016
Dotson, Alphonse—September 8, 2015
Douglas, Karl—July 24, 2015
Douglas, Marvin—January 13, 2016
Dowler, Boyd—June 9, 2015
Dunlap, Leonard—March 9, 2016
Ellison, Willie—March 22, 2016
Everett, Billy Don—March 10, 2016
Fairbanks, Chuck—December 4, 2007
Farr, Mel—December 21, 2007
Felts, John—March 10, 2016
Ferguson, Charlie—May 18, 2015
Fields, Leonard—January 13, 2016
Fleming, Marv—August 17, 2015
Fore, Von—April 27, 2016
Frazier, Charlie—April 10, 2015
Frazier, Dyain—March 11, 2016
Gafford, Jimmy—September 28, 2016
Garcia, Charles—May 16, 2015
Garcia, Lacy—February 28, 2016
Garrett, Carl—May 21, 2015
George, Phil—May 18, 2015
Gilliam, Frank—July 19, 2016
Glosson, Clyde—July 21, 2015
Gonzales, Ramon—August 20, 2016
Gonzalez, Philip—October 8, 2016
Gonzalez, Victor—October 5, 2016
Granato, Joe—August 25, 2016

Grandberry, Kenneth—August 17, 2015
Granderson, Rufus—July 6, 2015
Green, Charles—July 23, 2015
Green, Ernest—March 15, 2016
Gregory, Bill—August 6, 2015, September 11, 2015
Groman, Bill—April 10, 2015
Guillory, Tony—May 12, 2015
Gunner, Harry—March 29, 2015
Haggerty, Arthur—June 6, 2015
Harden, Roland—January 7, 2016
Hardin, David—August 25, 2016
Hardman, Cedrick—May 22, 2015
Harkless, Berkley—June 15, 2015, June 18, 2015
Harper, Willie—February 28, 2016
Harris, Bill—August 5, 2015
Harvey, Doug—May 20, 2015
Hawkins, Nate—March 18, 2016
Hayes, Wendell—August 17, 2015
Haynes, Abner—July 23, 2016
Hennigan, Charlie—April 10, 2015
Hentschel, Jerry—March 12, 2015
Herrington, Barbara—March 2, 2016
Herrington, Whit—March 3, 2016
Hilliard, Joe Mack—March 16, 2015
Hines, Percy—June 6, 2015, July 11, 2015
Hoelscher, Raymond—March 16, 2016
Hoggins, James—July 22, 2016
Hollis, Wardell—August 26, 2015
Hollomon, Gus—December 20, 2007
Holmes, Michael—June 4, 2015
Holmes, Robert—May 3, 2015
Hopkins, Andy—July 14, 2015
Horne, Buddy—June 7, 2015
Hornsby, Gentris—June 7, 2015
Houston, Ken—May 1, 2015
Howard, Leroy—March 8, 2016
Howard, Sherman—April 7, 2016
Hysaw, Guillermo—September 11, 2015
Jackson, Bobby—May 27, 2015
Jackson, Carl—April 12, 2015
Jackson, Cass—August 17, 2015
Jefferson, Roy—September 8, 2015
Johnson, Leo—February 12, 2016
Johnson, Rudy—January 21, 2016

Jones, Dub—April 5, 2016
Jones, Earl "Bud"—September 29, 2015
Jones, Homer—April 10, 2015
Jones, Leodia—June 13, 2015
Jones, Loman—September 28, 2016
Jones, Willie—May 8, 2015, March 12, 2016
Keeling, Jimmie—July 13, 2015
Kelley, Louis—May 28, 2015, July 11, 2015, April 1, 2016, July 8, 2016
Kelly, Alvetta—May 21, 2015
Kennedy, Tom—May 23, 2015
Keys, Brady—September 2, 2015
King, Lindley—August 18, 2016
Lacy, Herbert—October 3, 2016
Lawrence, Marshall—March 15, 2016
Levias, Jerry—October 5, 2016
Linton, Fred—August 30, 2016
Locklin, Billy Ray—March 10, 2016
Lott, James—April 17, 2015
Lundgren, Hal—March 12, 2015
Madden, Gerald—August 22, 2015
Malone, Otto—July 20, 2016
Manning, Rosie—February 23, 2016
Marchetti, Gino—April 3, 2016
Mascorro, Homer—August 17, 2016
McGee, Tony—September 18, 2015
McVea, Warren—November 18, 2015
McWilliams, Jerry—July 20, 2016
Menefee, Hartwell—August 22, 2015
Miller, James—November 17, 2015
Minor, Claudis—May 10, 2015
Mitchell, Willie—March 10, 2016
Mixon, Rayford—August 9, 2015
Moody, David—July 21, 2015
Moseley, Marcus—July 24, 2015
Moten, Bobby—August 16, 2015
Mueller, Wilbert—March 5, 2016
Nance, Ted—October 20, 2007
Neubauer, Buddy—August 16, 2016
Nobis, Tommy—August 2, 2015
Nobles, D. C.—June 7, 2015
Norris, Trusse—January 13, 2016
O'Barr, Billy—March 19, 2016
Oliver, Gale—May 26, 2015
Overstreet, Morris—November 3, 2015

Paschall, Willie—July 16, 2015

Payton, John—June 4, 2015

Pedro, Pete—May 22, 2015, August 12, 2016

Perez, Ines—May 3, 2015

Perez, Marcos—August 26, 2016

Perkins, Arthur—May 23, 2015

Pollard, Bob—June 16, 2015

Porter, Willie—May 16, 2015

Powers, Jody—January 11, 2008

Pruett, Perry—June 1, 2015

Pruitt, Greg—July 2, 2016

Ragus, Pete—April 26, 2015, July 11, 2015, July 23, 2016, August 23, 2016

Reed, Alvin—April 10, 2015

Reid, Joseph—April 3, 2016

Renfro, Mel—August 17, 2015

Ritcherson Jr., Lewis—October 3, 2016

Ritcherson Sr., Lewis—September 10, 2015

Roberts, Walter—August 17, 2015

Robinson, Floyd—February 25, 2016

Roby, Ed—August 20, 2015

Roland, Johnny—May 4, 2015, May 5, 2015

Sanderson, Reggie—August 31, 2015

Sapenter, Hensley—February 23, 2016

Searles, Joseph—August 16, 2015, May 1, 2016

Shanklin, Julius—June 18, 2015

Sharp, Harry—March 3, 2016

Shurmur, Peggy—October 8, 2015

Shurmur, Scott—October 12, 2015

Smith, Bobby—May 12, 2015

Smith, Bubba—December 21, 2007

Smith,Willie Ray—May 13, 2015

Sohenge, Judy—March 5, 2016

Sowells, Richard—June 15, 2015

Stanislaw, Hal—March 11, 2016

Stewart, Larry—July 25, 2016

Stokes, Jesse—August 4, 2015

Storms, William—May 14, 2015, March 12, 2016

Strahan, Art—May 17, 2015

Summer, Carl—March 17, 2016

Taliaferro, George—April 5, 2016

Taliaferro, Viola—April 5, 2016

Tansey, Donald—March 16, 2016

Taylor, Jack—September 23, 2015

Taylor, Leo—July 23, 2015

Taylor, Margie—September 23, 2015
Teaff, Grant—March 31, 2016, August 29, 2016
Thomas, Edward—August 21, 2015
Thompson, Sherwood—May 16, 2015
Toth, Zollie—April 3, 2016
Triplett, Leonore—April 5, 2016
Triplett, Wally—April 5, 2016
Tusa, Joe—July 26, 2008
Ugalde, Julio—March 17, 2015
Upshaw, Marvin—February 23, 2016
Vandergriff, Jerry—July 24, 2016
Varnado, Kenneth—March 19, 2016
Wade, Robert—July 30, 2015
Warner, Charles—September 6, 2016
Washington, Gene—April 30, 2015, May 5, 2015
Washington, Joe—April 6, 2015
White, Phil—September 24, 2015
Whitmore, Clarence—July 27, 2015
Williams, Delvin—January 20, 2016
Williams, Jerry—March 13, 2016
Woods, Glenn—June 9, 2015
Wooten, John—May 21, 2015
Worrell, Bill—June 3, 2008
Wright, Harry—June 2, 2015
Wright, Leroy—March 10, 2016
Yeoman, Bill—June 8, 2015
Young, Geraldine—April 4, 2016
Youngblood, Eltra—April 18, 2015

Newspapers

Abilene Reporter-News
Alamogordo Daily News
Albuquerque Journal
Amarillo Globe-News
Amarillo Globe-Times
Austin American-Statesman
Baltimore Sun
Baylor Lariat
Baytown Sun
Beaumont Enterprise
Borger News-Herald
Brownsville Herald

Brownwood Bulletin
Bryan-College Station Eagle
Cameron Herald
Canyon News
Carroll Daily Times Herald
Chicago Tribune
Corpus Christi Caller-Times
Corsicana Daily Sun
Cumberland News
Dallas Morning News
Del Rio News-Herald
Denton Record-Chronicle
Denver Post
Des Moines Register
East Liverpool Evening Review
Eau Claire Leader
El Paso Herald-Post
Estherville Daily News
Eugene Guard
Freeport Facts
Fresno Bee
Galveston Daily News
Garden City Telegram
Gilmer Mirror
Greeley Daily Tribune
Houston Chronicle
Houston Post
Huntsville Item
Indiana Gazette
Indianapolis Star
Iowa City Press-Citizen
Irving Daily News Texan
Jefferson City Daily Capital News
Jefferson City Post-Tribune
Jefferson City Sunday News Tribune
Kansas City Times
Kerrville Mountain Sun
La Crosse Tribune
Las Cruces Sun-News
Lawton Constitution and Morning Press
Lebanon Daily News
Llano News
Lubbock Avalanche-Journal
Lubbock Evening Journal

Lubbock Morning Avalanche
Marshall News Messenger
Maryville Daily Forum
Mason City Globe Gazette
McKinney Courier-Gazette
Mexia Daily News
Moberly Monitor
Muscatine Journal and News Tribune
Nacogdoches Daily Sentinel
New Philadelphia Daily Times
New York Age
New York Times
Odessa American
Ottawa Herald
Pampa Daily News
Paris News
Pittsburgh Courier
Pittsburgh Post-Gazette
Pittsburgh Sports Daily Bulletin
Pocono Record
Pratt Tribune
Raleigh Register
Salina Journal
Salina Journal Sun
Salt Lake City Deseret News
Salt Lake Tribune
San Angelo Standard-Times
San Antonio Express
San Antonio Express-News
San Saba News
San Saba News and Star
Superior Daily Telegram
Taylor Daily Press
Terre Haute Star
Tipton Daily Tribune
Valley Morning Star
Vernon Daily Record
Vidette Messenger
Waco News
Waco News-Tribune
Waco Tribune-Herald
Warren County Observer
Waxahachie Daily Light
Wise County Messenger

Books

Bloom, John, and Michael Willard. *Sports Matters: Race, Relations, and Culture*. New York: New York University Press, 2002.

Burns, Mike. *Night Train Lane: Life of Hall of Famer Richard "Light Train" Lane*. Austin: Eakin Press, 2000.

Bynum, Mike, ed. *King Football: Greatest Moments in Texas High School Football History*. Birmingham: Epic Sports Classics, 2003.

Cashion, Ty. *Pigskin Pulpit: A Social History of Texas High School Football Coaches*. Austin: Texas State Historical Association, 1998.

Demas, Lane. *Integrating the Gridiron: Black Civil Rights and American College Football*. New Brunswick: Rutgers University Press, 2010.

Dent, Jim. *The Kids Got It Right: How the Texas All-Stars Kicked Down Racial Walls*. New York: St. Martin's Press, 2013.

Eisen, George, and David K. Wiggins. *Ethnicity and Sport in North American History and Culture*. Westport: Greenwood Press, 1994.

Glasrud, Bruce A., ed. *African Americans in South Texas History*. College Station: Texas A&M University Press, 2011.

Glasrud, Bruce A., and Archie P McDonald, eds. *Blacks in East Texas History: Selections from the East Texas Historical Journal*. College Station: Texas A&M University Press, 2008.

Glasrud, Bruce A., and James M. Smallwood, eds. *The African American Experience in Texas: An Anthology*. College Station: Texas A&M University Press, 2007.

Harris, Jack. *A Passion for Victory: The Coaching Life of Texas Legend Joe Kerbel*. Dallas: Taylor Publishing, 1990.

Jacobus, Robert. *Houston Cougars in the 1960s: Death Threats, the Veer Offense, and the Game of the Century*. College Station: Texas A&M University Press, 2015.

Ladino, Robyn Duff. *Desegregating Texas Schools: Eisenhower, Shivers, and the Crisis at Mansfield High*. Austin: University of Texas Press, 1996.

Lapchick, Richard. *Broken Promises: Racism in American Sports*. New York: St. Martin's Press, 1984.

Levy, Alan. *Tackling Jim Crow: Racial Segregation in Professional Football*. Jefferson, NC: McFarland Press, 2003.

Linden, Glenn M. *Desegregating Schools in Dallas: Four Decades in the Federal Courts*. Dallas: Three Forks Press, 1995.

McKone, Jim. *Lone Star Fullback*. New York: Vanguard Press, 1966.

McMurray, Bill. *Texas High School Football*. South Bend, IN: Icarus Press, 1985.

Miller, Patrick, and David Wiggins. *Sport and the Color Line*. New York: Routledge Press, 2004.

Olsen, Jack. *The Black Athlete: A Shameful Story*. New York: Time-Life Books, 1968.

Patrick, Latrina. *The Brady Keys Jr. Story: Overcoming Adversity by Staying within the Blessing.* Albany: The Keys Group, 1999.

Pennington, Richard. *Breaking the Ice: The Racial Integration of Southwest Conference Football.* Jefferson, NC: McFarland and Company, 1987.

Robins, Thurman. *Requiem for a Classic: Thanksgiving Turkey Day Classic.* Bloomington: Author House Press, 2011.

Ross, Charles. *Mavericks, Money, and Men: The AFL, Black Players, and the Evolution of Modern Football.* Philadelphia: Temple University Press, 2016.

Sailes, Gary, ed. *African Americans in Sport: Contemporary Themes.* New Brunswick: Transaction Publishers, 1998.

Shabazz, Amilcar. *Advancing Democracy: African Americans and the Struggle for Access and Equity in Higher Education in Texas.* Chapel Hill: University of North Carolina Press, 2004.

Shanahan, Tom. *Raye of Light: Jimmy Raye, Duffy Daugherty, the Integration of College Football, and the 1965–66 Michigan State Spartans.* Middleton, WI: August Publications, 2014.

Smith, Tommie, with David Steele. *Silent Gesture: The Autobiography of Tommie Smith.* Philadelphia: Temple University Press, 2007.

Taylor, Otis, and Mark Stallard. *The Need to Win.* Champaign, IL: Sports Publishing, 2003.

Articles

Borucki, Wes. "You're Dixie's Southern Pride: American College Football and the Resurgence of Southern Identity." *Identities: Global Studies in Culture and Power* 10 (2003): 477–94.

Marcello, Ronald. "The Integration of Intercollegiate Athletics in Texas: North Texas State College as a Test Case, 1956." *The Journal of Sports History* 14 (winter 1987): 286–316.

_____. "Integrating New Year's Day: The Racial Politics of College Bowl Games in the American South." *The Journal of Sports History* 24 (fall 1997): 358–77.

Smith, John Matthew. "Breaking the Plane: Integration and Black Protest in Michigan State University Football in the 1960s." *The Michigan Historical Review* 33 (2007): 1–21.

Index

Page numbers in *italics* refer to images and photos.

7–8; attacks on black players, 6, 7, 12, 63, 64, 66, 80, 83, 95–97, 104, 110, 120, 121, 139, 144, 146, 150, 160–61, 207, 214; benching of black players, 220–21; and boycotts, 197, 198, 199–201, 221–22; camraderie in, 4–7, 68, 80, 88, 93, 96–97, 99, 108, 111–12, 115, 116, 123–24, 126, 128, 139, 143–44, 152, 207; cancellations of games, 12, 35, 42–60; 88, 98; courage of black players, 136–37; Hispanic players, 156–57, 213; vs. other integrated teams, 115–16; protected by the Military Police/FBI, 104, 214; racist coaches, 187–93; at restaurants, 62, 64, 83, 89, 96, 106, 111, 115, 116, 119, 126, 143, 152, 127–28, 99–100; sundown towns, 68–69, 120, 142; threats against, 69; travel difficulties, 33, 43, 44, 63, 80, 83; and white parents, 115

integration: in the American Football League, 22; in Austin, 10; in the Bay Area, 40–41; and Ben Kelly, 3; the black community and, x; in California, 31–32; in Catholic schools, 42–44; in Central Texas, 102; in the Coastal Bend, xv, 11, 61; college resistance to, 90; in Corpus Christi, 10, 73, 117–33; in Dallas/Fort Worth, xv, 10, 23, 42; and demographics, xv; in East Texas, xv, 10, 42; and football team camraderie, 4–5; in Friona, 9, 42; and game cancellations, 203; and geography/demographics: 9–11; in Houston, xv, 10, 42; in the late 1960s, 217–36; on the Louisiana/ Texas border, 10–11; in the military, 28, 102–3; in the National Football League, 22, 28; outside of Texas, 31–41; in the Panhandle, 102, 111–16; in the Rio Grande Valley,

102, 104–6; in San Antonio, 10, 12, 74–84; in South Texas, 12; in the Southeastern Conference, 178; in the Southwestern Conference, 178, 203–16; in Texas colleges and universities, xiii, 85–100; in Texas high schools, 61–84, 117–33; in the Texas Panhandle, xv, 9, 10; in Texas schools, xiv–xv, 9–11, 42, 102–16; and violent protests, 148; white reaction to, ix–x

interracial couples, 83

Iowa State University, 195–96

Jack Yates High School, 12, 31

Jackson, Cass, 37–38

Jackson, Leon, 104–5

Javelina Hall of Fame, 107

Jefferson High School, 75, 77, 79–80, 82–83

Jefferson, Roy, 36–37

Jernigan, Clark, 140

Jim Crow. *See* segregation

Johnson, Charlie, 100

Johnson, Clifford, 77

Johnson, Rudy, 134, 175–76

Johnston, Max, 4

Johnston, Rex, 3

Jones, Earl "Bud," 187–93

Jones, Joe "Turkey," 220

Jones, Loman, 5–6

Jones, Ron, 39

Jones, Willie, 51–52, *52*, 63, 66, 134, 168–70

Kansas City Chiefs, 77, 107, 135

Kansas City Monarchs, 40

Kansas State University, xvi, 103

Kelley, Ben, 1–9, *5*

Kelley, Louis, xiv, 18, 85–87, *86*, 99–100

Kelley, Robert, 85, 86

Kelly, Ben, xiii, 12, 42, 134

Kennedy, John F., 193

Roberts, Walter "The Flea," 37
Robinson, Eddie, 168
Robinson, Floyd, 63–64
Robinson, Jackie, 29–30
Robinson, Joe, 165
Robstown High School, 51, 53–54,
    56–59, 61, 66
Rockdale High School, 46–48, 50, 51
Rockefeller, Nelson, xvi
Roland, Johnny, 103, 129–31, *130*,
    132, 176–77
Rose Bowl, 170
Ross, Ollie, 140–41, 145
Rutledge, D. W., 235
Ryan, John, 197
Rydolph, Kennard, 66, 67, 68–69

Sacramento State College, 118
Sam Houston High School, 1, 78, 111
Samuel Huston College, 27–28, 29
San Angelo College, 1, 2–3, 12
San Angelo Independent School
    District, 45
San Antonio Brackenridge High
    School, xiv, 77, 78–79, 107, 140,
    153–66
San Antonio Jefferson High School,
    102
San Antonio: integration in, 74–75
San Antonio Wheatley High School,
    74, 75, 76–77, 82
San Diego Chargers, 173
San Felipe High School, 110–111, 137
San Francisco 49ers, 8, 107, 175
San Saba High School, 46–48, 50, 51
Sanderson, Reggie, 40–41
Santa Rosa Junior College, 118
Sapenter, Hensley, 74–76
Searles, Joseph III, xv–xvi, 103–4
Seattle Seahawks, 171
segregation: in Arizona, 37; in Austin,
    27–28, 74; back door entrances,
    23–24; and the black community,
    xiv, 15–16, 21, 22, 190, 218; in

clothing stores, 19–20, 21–22, 26,
    27, 109; "colored" water fountains,
    67; in Dallas/Fort Worth, 42; in
    East Texas, 54, 88; in El Paso,
    35; firsthand accounts of, 15–30,
    40–41, 72, 79–80, 91, 103, 109–
    110, 215–16, 219–20, 224–25,
    227–28; at football stadiums, 20;
    and historically black colleges and
    universities, 134; in Houston, 32,
    42; in the military, 28; in movie
    theaters, 20, 23, 25, 26, 27, 49,
    109; in the National Football
    League, 16; in New Mexico, 34;
    protests against, 18–19, 81–82, 122;
    in restaurants, 49; in San Antonio,
    79–80; in stadiums, 39, 78, 91; and
    substandard equipment/facilities,
    11, 15, 17, 20, 21, 23, 25, 61, 84,
    135, 218–19; in Texas, 15; in Texas
    football, ix; and West Texas, 15;
    and violence, 16, 20, 22, 33
Shannon, Pat, 76
Shell, Art, 38
Simmons, Ozzie, 167
Sims, E. A., 85, 100
Sinton High School, 61
Sly and the Family Stone, 92
Smith, Bobby, 51, 117, 118–22, *122*
Smith, Bubba, xi, xiii, 18, *182*, 182–83
Smith, Tommie, 193
Smith, Treilis, 62–63
Smith, Willie Ray Jr., 170–71
Smith, Willie Ray Sr., 18, 168
Soehnge, Judy, 59
Solomon Coles High School, 70–71,
    123
Southern Methodist University, 13,
    152, 210–16
Southwest Conference, 203–16
Southwest Conference: and
    integration, 13
Sparkman, Jim, 113
Speegle, Cliff, 188